DAVID CONN

THE FALL OF THE HOUSE OF FIFA

The Multimillion-Dollar Corruption
at the Heart of Global Soccer

NATION
BOOKS
New York

Library of Congress Control Number: 2017905020
ISBN: 978-1-56858-596-3 (hardcover)
ISBN: 978-1-56858-597-0 (e-book)

10 9 8 7 6 5 4 3 2 1

Dedicated to

Brian Lomax, 1948–2015, founding father of Britain's football club supporters trust movement

and

John Potts, my school PE and football teacher

and all the many good and inspiring people I have come to know through football.

I have spread my dreams under your feet;
Tread softly because you tread on my dreams.

From 'He Wishes for the Cloths of Heaven', by W. B. Yeats

'Say it ain't so, Joe.'

Reportedly said by a small boy to 'Shoeless' Joe Jackson, a Chicago
White Sox baseball player accused of throwing the 1919 World Series.
Now believed to have been a myth.

Contents

CHAPTER 1

The People's Game

All the people who love football, the uncountable, ever-expanding millions or billions of us, will forever remember their first World Cup. For children, watching on television the faraway stars and splendours of the rolling matches, it is greater than entertainment and remembered with more than fond nostalgia: it is a formative experience. At the risk of blurting out a near-religious affinity for football, a simple, natural sport, so early in this account of how its world governing body, Fifa, crumpled into a mire of corruption and lies, I do believe there is in the World Cup something transcendent.

My first was 1974, the tournament played in the west of divided Germany, won finally by the host country whose strong and capable team, helmed by the visionary and rarefied skills of its captain, Franz Beckenbauer, overcame the fabulous, elaborate Holland of Johan Cruyff.

I was nine. I watched the whole spectacle, transfixed, on a big wooden lump of a colour telly in the living room of our house in north Manchester, where football was all around, woven into childhood. One of my earliest memories is of walking to infant school with my friend Anthony, and seeing the big boys in the junior school thundering through a mass game in the playground. As we passed by, a boy scored a neat, side-footed goal between the lines in the tarmac which passed for goals, and he wheeled sprinting away with an arm in the air and all his team running after him. I always wanted to be in the thick of that tumult, to play the game, and to be good at it.

Being taken to see United at Old Trafford and City at Maine Road, my head waist-high to the enormous crowds gathered there, connected our scamperings in the playground, park and garden to a much wider experience. I remember a friend of my dad's pointing to some mass synchronised singing, swaying and clapping on the Stretford End at United, and I instinctively understood there was a deep swell of passion and tradition formed for football long before I was born into the swim of it. When it came to the challenge every Manchester boy faces, sometimes demanded with menaces – City or United – my dad, a lapsed Bolton Wanderers supporter, gave no direction to follow, and with my freedom to choose I opted for City. The club was not the corporate, mega-wealthy, Abu Dhabi-owned, multinational City Football Group of today, nor were City the underachieving poor relations of United then; in the early seventies City had international stars and were the superior Manchester club. Bobby Charlton, the great engine of United's recovery as a football club from the human tragedy of the 1958 Munich air crash, star for England in the 1966 and 1970 World Cups, was exhausted by then. The bright-eyed Belfast boy George Best, who unfurled his playground skills in the grandest stadiums, was already being scooped up in drinking basements in town. Denis Law, the other maestro in United's triumphant trio, was a City striker for a final season or two by the time I emerged into football consciousness.

The gruff, tough pride Manchester men had for football was stamped into the city's character, and I think I was dimly aware of the general impression that we, in England, even 'invented' the game. I never gave that much credence because the people who made a point of it only seemed to do so when they were angry, in bad-tempered exasperation at a modern game or world gone wrong, and with some implicit hostility to 'foreigners' thinking they owned it.

It was only as an adult, a journalist researching the roots of football to understand its hyper-commercially exploited modern incarnation, that I read into the game's history properly and discovered that this claim of British national pride is actually, remarkably, true. Football, its proportions, layout of the pitch and rules, which allow for its endlessly thrilling expression, were indeed first established and agreed at the historic meetings of the newly christened Football Association at the Freemason's Tavern in London's Lincoln's Inn, in 1863.

Now I believe that these fascinating and cherished origins should be taught to young people as a valuable part of learning football, and history, but they are not, and many of football's adherents love the game all their lives without ever knowing how it all began. Growing up, we experienced these roots not as explicit history lessons but as a received sense of heritage, with innate values, from teachers at school and the dads who ran our clubs in the Sunday leagues. They strove to impart the understanding that along with the human instinct to get hold of that ball and run with it, dribble, boot it into the goal, came a necessary teamwork. When I started to play the game properly, on an actual grass pitch, I was quite startled to discover the degree of effort and fitness it demanded, and the challenge of sustaining it. There were the obvious rules of the game itself, against fouling, bullying, cheating and other thuggery – not always observed in the snarling confrontations, which passed for football, we grew up to encounter in some of Manchester's badlands. There was a decency we all soon understood in not lording a victory too cockily, and in having to scrape ourselves up after a defeat and shake hands with the boys on the other side. There were, to acknowledge the words now proclaimed as global commandments by Fifa and Uefa, fair play and respect, inherently required in the essence and conduct of the game.

Before the World Cup magically turned up on television in the summer of 1974, I am not sure I knew much about it at all. I can remember watching only two international matches before that tournament, both famous defeats for England, who were sinking into what would be a prolonged hangover following their victory at Wembley in their home World Cup of 1966. The first match was a 3–1 evisceration by Beckenbauer's West Germany at Wembley, in which Günter Netzer seemed to play uncontested in midfield, and which I did not even realise was the quarter-final of the 1972 European Championships, ultimately won by West Germany. The second was the generation-defining 1–1 home draw with Poland in October 1973, which meant England had not even qualified to play in the World Cup finals, when their goalkeeper Jan Tomaszewski was extraordinary and ours, Peter Shilton, let their goal through his legs. I couldn't quite take in what it all meant at the end, but remember running out of the lounge, crying in dismay.

I could, of course, regret that timing now, wonder what it might have been like had my first World Cup experience been the self-congratulatory national glow of England's 1966 triumph. Or 1970 in Mexico, the first World Cup on colour television, illuminated by the golden, trophy-claiming brilliance of Brazil. I educated myself about it years later, watching repeatedly the wonder of that goal in the final scored by the captain Carlos Alberto, surely still the greatest team goal ever scored. It is decorated by the short square pass played into his stride by Pelé, so easy looking, which somehow encapsulates the very beauty football can craft from its simple elements. There is the picture from that tournament which Fifa itself used as the signature image for its 2004 centenary publication, as the essence of football's achievement: England's Bobby Moore and Pelé, embracing and congratulating each other after Brazil's 1–0 win in the group. A white man and a black man, both great stars, united through sport in mutual admiration.

But I never really thought that at all; a child doesn't: you grow into the era which is yours. The 1966 triumph was bored into us with a load of other landmarks from before our time, which, we were endlessly told by our elders, showed why things weren't as good as in their day. England's absence was all we knew, so we accepted the World Cup without them; Pelé had retired from international football, Brazil were famously and jarringly stolid in 1974, and my generation had to wait until the 1982 World Cup in Spain to see a Brazil of marvellous talents.

So the 1974 tournament came on television, and I just watched it, agog, all this splendour laid out, on school nights in north Manchester. The memory of it is somehow draped across years of general impressions from my childhood: often I picture myself watching it in the next house we moved to, but that is not possible because we didn't go there until 1976. I watched the historic East Germany versus West Germany group game, which east won 1–0, as a football match, without any understanding of the profound political meaning with which the contest was freighted. I always remember seeing live the arcing, swerving volley from the edge of the penalty area scored by the centre-forward Ralf Edström, for Sweden, and the way the raindrops fell off the back of the net as the ball bulged into it.

As a nine-year-old I was strangely and somewhat ungratefully underwhelmed by Cruyff. Of his forever celebrated backheel swivel turn against Sweden, I pronounced myself unable to see what all the fuss was about. My uncle Stephen, fourteen years younger than my dad and still playing Sunday league football when I was a boy, had taught me a similar move in the back garden not long before that. The Conn turn involved putting the sole of your foot on top of the ball, rolling it backwards, then turning round and running on with it. I got it into my head that what Cruyff had done was as basic a trick as that. When Cruyff died in March 2016 of cancer aged sixty-eight – a smoker's premature age, two months after David Bowie, another icon of my generation and another smoker, died aged sixty-nine – the Cruyff turn was shown endlessly with the tributes, and I gazed on what I had failed to appreciate as a kid.

It was truly a feat of wonder. It was elegant beyond imagining. It was conducted in front of a live, global television audience of hundreds of millions, on the highest platform of the world's most popular sport. You can see that Cruyff knew exactly what he was going to do. He disguised the turn with an extravagant swing of his right foot, as if to pass long across the penalty area. His drag back was just a little more finely wrought than the sole-on-ball trick Uncle Stephen had shown me to bamboozle my friends in the playground. But watching the turn now, with an adult appreciation from a life of playing and watching football, understanding how deceptive the game's simplicity is and how infinite the task of mastering it, I love most what Cruyff did next. It is his emergence from the turn, how he runs on so effortlessly, controlling the ball so easily with his left foot, the perfection of his balance, which gets you every time.

The Sweden defender caught as the bemused foil for this brilliantly executed sporting achievement, which was done in a couple of seconds and is still being watched all around the world forty-two years later, gave a lovely interview about it after Cruyff passed away. Jan Olsson said he knew when it happened it would become famous, that there was nothing he could have done in the face of such genius, that he remembers it every day, that he was 'proud to have been there'.

'After the game,' Olsson said, 'I thanked [Cruyff] for the match and said congratulations. Even though it was 0–0, it was right to say congratulations.'

Beckenbauer, the other great player of that tournament and era, was different. He was class in footballer form. He had carved out the exotic role of sweeper and shaped it into a means of controlling the pace and direction of the whole game from the back. He was always upright, never under any pressure, forever in space. The game seemed to stop and form itself for him. Even at nine years old, I could not get enough of the way he stroked the ball with the outside of his right foot; it was so unnecessarily exquisite. I have since seen the film of him playing in the World Cup of 1966, up to the final defeat to England, and scoring against England in West Germany's 3–2 victory in 1970, and it still seems odd to see him in midfield, young, dribbling, attacking at speed. In 1974, his bouncing black curls were receding a little; he was wearing the captain's armband, he calmly played and prodded Germany back into the final after the shock of Holland's first-minute penalty, won by Cruyff. His authority looked effortless. At the end of the final, he even lifted the schlock golden trophy – newly forged because the old Jules Rimet version was given permanently to Brazil in 1970 after their third victory – with style and poise; his smile the consummate combination of pride and humility.

As many football lovers of my generation have said, partly we were so entranced because we were watching live, full football matches on television. There were no live matches besides the FA Cup final and internationals because of the authorities' fear that this would reduce the numbers of people going to the matches, when supporters' money was more necessary to each club than the small sums paid by the broadcasting companies. Then the World Cup came on and suddenly we were served up the greatest football which could be played, by these astounding stars, in colour, on television, night after night. My dad had grown oblivious and borderline hostile to football by then, and neither of my brothers was interested, so I watched it all on my own, just me and the telly, opening out to an altogether more splendid world.

The World Cup, I think, was transcendent because it connected the local efforts we made playing football and the grand feats of our proud Manchester clubs and their national contests, and broadened them, showing us that this game was beloved worldwide. We were graced by being part of something much bigger than we had imagined, greater than ourselves.

If pushed, I would say that the name Fifa did seep to some extent into my perception of the tournament, even then. The organisation was branded into the World Cup which it organised and in effect owned, and I think I was faintly aware of that, just as I understood that the FA was there as a disembodied presence in England, somehow overseeing the sport. Of course I did not know anything as a nine-year-old boy, captured for life by football and the World Cup, of Fifa's structure, its committees, or the ambitions of the men seeking to inhabit them. I didn't know anything and never gave a second's thought to money in football; I would have been quite baffled if told that the broadcasters had to pay Fifa for the right to beam the football into our homes.

Yet now that Fifa, the Fédération Internationale de Football Association, has been brought low by proven corruption on a dizzying, entrenched scale, it is ever clearer that 1974 was, coincidentally for me, the year of seismic change for the organisation. In the contested election of the president at the Frankfurt congress just before the World Cup, the Brazilian businessman João Havelange finally and controversially supplanted the seventy-nine-year-old English administrator, Sir Stanley Rous.

Contemplating the major and surprising influence we now know was brought to bear on the politics of Fifa and other sporting organisations by the boss of the sportswear firm Adidas, Horst Dassler, it is startling how dominant the brand is when you see the 1974 World Cup again. The sponsorships worked on me as they did on millions of others, as Dassler intended them to, subliminally: I found as I grew up that the three stripes of Adidas denoted coveted style and glamour, without noticing consciously that Beckenbauer was wearing their boots. Holland, too, were wearing Adidas, although famously Cruyff himself had a deal with Puma, the rival company created after a Dassler family split, and he wore two stripes on his shirt rather than the Adidas three. In the game played between East and West Germany, Adidas transcended the political divide, the wall between repressive communism and socially enlightened capitalism, and managed to have both teams wearing their boots. Even Zaire, the single representative of Africa's growing and restless football-playing countries, wore Adidas.

In 1974, as a child, I fell like so many other people for the miracle of football, the World Cup, which Fifa had organised and delivered impeccably. Of course I was not to know that the election of that year, and that tournament, was a watershed, marking the beginnings of the culture which would culminate forty-one years later in Zurich, in arrests, indictments and Fifa's traumatised, toxic implosion.

CHAPTER 2

Fifa's Smiley Face

It was exactly thirty-five years later, when I had grown up a bit, and become a journalist drawn into investigating modern football's entanglements with money, that I first encountered the American Fifa chief, Charles 'Chuck' Blazer. It was in the Gulf, in Abu Dhabi, in the summer of 2009. I was there because I was inquiring for the *Guardian* into the improbable takeover of my boyhood football club, the beloved sky blue of Manchester City, by the scion of that far-flung country's ruling family, Sheikh Mansour bin Zayed Al Nahyan. Mansour's executives had suggested that to understand Abu Dhabi, and its intentions for City, I should come and see the country when preparations were stepping up for the Fifa club world championship, which they were hosting as part of their broader nation-promoting activities. There was to be an update and a press conference, some excitements at the country's one big football stadium, and the local Al Jazira football club, which Mansour also owned.

That was why Blazer was there: he was the Fifa executive committee member with responsibility for overseeing the club world championship. A New Yorker, he had in 1996 garnered this position of power among the twenty-four men of the world governing body's highest decision-making forum, whose responsibility extended to voting on which country should host the World Cup. His ascendance came six years after Blazer had been appointed the secretary general, like a chief executive, of his geographical football region, Concacaf: the Confederation of North and Central America and Caribbean Football Associations. In that position, he had worked intimately for twenty years with Jack Warner, a former college history lecturer in his native Trinidad whom Blazer had supported to become the Concacaf president in 1990. Warner had since, as the two of them planned, led a coalescing of power for the small Caribbean islands, uniting to cast their votes as a block of thirty-one among Concacaf's forty-one countries, which included much bigger nations, principally the US, Canada and Mexico. In the election of a president, all Fifa's 211 countries' FAs vote, so Warner could become a man of influence, wielding the block Concacaf and Caribbean numbers.

Concacaf were entitled to elect or appoint three members to the Fifa executive committee, the same number as the South America football confederation, Conmebol. Oceania, representing New Zealand and mostly Pacific island countries, had one representative, the Confederation of African Football and Asian Football Confederation had four each. Uefa, representing Europe, the richest, strongest and oldest football region, had, through the politics and compromises which shaped Fifa over the years, retained eight representatives. The president, Sepp Blatter, elected by a majority of the member FAs in 1998, 2002 and unopposed in 2006, made it twenty-four, sitting around the top table at Fifa headquarters, the so-called 'House of Fifa', in Zurich.

Jack Warner would become a great deal more notorious after 2009 but he was already infamous then for his fiery, declamatory manner and for his involvement in ticketing scandals over the years. The first, in 1989, concerned the crucial World Cup final qualifying match for Trinidad and Tobago, which his home country had only to draw with the USA to claim a place in the 1990 World Cup. Terrible overcrowding outside and inside the stadium led to the accusation that Warner, the president of the Trinidad and Tobago FA, had had 15,000 too many tickets printed and sold, leading to a judicial inquiry which never reported. Watched from the packed stands the USA won the match 1–0, and they, rather than a devastated home side, went through to play at the World Cup in Italy. In 2006, Warner was found by Fifa's own inquiry, conducted by the consultants Ernst & Young, to have had tickets for that year's World Cup in Germany picked up by his son, Daryan. They were then provided to a travel company, Simpaul, owned by the Warner family, which sold them at a premium, above face value, in breach of Fifa's rules. Fifa's disciplinary committee reprimanded Jack Warner but took no action against him because, they concluded, it could not be proved that he knew about the resale of the tickets. Warner had declared himself 'vindicated'.

Blazer had not been exposed for major wrongdoing then; far from it, he was still an undisputed master of the football universe. He was known for his unashamed big-ness, his outsized personality and social life which he exhibited on a blog, proudly titled *Travels with Chuck Blazer and Friends*. Pride of place at the top of the blog was a picture of an elderly Nelson Mandela, presumably being displayed as one of Blazer's friends, in a private plane with a rug over his legs. It was taken when Mandela made the long and, to him, arduous journey from South Africa to Trinidad at Warner's request in 2004, when South Africa were entreating Warner to vote for the country to host the 2010 World Cup. Blazer and his girlfriend, Mary Lynn Blanks, are smiling, facing the camera, their expressions saying: get us, on a private plane with the living legend, Mandela.

When I went to Abu Dhabi, it was August, impossibly hot, 40 degrees, and shirt-soaking 80-degree humidity. The locals, the Emiratis, and their visitors and expatriate professionals, lived their whole lives in air-conditioned buildings, linked by journeys in air-conditioned cars. When I went outside, the heat and humidity immediately steamed my glasses up, the reverse of home where that happens when you go indoors from the cold. Mansour's people showed me some projects the country was building to fulfil the plans of Sheikh Zayed, Mansour's father, to develop an economy beyond reliance on oil, and to attain influence through cultural and sporting investment. They took me to Yass, to see the Formula One racetrack built at great cost for an Abu Dhabi Grand Prix, and the Ferrari visitor attraction adjoining it; to the Sheikh Zayed Stadium, and they talked me through the country's wealth, and plans. I noticed, as all visitors presumably must, that the only people actually outside on the streets in that heat were Indian, Pakistani or Bangladeshi workers, in thick overalls and heavy boots, toiling to build the Emiratis' towers, malls and hotels. I was aware of the campaigns by Human Rights Watch and Amnesty International highlighting the poor wages, living conditions and lack of employment rights for these people, and I sought some out to talk to. They were not the worst treated; their pay was modest and accommodation communal, but they told me others had it worse. Their greatest lament was being away from their families, many with babies and very young children whose pictures they showed me, for so many months at a time. After the majority of the Fifa executive committee, fourteen members, made the shock and far-reaching vote on 2 December 2010 to send the 2022 World Cup to another, rival Gulf emirate, Qatar, I often wondered if on their chauffeur-driven, red-carpet visits to the region, through their darkened windows, they much noticed the immigrant workers at all.

I first saw Blazer in the Emirates Palace Hotel, a vast, lavish kingdom of a complex, reported in the Dubai press to have cost $3bn to build, the second most expensive hotel in the world. The wide and long floors from the entrance to the room where Blazer was giving his audience were paved in endless marble. The domes in the roof were decorated with gold. The Al Nahyan family used the hotel partially as a seat, and the country's ruling council, I was told, met there. There were expatriate professionals, in suits, walking briskly through the complex on business, while groups of Emirati men were often sitting serenely in the lobby in traditional ankle-length dishdasha robes and headdress, running their beads through their hands and chatting.

Blazer came crashing through this scene as if he, not the Al Nahyans, owned the place. He is a big man, with a very red face set into a bushy white beard and curly white hair. Some have said he is like Santa Claus, and so he was, a dystopic American version of Father Christmas. He was, it has unavoidably to be observed, grossly overweight, on a scale of obesity so beyond a normal sight that it took a moment to adjust the eyes to it. He was so sadly enormous that he could not walk except with great difficulty, and he was in a large mobility scooter, which he was riding like a giant dodgem car, hovering cheerfully around the marble floors of the Emirates Palace. He was quite brazenly unembarrassed about the spectacle he presented; he had assistants and Fifa staff always in attendance, and he was barking orders at them, like a cartoon bad boss in a caper movie.

It would be nice to be able to describe the attention being paid to him differently, but it can only be properly expressed as bowing and scraping. This was not because the young Fifa or Abu Dhabi football officials were natural sycophants to a character like him; far from it, they came across as very professional, preparing to expertly organise another international tournament in a new host country. Their obedient respect to him was clearly because his position demanded it. He was the Fifa boss; his executive committee had bestowed the tournament on this country, and now when he was here, everybody had to scurry. His status meant that he was routinely accommodated in luxury like the Emirates Palace Hotel, which has suites for presidents and princes; he would be met in a limousine at the airport, and never leave air-conditioning during his stay. One of those whose job it was to give a positive account of Fifa's work and its people said Blazer was a football enthusiast who worked very hard – which did seem to be true – and even suggested his weight may have been due to some kind of illness, rather than a propensity to overindulge at a buffet. There was just one member of the entourage who could not help but articulate the thoughts of the honest child seeing through the emperor's fine clothes, and he muttered, out of the corner of his mouth, that Blazer was an odd sight to be the public face of promoting the world's greatest sport.

In my work up to then I had dug predominantly into English football, the Premier League club 'owners' who had previously been termed 'custodians'; their great commercial carve-up for their clubs and the FA's modern inadequacy in restraining it. This journey of investigation had led me into discovering and understanding the historic origins of football itself, and that the owners' modern banking of vast personal profits was indeed as it felt: contrary to the traditions and ethos insisted upon for a century by the FA. The governing body had from the beginning sought to incorporate core sporting values for its game, before the FA was finally overwhelmed in the new moneyed era and lost administrative clarity.

I had learned that the roots of the modern, refined, global sport were indeed in the rough folk games which English villagers used to battle over in the Middle Ages, literally fighting to carry a ball miles into the 'goal' of forcing it into the opposition territory. Some of these muddy, heaving, steaming free-for-alls survive today, most famously the Shrove Tuesday and Ash Wednesday sprawls between the 'Up'ards' and 'Down'ards', across fields, a river and through the town of Ashbourne, in Derbyshire. The phrase 'local derby', for near-neighbours clenched in an intense rivalry, derives from the grapples of old between two parishes, All Saints and St Peter's, in the city of Derby.

These battles had been gradually shaped into more recognisable tests of athleticism and skill in the 1840s, the civilising years of the English public – in fact fee-paying, private – schools, while farmworkers and country labourers were being crammed into mines, mills and factories in smog-filled new industrial cities. When the public schoolboys left for university, work or the army, they wanted to continue playing the games, so the early clubs were formed.

Each school, however, had developed its own rules, so on 26 October 1863, twelve clubs met, at the Freemason's Tavern in Lincoln's Inn, London, to agree one common form of the game, and establish what they called the Football Association. These clubs, whose names are forever imprinted into the history of what would grow so phenomenally into the world's most popular sport, were former graduates and army officers enjoying their Victorian leisure time in London and its then plusher suburbs: Barnes, the War Office Club, Crusaders, Forest of Leytonstone, No Names club of Kilburn, Crystal Palace, Blackheath, Kensington School, Percival House (Blackheath), Surbiton, Blackheath Proprietary School and Charterhouse – the only public school represented at the first meetings.

Blackheath would famously walk away because the other clubs decided to outlaw 'hacking' – booting the opposition in the shins – as an integral skill of their game, and that south London club, still playing today, threw its future in with the code developed by Rugby school. The first football match ever under the new rules was played on Saturday 19 December 1863, a 0–0 draw between clubs housed in south-west London suburbs still leafy and well-appointed today, Barnes and Richmond.

'The game was characterised by great good temper,' the *Official History of the Football Association*, written by the revered journalist and BBC radio commentator Bryon Butler, cites from a contemporary match report, 'the rules being so simple and easy of observance that it was difficult for disputes to arise.'

Football was gradually taken north and into the rowdy, grim industrial cities by former public schoolboys, whose families owned mills or other businesses, and they enlisted local men to make up the numbers. As the game's presence and popularity grew, churches and enlightened employers began to see its benefits, physical and moral, and to form clubs themselves. So, some of England's most famous great clubs, now Premier League corporations mostly owned by financial investors with no previous connections to them, have their origins in the search for spiritual space and greater church attendance in gin-soaked cities. Arsenal, Manchester United and West Ham United were formed in heavy industrial workplaces; Tottenham Hotspur was a schoolboys' club, whose founder members first met under a street lamp on Tottenham High Street. The remarkable number of church clubs, which seized on football passionately enough to become serious and professional as the game became a mass popular spectacle, included Everton (St Domingo's Church, Liverpool), Aston Villa (Villa Cross Wesleyan Chapel, Birmingham), Southampton (St Mary's), and Bolton Wanderers (Christ Church). My own club, which so entranced me through my growing up, also began as a church team: St Mark's, in Gorton, the stinking east of the world's first industrial city, Manchester.

The early efforts found a vast, untapped public appetite for the game – perhaps, I always think, the folk memory of rough, rambling countryside contests had survived as a longing in the mines, mills and factories – and crowds began to gather to watch and roar. The FA established its cup competition, the world's first, in 1871, and it was won for its initial eleven years by upper-class clubs before Blackburn Olympic, from the hard Lancashire cotton town, beat Old Etonians in 1882, 2–1 at The Oval in London. Forever after that, clubs predominantly fielding and supported by working-class men overtook the amateur aristocrats.

Inexorably, competition between the tough, ambitious new clubs in the north and Midlands had led to good players being paid, which the FA banned at first, as contrary to its spirit and ethos. Threatened by the clubs with a split, however, the FA agreed in 1885 to live with professionalism, and sought to protect football in other fundamental ways from outright takeover by commercialism.

After Fifa was formed in 1904 by seven European football associations – not the FA, by far the world's strongest and longest established, which spent two years condescending before joining in – the new world governing body also drew an innate distinction between its sport and purely commercial entertainment. At the 1906 congress in Bern, by which time the English FA had joined and sent a delegation, among seven key founding rules was one which stated that international matches had to be between teams representing national associations, that the associations had to agree to matches being played between clubs from different countries, and that 'No person should be allowed to arrange matches for personal profit.'

The English Football League, the world's first, was formed in 1888, a more brass tacks business held at the Royal Hotel, Manchester, than the public school old boys' recreational rule-setting in London twenty-five years earlier. For a competition which would inspire similar leagues all over the world and create such enduring glories, the league's founding motivation was basic: to provide regular fixtures for clubs which now had the financial commitment of paying players and catering to supporters. The twelve clubs, six from the north, six from the Midlands, which have in their histories that they were the original, founder members of the Football League, were Accrington, Aston Villa (whose chairman, William McGregor, a draper and devout Christian, was the league's initiator), Blackburn Rovers, Bolton Wanderers, Burnley, Derby County, Everton, Notts County, Preston North End, Stoke City, West Bromwich Albion and Wolverhampton Wanderers. At that very first meeting in Manchester, the representatives understood that clubs based in the cities could attract bigger crowds and so make more money than the clubs in the smaller towns. They agreed that, in order to ensure genuine competition between them, clubs should share the attendance money, the only source of income they had then, otherwise the big clubs would make more and therefore pay high wages to the best players, and dominate. So, the fair distribution of money was embedded as a principle in professional football from its very beginning.

A key discovery for me was that the Victorian gentlemen of the Football Association had also sought to restrain the potential for individuals to profit personally from the bristling commercialism of the industrial clubs. The FA allowed the clubs' founders to form limited companies, to raise money and protect themselves from the liabilities of paying wages and building grounds, but introduced rules to prevent the shareholders making money for themselves. This bargain, between business and football's founding principles, not perfect, perhaps too amateurish, but insisting on a core sporting purpose, was the basis for the Football League and its clubs' remarkable growth into and through the twentieth century. It had grown to four divisions after the First World War, included ninety-two clubs throughout England and Wales, and marked an extraordinary 100 years of story-making in 1988.

The big clubs' breakaway from this and the other essential bases of the sporting constitution came as the amounts of money available, principally from television, grew in the 1980s. In 1992, the First Division clubs broke away, to form the Premier League, so that they would not have to share the bonanza of a new payTV deal with the rest of football. A small group at the head of the FA somehow persuaded themselves that they would become pre-eminent in English football and deliver a blow to a Football League they had come to see as administrative rivals, by backing this big clubs' breakaway. The FA also allowed the clubs' shareholders to form holding companies to bypass the old rules limiting the cash they could make out of them, and as the money and exposure of the Premier League soared, the 'owners' began to make fortunes by selling the clubs.

Sheikh Mansour, an oil-rich prince with an enthusiasm for football, had in the 2000s seen overseas investors taking over Premier League clubs, paying the British shareholders tens or hundreds of millions of pounds, and began to consider a purchase of his own. When Manchester City arrived as a proposition, he considered it just right: a historic, big-city club, with many fans grown loyal over decades and a new stadium built for the 2002 Commonwealth Games and converted for City – not a club with an old ground, like Tottenham's, which needed work. The Abu Dhabi takeover took the forces assailing modern English football into a different dimension. In Mansour, we had an education into the mega-wealth of the Gulf states and, in the absence of elected governments, their ruling dynasties; the Al Nahyan family had ruled in Abu Dhabi since the eighteenth century. The countries were sophisticated; their modern rulers agreed strategies to develop rapidly, looking also to a future when the oil or gas propelling their fortunes would run out. 'Soft power', the association with culture, sport and the media, for the countries to become a presence, economic partner and accepted part of the conversation in the developed West, had become integral to the strategies. In Qatar, Abu Dhabi's neighbours and entrenched religious and political rivals, such a strategy resulted in the bid, which always looked spectacularly overreaching, to host the 2022 World Cup. Their stunning success in gaining enough votes was the catalyst which many people, Sepp Blatter included, believe heralded Fifa's unravelling, because it appeared that its sole reason could only be money.

The Abu Dhabi nation-building strategy was a phenomenon, but had been steadier, over a longer term than Qatar's. Sheikh Zayed bin Sultan Al Nahyan, Mansour's father, was revered as the visionary, having taken over as ruler in 1966 and begun the process of shaping Abu Dhabi to a modern strategy. In Qatar, the Emir who strove for a similar plan to that of his rivals in the UAE, Hamad bin Khalifa Al Thani, finally overthrew his conservative father in a bloodless coup as late as 1995, and appears to have believed he had to catch up fast. In Abu Dhabi, they had built modern housing, hotels, offices and malls and more recently begun the soft power cultural acquisitiveness: buying prestige attractions such as branches of the Louvre and the Guggenheim, and building the Formula One racetrack at Yass. It was a part of this broadening out which led the country to consider bidding for Fifa events, but Abu Dhabi decided against the World Cup, which would have required a multi-stadium building programme on the same startling scale, in a tiny country, with which Qatar has now saddled itself. Instead, they bid for the 2009 and 2010 club world championships, played between the champions of Fifa's six global confederations, which would still showcase the country on television around the world, and bring supporters to it. Abu Dhabi, they told me, had to actually pay Fifa for the right to host this championship, then pay to put it on – and, as part of the package, to host Chuck Blazer in the manner to which he had become accustomed.

At the Emirates Palace I interviewed him briefly; he was incidental to the story I was working to understand, but I talked to him for form, politeness almost, because he was there. From memory, I don't think Blazer scooted over to me; I think at the appointed time, after his press conference, I was ushered to where he was sitting in his mobility scooter. He was jolly, very loud and bullish, about the merits of the tournament Abu Dhabi were staging for Fifa. It was getting good coverage, he said, and would be shown in more than 200 countries.

'Our sponsors participate as well,' he said.

I asked him how much it was all costing the country, as it has billions to spend on sporting and cultural assets like Fifa tournaments and Manchester City, and whether it was making a huge loss to put the championships on. Blazer essentially said it was, but it was worth it to Abu Dhabi:

'Budgets and profits are strange things. How you measure them isn't clearly defined, between governments and sponsors; the lines are fuzzy. In the end, it's an investment they are making for the public. They end up with training facilities and infrastructure, trained people, then become integrated into other sporting events and they recognise it. Where else do you get a laboratory as perfect as this? You shouldn't talk of it in terms of profits and losses – they are investments. Everybody is excited, so can you call it a loss?'

I asked him about himself and he told me, eagerly and a little boastfully, about having been the secretary general of Concacaf for nineteen years, a remarkably long tenure, and on the Fifa executive committee for thirteen. They had just finished the Concacaf Gold Cup, he told me with great satisfaction, at which a crowd of 80,000 at the Giants Stadium in New Jersey had watched Mexico beat the USA 5–0 in the final. The Concacaf club Champions League was now kicking off, he said; it was all doing very well.

I asked Blazer what his background was, what he did before attaining his positions at Concacaf and Fifa and becoming such an evidently great success story. He asked me straight away if I was familiar with the smiley face. Of course, I said, instantly. It was everywhere when I was young; I always associate it with my auntie Sharon and uncle Alan, who were teenagers in the 1960s and whose house in the seventies was filled with fun, LPs and frisbees.

'I made the smiley faces,' Blazer told me.

He left me with the distinct impression that he was saying he designed and owned the whole copyright on the smiley face, but

I have dug out my notes of the conversation in Abu Dhabi and he seems in fact not to have gone that far. I just wrote down that he'd said he made them, that he had had a factory making smiley face buttons – badges, as we call them – from 1968 to 1972. He told me that he had made his fortune on that worldwide craze, sold the factory and had enough money to retire at twenty-seven. Before that he had been a prodigy, he told me; he had graduated from college at nineteen. Then he went into business, and he had done his first leveraged buyout at twenty.

It was a dizzyingly good and perfect story to tell; it certainly floored me. It declared his genius, that he was a man of wealth and substance, his fortune made from something cool and universally recognisable like the smiley face. His story also explained how he could be here, spending all his time on football, when it was not clear or yet public that the barons of Fifa, like him, were making huge money out of the game's governing bodies. This large and booming character was, he was telling me cheerfully, a living embodiment of the American dream, and football was clearly very lucky to have him.

It was only years later that I learned with a start, feeling an anger which surprised me, that his smiley face story was a calling card of his, but that it was a trumped-up story. The truth was set out in the book *American Huckster,* written about Blazer by the New York *Daily News* journalists Mary Papenfuss and Teri Thompson, who broke the story in 2014 that Blazer, having been found to have committed tax evasion, fraud and money laundering on a gigantic scale at Concacaf, had in 2011 agreed to wear a wire for the FBI, to see if he could implicate some of his colleagues at Fifa. The book also found that having in his early years been a hustler in Queens, New York, Blazer went around telling people he invented the smiley face badge. In fact it was designed by graphic artist Harvey Ball, and marketed, on posters, mugs and dozens of different products including badges, by two Philadelphia entrepreneur brothers, Bernard and Murray Spain. Blazer had, it was true, been contracted by the Spains to manufacture the badges, when he was running a factory in Queens. The book said that in fact Blazer had defrauded the Spains, selling badges out of the factory back door to other retailers who had no licence for the smiley face, rather than keeping to his exclusive contract with them.

Via his daughter, Dana Spain, who recently stood to be mayor in Philadelphia and was easy to track down, I talked to Bernard Spain. He told me that he and his brother Murray, the sons of Russian immigrants, had opened their first Hallmark store, selling gifts and gimmicks, with 'a bit of borrowed money', in 1959. He said they hit on pop culture fads, Andy Warhol's Campbell's soup can design, the student craze for traffic signs – 'Our motto was: Why Steal Them Off the Street?' he said – and built up the business 'bit by bit'. In 2000, the Spains, who had moved into dollar stores, sold their whole chain of 101 stores to Dollar Tree, a Nasdaq-quoted company, for $300m.

'We are a true American dream,' he said, 'not like Chuck.'

Remembering the smiley face, he said they had learned to expand the range of products on which a design would go, to maximise the sales while a craze lasted, and when the badges took off in popularity 'We needed somebody who could pump them out in big quantities. Somebody said there was a company in Queens, New York, so I went there with my brother, met Chuck Blazer. I think the factory was owned by his wife's uncle, not by him, and he was running it. He said he could do our order, and we paid him three cents a button, which we sold for ten cents.

'Then when we were up to our ears in orders all over the world, we heard from one of our drivers that he saw buttons going out the back door of the factory, to other people. We realised he was making additional buttons and selling them on his own, or stealing from our own orders and short-shipping us. We complained all the time – "Where the fuck are our buttons?" – and he had his excuses. We didn't sue; we're pragmatic businessmen; in fact we never sued anybody in business, period, we weren't litigious.'

I had not quite been prepared for how personally affronted the Spains would be, to hear that Blazer used their product as a claim to his own brilliant achievements.

'We think nothing of him; he's a cheat and a fraud, a bad guy, and if that's all he can do, steal anyone's thunder ...' Spain said, his wife calling out further insults of Chuck in the background. Spain also said that he and his brother, who did own the copyright on the smiley face and made a mini-industry out of it, did not make enough money out of it to retire when the craze fizzled out, and there was no way

Blazer could have done by selling the factory, even if he did own it, which they believed he didn't.

When he heard that Blazer had been caught up in the fall of Fifa, Spain said that after all the years, he and his wife were not surprised.

'I thought he must be involved in criminal activity up to his neck when I heard.'

Looking back, the summer I met Chuck Blazer in the Emirates Palace Hotel in Abu Dhabi was the high point for him before the fall, for many of the men who had been rulers of their football empires for decades, for Sepp Blatter's Fifa itself. They were making fortunes for themselves, whole countries had to bow down in homage, they had the World Cup in South Africa to come in 2010, which would be feted for remaking Africa's very image and for being a fitting tribute to Nelson Mandela's humanity and heroism. Blatter's ascendance from a childhood spent in the provincial Valais region of Switzerland in the Alps was still so stratospheric that he was said to be angling strategically for the summit of a Nobel peace prize. Fifa's executive committee had not yet staggered the world with the majority votes for Russia and Qatar, Mohamed bin Hammam had not yet fatefully challenged Blatter for the presidency of Fifa in 2011, some of the chief power-brokers had not yet self-destructively turned on each other. The FBI had not yet decided that Fifa itself, the world governing body of football, might in fact be a RICO – a racketeering influenced criminal organisation – and begun to investigate. Chuck Blazer was not carrying a recording device, as he would in the fine hotels of the dignitaries at the 2012 Olympic Games, in his key fob, reportedly because he was too obese for a wire to be run in the standard way up his stomach. He was still a carefree baron then, free to bark his way merrily on his mobility scooter around a seven-star palace in the Gulf, every door opened for him, his every want fulfilled, cheerily telling the world that it had him to thank for the smiley face.

CHAPTER 3

1904: 'A Pure Sport'

Contemplating Fifa's modern disgrace, the shocking arrests and charges of nine senior figures in May 2015 in Zurich, days before Sepp Blatter's re-coronation as president, Chuck Blazer's and others' pleas of guilty to huge frauds, it is natural to look back at the founding fathers and imagine them turning in their graves. Like the beginnings of football itself in England's market towns, schools and inner-city churches, the origins of Fifa are heroically small scale. The organisation was formed at a meeting on 21 May 1904 at 229 rue St Honoré, Paris, in a back room of the offices of the Union des Sociétés Françaises de Sports Athlétiques, an amateur French sports association. Representatives of only seven countries' fledgling football associations were there, wanting to facilitate international matches between their teams: Holland, Switzerland, Denmark, Belgium, France, Sweden and Espir FC Madrid, representing Spain, with Germany wiring their intention to sign up. That these associations solemnly and grandly called themselves the Fédération Internationale de Football Association after such a threadbare meeting was a statement of sporting cooperation and ambition. Yet the men in the room can have had no idea how remarkably football, and their organisation, would grow throughout their century.

The English journalist Guy Oliver, editorial director at the Fifa museum in downtown Zurich, a diplomatic distance from the organisation's bunker-like headquarters up the hill near the zoo, cherishes these founders' original mission and achievements, but cautions against overidealising their motives. It was not consciously, Oliver has found looking through the archives, all about world peace, diplomacy through sporting endeavour or any other of the vaulting political hyperbole indulged in by Blatter in his pomp. Oliver contrasts the formation of Fifa in that sparse back-room huddle with the re-establishment of the Olympic Games ten years earlier in 1894, also in Paris, at a conference held in the amphitheatre of the Sorbonne. Pierre de Coubertin, the initiator, was explicitly inspired by ideals of internationalism, pacifism and peace among nations, and seventy-eight delegates attended, from countries in Europe, the USA and New Zealand. The modern Olympics were draped from the beginning in such proclaimed virtues, but Oliver has learned that the founding principle of football's international federation was more grounded: to play the game and organise competition between countries.

While acknowledging that, you can still recognise there was idealism and innocence in these beginnings, that exactly ten years before Europe would be torn apart in a terrible war, men from different countries were gathering for the simple purpose of agreeing the rules for a game to play with each other. Money does not seem to have been any part of the motivation; there was very little to be made from football then, in those European countries. Later, after the First World War, Jules Rimet served as president of Fifa from 1921 to 1954, a thirty-three-year era of determined globalisation including his landmark foundation of the World Cup in 1930. He was a religious Christian who did subscribe to de Coubertin's view of sport as a force for peace and goodwill between nations. Rimet talked of Fifa at the end of his tenure as 'a spiritual community to which we all adhere with one heart and one will', and of football as 'a channel for imparting the finest human qualities', listing discipline, moderation and solidarity among its virtues.

'Loyalty to the spirit of the game, fairness to the adversary, is perhaps the most remarkable quality of football,' Rimet said, in his noted address to the Fifa congress in Rio de Janeiro before the start of the 1950 World Cup held in Brazil. 'Without it a match would be devoid of all meaning and would return to the condition of the barbarous games of antiquity.'

He concluded that football had moral benefits it should impart to the world: 'Our aim must be to transfer these idealistic qualities of the game to our everyday life.'

The founders had tried and failed at the beginning to involve the English FA, by far the strongest and longest-established football association, which had its flourishing professional league by then, a bristling population of clubs at all levels. The British had codified the game and given it to the world – literally, as many clubs in Europe, South America, Africa, Asia and Oceania were founded on the initiatives of British expatriates or commercial travellers. Robert Guérin, the Frenchman who initiated Fifa, approached the gentlemen of the FA by letter and went to London twice in 1903, but found Lord Kinnaird, the chairman, and Frederick Wall, the top-hatted, frock-coated secretary, sniffy. Guérin complained, in a famous phrase cited in all the histories, that dealing with the English was like 'slicing water with a knife'.

For an English lover of football, to understand this early history is a wincing, at times embarrassing journey, with uncomfortable parallels to growing British isolationism today, a recognition of lessons not learned. The FA wrote to Guérin after he had taken the trouble to see them, replying in November 1903 that its council 'cannot see the advantages' of an international federation. The FA did not take part in that inaugural meeting in Paris, sending a letter of apology instead of a delegate. Then, bizarrely and insultingly, the year after the seven European countries formed Fifa, the English FA held its own conference at the Crystal Palace in London, on April Fool's Day 1905, and resolved that some new international union should be formed.

Guy Oliver's delvings into the Fifa archives have led him to seek some rehabilitation for the English attitude, though, and plead also for some understanding and perspective.

'In 1904 [when the FA was invited to be part of Fifa's founding] the four nations of the United Kingdom were the unrivalled powers in football,' Oliver has written.

'So an international body created by anyone else faced a Herculean task of being taken seriously by the British. Consider the following parallel. Imagine American football enthusiasts today in France, Denmark, Belgium, Sweden, Spain and the Netherlands decided to set up an international federation for American football. That such a body could become the pre-eminent body in American football within a decade would seem absurd, but that is exactly the scale of what Fifa achieved in association football.'

Oliver reads the correspondence from the English FA, with the fact that the football associations of Argentina, India, Canada and South Africa were already affiliated to the FA, and the Crystal Palace conference, less as insularity and more as illustrating a keenness to be a dominant force in organising international football. By 1906, the FA decided to become fully involved in the new Fifa organisation, and sent a delegation to the June conference in Bern, Switzerland, including Daniel Woolfall, the FA treasurer and Blackburn Rovers committee member. He was elected Fifa president at the meeting, a recognition of the English FA's size, history and know-how, and he served until 1918. Woolfall was the first of three English Fifa presidents out of just six in total during the seventy formative years of Fifa, before its culture irrevocably changed after the Brazilian João Havelange was elected president in 1974.

For forty years after that, British influence waned and sank, as the organisation widened its activites far beyond its founding European focus. Fifa had only two more presidents: Havelange, for a monumental twenty-four years until 1998, when his protégé and former secretary general, Blatter, achieved the reward for a lifetime's ambition and obsessive self-advancing by ascending himself, and he held on for seventeen years.

The 1906 Bern congress laid the foundations for Fifa's status as the undisputed international federation, and for football's global growth. The delegates agreed that the laws of the game should be those of the English FA, that only one national association from each country, truly controlling football there, would be recognised and admitted to Fifa, and that international matches be arranged at Fifa's annual congress. Woolfall and Wall reported back to the FA's constituent members in its council that its game was evolving steadily beyond British shores. They cited 'the importance of continental football', and 'the opinion that in a short time clubs under the jurisdiction of the Football Association will consider continental football a part of their arrangements and will regularly visit and receive continental clubs'.

They continued, with a landmark view: 'The Football Association should use all its influence to regulate football on the continent as a pure sport and give all continental associations the full benefit of the many years' experience of the Football Association.'

The strength and depth of English football compared to the nascent game developing in other European countries is illustrated by the fact that, to play international matches and give other countries a chance, the FA formed and fielded an amateur team. Still, the team was so strong that England's amateurs won the first two football tournaments played at the Olympic Games, in 1908 in London, beating Denmark 2–0, and Stockholm in 1912, again defeating Denmark, this time 4–2. Oliver has argued strongly that these and the three subsequent Olympic football tournaments were in effect the first World Cups, which explains the twenty-six-year gap between Fifa's formation and the first World Cup, played in Uruguay in 1930.

Sadly, England had flounced out of Fifa twice by then, after rows in which the English high-handedness looks dismal yet painfully familiar. First, in 1920, after the slaughter of the war was over and when other European countries' football associations were slowly resuming sporting relations, the British FAs resigned because they did not want to recognise associations which authorised matches against Germany and the other defeated countries' teams. The British FAs rejoined in 1924, but then had another dispute with Fifa, this time disagreeing over the purity of amateurism in the Olympics, which argued that players should be compensated for time taken off work. This was in 1928, for the second time in four years, and two years before Fifa would first organise the greatest international football tournament in the world.

In his excellent book *Fifa: The Men, the Myths and the Money*, Professor Alan Tomlinson winces at the condescending, 'British know-all fashion' with which Frederick Wall delivered the decision to Fifa's then secretary, the Dutchman Carl Hirschman: 'The great majority of the Associations affiliated with the Fédération Internationale de Football Association are of comparatively recent formation,' Wall sniffed, 'and as a consequence cannot have the knowledge which only experience can bring.'

Rimet is credited with marrying his religious idealism for football's human potential with a real-world recognition that working men had to be paid for their time. He absorbed football associations from Africa – Egypt, in 1923, was the first – Asia and Central America, extending Fifa well beyond Europe during his tenure. And he steered an acceptance of full professionalism, which meant football breaking with the Olympics and founding its own World Cup. Oliver argues that this pragmatism by a Fifa visionary spared football the oppressiveness and pettiness with which amateurism was piously enforced at the Olympics and in other sports for far too long, and partly accounts for the game's great growth and accelerated capturing of the world's imagination.

England, still not members of Fifa after storming off, did not play in the Uruguay World Cup, won by the host country which had secured the right to stage it partly by promising to cover the other national teams' travel expenses. Nor did England deign to participate in the World Cups of 1934 and 1938, both won by Italy, before Europe was convulsed by war again.

Fifa moved to Switzerland in 1932 after it was plunged into financial crisis by precipitous losses Hirschman had made on investments in the Great Depression. Initially, and for twenty-two years after that, Fifa ran world football's affairs and organised the World Cups from just two rooms in an office building on Zurich's main Bahnhofstrasse, which runs through the centre of the city from the grand old train station. To professionalise the operation after the Hirschman debacle, Fifa took on its first actual employee as secretary, the German former player Ivo Schricker, who administered the operation from those cramped rooms, with just one assistant, for twenty years.

In 2006, seventy-three years later, Fifa moved into its current headquarters, an impenetrable-looking black block of predominantly Brazilian granite, set high on a hill, in grounds with manicured football pitches, the flags of all its nations, and plants and foliage in the gardens from football's six global regions. With floors sunk underground, although predominantly for parking, it is perennially described as a bunker, and looks inescapably like a building an organisation would choose if it had plots to hatch, secrets to hide. To build this House of Fifa, from the fortunes it was making principally from selling TV and marketing rights to the modern World Cup, Blatter's organisation had spent 240m CHF ($235m).

The move to Switzerland had partly been prompted by the basic need to have a permanent base somewhere; for years the address of football's world governing body had been Hirschman's home in Amsterdam. Switzerland was neutral in the war and an agreeable, well-appointed country in which to settle; de Coubertin had moved the International Olympic Committee to Lausanne, in 1915, while the First World War was raging. Switzerland's welcome extended to a generous legal status for sporting associations, which are spared taxation on their profits as they are considered to be dedicated to the public good. This freedom from tax and the transparency required of commercial companies – Switzerland was home to discreet, private banks which would be accused of accepting deposits of Nazi gold during the war – was no doubt helpful in 1932, but the privileges became the focus of fierce criticism as Fifa rang in multi-billion dollar television and sponsorship deals in the modern era.

Looking back from the current mega-money and scandal-strewn incarnation of Fifa, it is remarkable to think that the president, for thirteen years from 1961, was an Englishman as rigid and imbued with the amateur spirit as Sir Stanley Rous. Viewed with a jaded eye today, it is easy to lampoon Rous as a stiff-backed man out of his time, obsessed with protocol and the rulebook, as the world changed around him. He was, it is true, the ultimate FA blazer, although he began his career as the FA's secretary in 1934 being ticked off for not wearing a top hat and frock coat to his first match, as Wall, from whom he took over, had done. Rous had opted, he recalled in his memoir, *Football Worlds*, for 'a dashing pair of plus fours'.

Written in 1978, four years after he lost the election to Havelange, *Football Worlds* is actually a priceless historical document, chronicling a prodigious life in sport, from his birth in Mutford, a tiny Suffolk village, in 1895, at the beginnings of football itself, to Fifa president, organising the World Cups on colour television of Pelé, Cruyff and Beckenbauer. His childhood reads like a football administrator's version of *Cider with Rosie*, Laurie Lee's classic evocation of isolated English village life before cars and technology changed it forever, only without the flushed sex under a cart with a girl like Rosie – and without any cider, either. In just the third paragraph of the first page, young Stanley, aged fifteen, is lining up grown men, 'assembled farmhands and off-duty fishermen', and organising them into a football team. Rous wondered if it had been 'my own fervent enthusiasm' or 'the fortunate accident' of being six foot tall, 'which gave me a certain air of authority beyond my age'.

The most lasting image in his remembrances, which took in a career as a top-class referee, twenty-seven years as the FA secretary, thirteen as Fifa president, organising the 1948 post-war London 'austerity' Olympics for which he received his knighthood, and unquantifiable voluntary work in the service of sport and charity, was a reminiscence from his youth. Rous used to cycle the twenty-five miles, two hours there and back, from his small village to watch Norwich City at their then ground, The Nest. He wrote that he had an extra step fitted to the back axle of his bike so that 'the keenest of my village boys' could stand on it, with hands on Rous' shoulders, and so he would be able to cycle there taking a passenger, too.

'We had to be keen to do that journey on a rainy day,' Rous wrote, 'but we thought it well worth the effort when any of the contemporary heroes was in form.'

Rous' was, when you consider it, a remarkable life and career of dedication to sport, which can be argued to have been in the best of English traditions. True to the British integration of sport into schools, Rous qualified as a teacher and had impressed with his coaching methods and organisational skills at Watford Grammar School when he applied for and got the job of succeeding Wall at the FA. Among the other many careful modernisations he introduced to football's first ever governing body was to rewrite the rules of the game, which he completed in 1938. The rules had been first written in the Victorian English of 1863, and then their additions and modifications had become sprawling and sometimes difficult to understand, as Rous had found as a referee. So he unscrambled and collated them, producing a newly streamlined set of rules so clear that they lasted without a further overhaul for almost sixty years, until 1997. Rous wrote in his memoir that a member of the FA staff arranged to have the new laws copyrighted in his name, but he never charged any fee in the forty years the copyright lasted. He said: 'My object was simply to ensure they could not be tampered with, without my being consulted.'

When his successor, Denis Follows, was understood to have suggested to Fifa that the FA should charge a fee for use of the rules which the English body had developed, Rous said: 'Privately I warned him off a course which would have lined no pocket but my own.'

In the Fifa museum in Zurich, they have an extract of Rous' original rules as an exhibit in one of the glass cases. It is his first page, noting from rule one: Number of Players:

'The game shall be played by two teams each consisting of not more than eleven players.'

Then he noted the dimensions of 'the ground', the markings, the size and position of the goals 'joined together by a horizontal cross bar 8 feet from the ground'; and below that, rule number three: The Ball.

The rules in the Fifa glass case were handwritten by Rous on a basic, now yellowing piece of lined A4 paper, which looks as if it came from a standard school exercise book. Seeing it there was a surprisingly emotional experience, far more stirring than the caps and cups of legendary players housed in other cabinets and even the huge, actual World Cup trophy, whose lump of gold looks just a little gross and over the top, while still redolent of heroic feats. It was not just the simplicity of Rous' rules, forming the basis for so extravagantly successful a world sport as football. There is something almost child-like in them, as if he did it for homework; you could imagine Rous leant over his desk, sucking his pen, frowning hard, then making his best effort at the rules in his neatest handwriting.

His ultimate supplanting by Havelange, a formidable and icily ambitious Brazilian businessman, and the global development work and commercialisation of Fifa after that have cast Rous as a stuffy, incongruous, stuck-in-time colonialist, overtaken by modernity. But that is a caricature; his achievements merit a more generous assessment, and he was more forward-looking than superficial hindsight suggests; indeed at the time, he was described in the press as a moderniser and internationalist. He had the view of the FA's purpose expressed by Woolfall after that 1906 Fifa congress, that it should be part of and seek to influence football worldwide rather than turn away from it. Rous was always involved in international cooperation, even as a referee, and he criticised the 'aloof' FA which 'withdrew into ourselves' and flounced out of Fifa. Of the FA's absence from the world governing body, he wrote: 'I certainly had no thought that this was splendid isolation. To me it was a matter of regret and a constant cause of difficulty that we were not more closely associated with Fifa.'

He became determined to lead the FA back into Fifa as soon as he could after the war, and as early as November 1945 went to an executive committee meeting in Zurich with Arthur Drewery, the FA chairman. They found a welcome there, the FA and other British associations were readmitted in 1946, and Drewery, a fish-processing businessman and former chairman of Grimsby Town, would become Fifa president in 1956. Those were still the days, despite an increasingly internationalised organisation which included many more South American and Asian countries' FAs – the African FAs mostly joined after their countries gained independence in the 1960s – of European domination at Fifa. It seems to sum up how different an age it was, to think that the president of Fifa, administering the sport for the whole world, was the former chairman of a northern provincial English football club like Grimsby.

Rous' steady, sterling work at the FA and Fifa, his organising competence, attention to detail and commitment to progress, led to him being asked to take on the role of president in 1961, although he too had to win an election over two other candidates. He was always unpaid at Fifa, and says in his book that he did the job on his pension from the FA, which must have been modest. He was already sixty-six when he took this on, describing his presidency at Fifa as 'the most exciting and the most exacting 13 years of my life'. Rather than seeing it as being 'pensioned off,' he said:

'Here was the chance to use all my experience and to indulge my lifelong interest in international cooperation … I was determined Fifa should take the broadest view looking at problems from a world viewpoint, not from Europe's or South America's. I was determined too that Fifa should keep the game moving smoothly on without undue checks in the pattern of development.'

In modern times, Rous is remembered for his stance on the whites-only Football Association of South Africa (FASA), standing firm against the boycotting of the apartheid country demanded from the early 1960s by the growing number of post-colonial, independent black African nations which were members of Fifa. Rous gave the impression of being instinctively sympathetic to apartheid and hostile to African football development, and the votes against him by some African football associations made the crucial difference to Havelange winning the 1974 election. Rous himself resented that suggestion, and seems to have been genuinely bewildered by it, and he was aggrieved at the loss of so many African votes in the election.

Rous maintained that his view on South Africa was consistent with a principle he repeatedly restated, that sport itself should not indulge in politics. He argued that if a country was internationally recognised, Fifa should accept its football association and not set itself up as a judge of its politics or social conditions. That was, for example, the basis of his backing the readmission of German FAs to Fifa after the war, which was opposed by members of some countries which had particularly suffered under the terror of the Nazis. 'That was successfully achieved in 1950,' Rous wrote, 'and what a major contribution Germany has since made to international football.'

But his stance on embracing FASA within Fifa was never accepted by most African countries' FAs. The Confederation of African Football (CAF) had banned FASA for refusing to send a racially mixed team to the first African Cup of Nations, the year of CAF's formation, in 1957. After FASA were suspended in 1961, Rous decided to conduct a fact-finding commission in South Africa in January 1963, taking with him a white USA representative, Jimmy McGuire. They concluded that 'notwithstanding the [South African] Government's policy of separate development, FASA was not itself practising racial discrimination'. He based this on arguing that FASA was only following its government's policies, which it was not entitled to defy, and that it was allowing associations representing football played by other racial groups to affiliate: the Bantu, Indian and 'Coloured' associations. He argued that FASA was working towards integration despite apartheid, which he said he always 'disliked'.

This was a very long way from good enough for the African FAs and a majority of the countries populating Fifa. At the Tokyo congress the following year, FASA were suspended again, for twelve years, until the 1976 congress in Montreal, when the FA of the still-apartheid country was expelled. Some African FAs wrote to Rous accusing him of condoning apartheid, and then, furious at the lack of places available for African countries at the 1966 World Cup, CAF organised a boycott of the tournament. Rous' insistence on a fine separation between sport and politics, and perhaps his cultural perspective as a product of colonial Britain, seems to have led him to underestimate, and not himself feel, the visceral repulsion and opposition of the black Africans to apartheid.

He also took a position on Chile in 1973 which looks ludicrously blind to political reality: refusing to allow the Soviet Union to play their World Cup qualifier in a neutral country, because, they had complained, the national stadium in Santiago had been used to torture and kill left-wing targets after the brutal coup of General Augusto Pinochet that year. Rous is identified with the refusal to agree to this request, and to insist the Soviet Union play the game in Chile, although it was a majority decision of the relevant committee, which sent two representatives to look, and received the report that 'based on what they saw and heard in Santiago, life was back to normal.' Rous believed he was offering a special privilege to suggest the game be played in Chile but at a different stadium, and he was nonplussed at the Soviet Union's refusal. He oversaw their automatic elimination from the 1974 World Cup for refusing to play the qualifier, then pronounced himself bewildered at the 'political vendetta' he complained the Soviet Union waged against him afterwards.

But it is a mistake to judge Rous' entire tenure and character by these two episodes when his approach appeared to jar seriously with decent thinking. His insistence that Fifa should not take a political stance was elsewhere robust and admirable: he stood up against China's demands that breakaway Taiwan should be banned from Fifa, on the same basis, that it was an internationally recognised independent country, and Fifa should not be used to fight a political battle. Often described as 'paternalistic', he was internationalist at Fifa and believed he always did his best to encourage development of the game everywhere around the world.

Rous pushed for the development of confederations, the groupings of countries' football associations by region, including CAF, because, he argued, it was 'essential that Fifa decentralise rather than become a vast bureaucracy based in Europe and out of touch … and unsympathetic to the needs of other continents'.

This encouragement of the confederations looks innocent now. Rous saw them as a necessary buffer between the national football associations and Fifa in the running of the game, on which he argued everybody involved must be wholly focused. He drafted the first statutes for Europe's confederation, Uefa, which was established in 1954, and as the FA secretary he supported the participation of English champions in the new European Cup, against the parochial objections of the Football League. Rous specifically encouraged the formation of Concacaf, and efforts to hasten the development of football in the US, which he always believed 'has the capacity to become a world leader in the game'. He also helped in 1966 with the formation of the newest confederation, Oceania, then including Australia, whose FA moved to the Asian Football Confederation in 2005. The secretary right back then was Charles Dempsey, a Scot living in New Zealand, celebrated still by Oceania as its founding 'father'.

In 1966, the year the detailed plans Rous left at the FA for the World Cup in England came to delirious fruition for the home country, he was, at Fifa, propounding a new system of making financial grants to African and other developing football countries. Rous believed in this initiative; he travelled the world to document the need for Fifa to help financially with development, and he worked hard to persuade the European-dominated executive committee to endorse the policy, and the finance committee to release 500,000 CHF to fund it. The aims were to provide direct financial support to confederations serving developing countries, in order to employ a full-time secretary, pay for and encourage coaching courses and conferences, make technical films, help with the administrative and equipment costs of improving courses, and with the cost of tournaments.

Havelange, when he challenged Rous, promised to fund more development programmes, and expand the number of countries playing in the World Cup from sixteen to twenty-four, to open it up to more developing countries, which has created the perception that Rous was against both. Guy Oliver has found in the archives that this standard view of Rous is unfair. In fact, Rous circulated proposals as early as July 1970 asking for the confederations' views on expanding the World Cup to twenty-four, or thirty-two teams, as it subsequently would be. Expansion to thirty-two, he proposed, would allow four countries from Africa, four from Oceania and Asia, and four from Central and North America, alongside, on merit, thirteen from Europe, five from South America, plus the host country and holders. He was suggesting this could happen as soon as the forthcoming 1974 World Cup in West Germany.

Rous received a virulently negative response from Uefa, always jealous of ceding European control and dominance of international football, and the proposal was blocked. The African countries still did not have a single guaranteed place at that World Cup, having to go through a play-off with the Asian Football Confederation qualifier to make it to the tournament. Havelange, ultimately having won the election casting himself as the patron of international development, was then able to push the proposal through given his mandate, expanding the World Cup from sixteen to twenty-four countries' teams for the 1982 tournament in Spain. Rous, when facing the rival candidacy of Havelange, declined to actively electioneer, issuing only a modest pamphlet saying he would stand on his record, which he believed was self-evident: thirteen years of achievements, development and admirable progress. Given the stories, then and since, that Havelange was dispensing cash and promises to win votes, Rous' final statement in what passed for his manifesto looks a little barbed: 'I can offer no special inducements to obtain support in my re-election, nor have I canvassed for votes except through this communication. I prefer to let the record speak for itself.'

As he acknowledged himself, it was not enough. In his memoir, Rous had reined in the bitterness he felt and had expressed in the immediate aftermath, but he still said:

'The major disappointment for me was the African reaction. They had 38 votes to Europe's 33 and their influence was decisive in Havelange's election. The hurtful part of this was that I had done so much for the development of football in Africa during my term as president. Indeed the Europeans who contribute the bulk of Fifa's money often criticised me for giving too much aid to African associations.'

It has been written that the reason Havelange secured the votes was bribery. One report of the time talked of 'small brown envelopes in large black hands', a phrase which has not travelled well down the decades. It may have been true, like many other allegations of bribery which have infested Fifa elections and votes since that key regime change of 1974, but no cases have been provably documented. David Yallop, in his book *How They Stole the Game*, is repulsed by Havelange and alleges, based on research, that he was corrupt in business and at Fifa. But an example Havelange volunteered himself, about the 1974 election campaign, can also illuminate a different dimension of world football politics at play.

Havelange told Yallop that a friend of his, who was a senior executive at the airline Lufthansa, had paid for the travel costs of six African delegates to go to the crucial congress in Frankfurt – and there they voted for Havelange. That looks like a suitable case of bribery, or at least a blatant conflict of interest, if Fifa had had any kind of structures to enforce an ethics code in 1974. But it also demonstrates that in 1974 significant numbers of African football associations had no money, not even enough for the air fare to send their president or another representative to a congress of Fifa as important as the one which would elect the president.

More recently, in April 2016, the Brazilian academic Luiz Guilherme Burlamaqui presented research at a Harvard University conference, 'Soccer as a Global Phenomenon', documenting further the poverty of the smaller football associations in Rous' time. The FAs had a small fixed fee to pay for their membership of Fifa, in addition to the levy on international match income which Fifa still charged as its basic means of income to run itself. Burlamaqui found that in 1974 the fixed fee was only $150 annually, yet 'for minor [African] federations, such as Togo or Chad, the $150 was significant and they were constantly late'. In February 1974, Rous' secretary general at Fifa, the long-serving Helmut Käser, wrote to CAF that as many as twenty-eight associations owed fees, and threatened to bar them from the congress if they did not pay up. Elias Zaccour, an agent and match promoter who was acting for Havelange's campaign in Africa and the Middle East – a long-term Fifa lobbyist and fixer – said in a televised 2004 interview that he paid the dues of fourteen African national associations who could not afford the fees. 'So I paid,' he said. 'And they were able to vote, otherwise "they" won't vote. These 14 vote with us.'

Havelange did, without question, help himself to bribes from Swiss marketing company International Sport and Leisure (ISL) in the 1990s and almost certainly earlier than that, and was therefore embroiled in instituting a culture of corruption in this governing body of world football which had such admirable and idealistic founding principles. Yet the overwhelming focus on this, and his use and exploitation of patronage, can obscure Havelange's attractions and talents which were also factors in his election victory and his career at Fifa. Born Jean-Marie Faustin Godefroid de Havelange in Rio de Janeiro in 1916 to a wealthy Belgian father, Faustin, who made his money in arms dealing, João died in 2016, having reached the age of 100. He was a strong athlete in his youth, made the swimming team for Brazil for the 1936 Olympics in Hitler's Berlin, and competed in the water polo team in 1952. He studied law, then became engaged with transport and other industrial companies – including arms, according to Yallop's investigations.

Havelange became involved with the Brazil sports confederation, the CBD, and was elevated to its presidency after the failure of Brazil's football team to win the 1954 World Cup in Switzerland, which was seen as unforgiveable. The tournament was won by West Germany, a historic, nation-building success dubbed 'the miracle of Bern' for the country recovering from the ashes of war and disgrace of the Nazi era. Adidas, started by and named after Adi Dassler, Horst's father, claimed some credit for the victory, having developed for the West German team a football shoe which was a revolution in lightness compared to the clumping football boots still worn by other teams.

Havelange served as the CBD president, running the confederation of twenty-three national sports governing bodies from 1958 until 1973, when he mounted his campaign to be Fifa president. While the world gasped in awe at the Brazilian players' 'natural' skills when, with a wonderful seventeen-year-old, Pelé, in the side, they won the World Cup in 1958, and again in 1962 and 1970, in fact Havelange had implemented a dedicated, professional operation for the team. It was financed by the government and business interests, seeing the prestige which a victory would bring to Brazil, and it facilitated medical and technical expertise to support the players, who would be thoroughly prepared for the tournaments. As early as 1962, the global ambitions of Brazil's business and political classes were beginning to press on Havelange the suggestion of standing as Fifa president.

Burlamaqui found in his research on the genesis of Havelange's campaign that it was aiming for an extension of the international acclaim and profile which Brazil accrued via its brilliant football talents. Brazilian business and the government – the military dictatorship, in the grimmest period of repression – supported Havelange's campaign as a vehicle for Brazilian nation-making. Havelange dedicated himself to electioneering, famously flying to eighty-six countries to talk directly to the voting delegates of Fifa's worldwide FAs, often accompanied by the Brazilian or Santos teams playing a friendly, or just by Pelé himself, sprinkling the candidate with the most golden of stardust.

Quoted by David Yallop in his book, Pelé said himself of his status in Africa: 'I represented to the blacks in those countries what a black man could accomplish in a country where there was little racial prejudice, as well as providing physical evidence that a black man could become rich, even in a white man's country.'

Havelange was white, and rich, but he successfully presented himself as being from a racially mixed, less well-off and non-European country, and as sympathetic to the complaints and needs of the African FAs, positioning himself in opposition to the struggles they had had with Rous over South Africa. He already had the support of the South American countries, and he listened to the aspirations of the African FAs, promising them more development programmes and an expanded World Cup.

Emmanuel Maradas, a journalist from Chad who edited the magazine *African Soccer* and covered the political struggles of the African FAs, says Havelange, and later Blatter, understood their needs and how to talk to them:

'South Africa was a big factor, at the time of national liberation movements,' Maradas says. 'João Havelange went round and lobbied the leading nations, Ghana, Nigeria, Egypt, whose delegates were vocal in Fifa congresses. He promised to help Africa, for them to have a seat on the executive committee, a slot at the World Cup, youth development. They knew how to use the right words with a strong message: that money was there, and they would be helped.'

The lament as written by Rous, that he just got on with his work and expected it to stand for itself, is not quite the full story either. He was supported by the tireless lobbying efforts of Horst Dassler, who had succeeded his father, Adi, as the boss at Adidas, busied himself relentlessly in the politics of sports governing bodies and would later set up the pure sports marketing company, ISL. Dassler, running a kit and boot company, worked to have presidents elected who would owe loyalty to him, and do deals for sponsorship with him, promoting the Adidas brand through their sports and teams. According to Patrick Nally, at the time a young English marketeer who worked in partnership with Dassler after Havelange's election, seeking sponsors for Fifa, 'Horst Dassler had seen the sense of collaborating with the federations, which would then do a deal on what kit would be worn, and what brands would be allowed to be seen ... He understood that rather than paying athletes to wear kit and boots, which was complicated and could result in problems, it was better to collaborate with the federations themselves.'

Dassler did maintain endorsements from the very best of German players, his executives concluding deals which would last a lifetime with Franz Beckenbauer, from his playing days at Bayern Munich. The Franz Beckenbauer tracksuit, with its three stripes down each arm, sported by the star player in 1967, was the first sports clothing made by Adidas, which previously had always concentrated on boots. But once Dassler saw that major brand dominance lay with the branding of the federations, he even developed an international relations arm of Adidas, which schooled young executives in sports politics, lobbying and scheming to have favourable presidents installed. Fedor Radmann, a German long-term operator in football politics and close adviser to Beckenbauer, decades later a key official with Beckenbauer in Germany's bid to host the 2006 World Cup, worked at Adidas in the 1970s, where from 1979 to 1989 he became a director responsible for 'promotion and international relations'.

At the 1974 World Cup which took place just after Havelange's election, Adidas certainly was showcased, the three stripes worn by Beckenbauer as he stroked the Adidas ball extravagantly to victory, and by so many other teams. But Dassler had, in fact, lobbied for Rous, already an ally, because he was comfortable at Fifa and saw a Rous re-election as continuity for European dominance of the key football federation. The night before the vote, Dassler held a large banquet in support of Rous' presidency, to which Havelange complained he had been refused entry.

Nally says that Havelange nevertheless respected Dassler from that time, because he believed Dassler's efforts had made the contest closer than it otherwise would have been. At the epochal vote, sixty-two FAs voted for Havelange in the first round, to fifty-six for Rous, then Havelange won the second by a decisive sixty-eight votes to fifty-two.

'Horst Dassler was made aware just prior to the election that Stanley Rous was going to lose because of the character of João Havelange, travelling the world with the Brazilian team, with a vision for sport to be significantly greater and more important, as it was in Brazil,' Nally says. 'Dassler was talking to people, lobbying them to stick with the existing structure, helping Rous. And despite all that work and going round the globe, Havelange nearly didn't win, which he put down almost entirely to Horst Dassler, whom he saw as a powerful and influential man. It created a bond between the two individuals, and mutual respect.'

Havelange had won, Sir Stanley Rous had lost, and he admitted to feeling 'rejected by old friends', and 'disillusioned', before regaining the restrained bearing with which he had made his way to the heights of world football from his little village in rural Suffolk. He had become in several crucial ways a man from another era, a patrician administrator dedicated, as he saw it, to the game he always loved and believed in, when the world had changed around him. He was also seventy-nine by then, and there is a strain in football admin-istration of powerful men whose absorbing and thrilling work has become their whole life, who do not recognise when they are too far past their prime, who do not really know what they would do with themselves if they retired. Blatter, elementally clinging on for a fifth term in 2015 despite the arrests of senior Fifa officials at the Zurich hotel days before, still spinning the political wiles he learned for years at Havelange's side, was the same age.

Havelange, for whom he found kind words in public, and with whom he did enjoy a continuing good relationship, as an honorary president, for years afterwards, offered Rous a pension, but he declined it. Rous reasoned that as he hadn't been paid when he worked for Fifa, he couldn't be paid for not working there, and he retired on his FA pension. In a famous passage reflecting on his exit, Rous wrote: 'There was in my defeat something symbolic of changing attitudes and standards. In football the talk was all of money, and my own lack of personal concern with it may have seemed outdated and amateurish.'

Amateurish is an ambiguous word, carrying within it the virtue of doing something for the love of it, for pure motives, as well as the failing of being unprofessional and bumbling, which Rous certainly was not. His lack of interest in money was, though, certainly outdated, and at Fifa, under Havelange, it was all going to change.

CHAPTER 4

1974

In 1974, the year I was nine, when football and Fifa's World Cup claimed me for life via a colour telly in the living room in Manchester, the Brazilian João Havelange was fifty-eight, and moving in to take control of the governing body at Fifa House in Zurich. By then, the headquarters had moved, from the two-room offices downtown on Bahnhofstrasse 77 to, literally, a private house. It was up at the top of a hill at 11 Hitzigweg, in Sonnenberg, a quiet, enviably comfortable suburb of detached, classic Swiss homes, looking smugly down on the lake. There were still only twelve staff, and people who worked there at the time say that during Rous' presidency Helmut Käser, the secretary general, would have his Labradors snuggled under the desk. Yet from there they organised sophisticated, modern World Cups, captivating spectacles broadcast around the world in colour, and tried and ultimately failed to manage the politics and demands of a globally expanding sport.

Havelange, clever, domineering, would remain in charge for a transformational era, celebrated by the establishment in Brazil and elsewhere in the world where he was considered a force for progress, suspected throughout by many others of lining his own and associates' bank accounts. When he died in 2016, his extraordinary life was hailed as that of a visionary, a moderniser and worldwide developer of the people's game, the strong-jawed general after whom stadiums were named, and he was denounced for corruption, his own and Fifa's infestation with it. Both of those sides of the Havelange legacy are true, although for decades he, his protégé Sepp Blatter and Fifa boasted about their development record while publicly denying and condemning as false the mounting allegations of corruption.

Installed as the boss of Fifa House, Havelange had to make good on his policy of development to the African and other national associations which had voted him in on those promises. He would repeatedly say later that the Fifa left him by Rous at that house in Sonnenberg was virtually penniless, which was unfair. Fifa's records show that it is another misperception to believe that Havelange, a commercially aggressive beast compared to the clerkish Rous, instantly transformed the finances. It was probably true that, like league football in Europe, the television rights for the World Cups were undervalued, but this was before the financial eruption of TV rights, and, for all his efforts and assertions, Fifa records show that under Havelange Fifa's annual income only increased gradually after 1974, before the huge increase which arrived towards the end of the 1990s.

They did need to find some more money to fund the election promises, and so began to seek corporate sponsorship for the development programmes. Two men who were crucial then, and whose influence over Fifa's direction seeps back for forty years to that turning point in its history, were Horst Dassler, the indefatigable boss of Adidas, and Joseph Blatter, his name always shortened to Sepp, a kipper-tied PR and marketing operator who came to Fifa from the Swiss timing firm Longines.

Dassler, according to Patrick Nally, saw Fifa's promised global development plan as a long worked-for opportunity to expand the Adidas brand, and further the entwined relationship with Fifa under Havelange. However, Adidas was stretched and while it would be a sponsor, providing kit and footballs throughout the world, his company did not have the money to actually fund the programmes. Nally, in partnership with Peter West, a renowned cricket commentator, had been pioneering in London the sponsorship of sport by blue-chip companies which understood the prime and benevolent association it bought for their brands to the massive audiences of sports fans. John Boulter, a British former 800m runner whom Dassler had hired to work at Adidas, was dispatched to meet Nally, who then joined Dassler in a joint venture to sign up sponsors for Havelange's new Fifa development programme.

Blatter recalled the background to this early part of his glistening ascent of Fifa in a long interview with me for this book. He agreed to see me in the summer of 2016, after he was banned from Fifa and football, devastatingly for him, and he was appealing his case to the Court of Arbitration for Sport. He talked about his early career and recalled his entry to the organisation as the marketing man responsible for delivering the promised development programme. Blatter said that, contrary to the common telling of the story, Dassler did not originally recommend him to Fifa. In fact, he said, he was first called by Thomas Keller, the president of Swiss Timing, in November 1974.

'He said the new president in Fifa is looking for a man who knows football but who specifically could sell a programme, because they had no money,' Blatter told me.

Blatter's take on the story is that Dassler 'had the file' – the Fifa development programme, which included a youth tournament, to sell to a sponsor – but in these early days of sponsorship, he and Adidas had not yet managed to sign any company up.

'Havelange tried in Brazil, made contact with different entities, banks and chocolate, insurance, whatever. I don't know if they were not good salesman,' Blatter said, with a glint of mischief in his eye, 'but nobody wanted it.'

The ultimate signing up of Coca-Cola to brand the Fifa development programme has become a well-rehearsed tale of Blatter's, a set-piece triumph in *United Passions*, the notoriously self-glorifying film his Fifa had made in 2015, and he rolled it out for me again in our interview. He said that Dassler had organised a meeting in a restaurant at the Parc des Princes, Paris, with Guinness, the treacly Irish beer company, before the 1975 European Cup final. Leeds United, the English champions, have always since complained about that match, the refereeing which denied them a blatant penalty and disallowed a Peter Lorimer goal for offside, Beckenbauer gleefully lifting the cup for the second of three consecutive Bayern Munich victories after a 2–0 win.

Blatter said that at his meeting before the match Guinness's executives told him the football sponsorship wasn't for them: they were an Irish and British drink of choice, not international, and an alcoholic drink was not the best fit for such a sporting programme. He says they gestured at his glass and said it was Coca-Cola – 'By the way I was drinking a Cuba Libre, with rum!' he grinned – and they pointed out that executives of Coca-Cola in the UK were at another table, accompanying a Leeds United party.

From that initial contact with Coca-Cola, Blatter said he had further discussions with a Dutch representative of the company, and with Nally doing the presentation of the project they went to Atlanta in November 1975 to pitch to the Coca-Cola board. One of the lawyers around the table, Blatter says, asked him how many bottles of Coca-Cola Fifa would be selling on the company's behalf, and Blatter says he replied: 'You are not going to sell Coca-Cola; you sell an idea. And we invite Coca-Cola to join us with the idea.'

Called Project 1, the proposed development and promotional programme was typed up between bright green booklet covers. It also coincided with a ramping up of Fifa rhetoric about operating as a global good, and the brochure had a motto on the front: 'Football is a universal language.'

For the 2015 congress in Zurich at which he was seeking his fifth presidential term – the coronation tarnished a little by the mass arrests at the Baur au Lac – Blatter had had the original Project 1 booklet reprinted. It was handed out to delegates from the national FAs to remind them of the president's very long, forty-year history at Fifa, and his roots in the very beginnings of the development programmes from which so many of them had benefited. I picked up a copy at the excellent, well-resourced library attached to the Fifa museum in Zurich, and it is a fascinating document.

At the top, under the heading 'The Idea', it explains its purpose both to sponsors and the FAs themselves:

'The Fifa Project No. 1, based on an initiative of its president, Dr João Havelange, has as its aim the development of football on a world-wide scale and should, above all, benefit the countries of the third world, generally called developing countries,' it states as an introduction.

Nally, recalling the landmark deal, said that Coca-Cola gained the association of their name and product with the image and glamour of a pure sport, penetrating deeply into countries around the world. Besides the money itself from the sponsorship, Fifa also gained the expertise and clout of a powerful US corporation. 'They had bottlers, distribution networks and relationships with governments in these countries, which were very useful for Fifa when setting up the programmes,' Nally recalled.

Project 1 proposed a series of courses to promote football and strengthen countries' national FAs, teaching administration, tactics and coaching, sports medicine and refereeing. The courses always included significant time doing physical training with the delegates themselves. Blatter says he presented the proposal to CAF in Addis Ababa in February 1976, and the African officials made it clear they wanted the courses tailored to the sporting culture of their countries, not imposed as a European blueprint.

The money sought was a total of $1.2m over three years of the programme. When Coca-Cola's board in Atlanta finally agreed and signed up, Havelange's Fifa could roll out a dedicated development programme to the national football associations which, although it looks rudimentary now, was then on a scale beyond what Rous' grant-aiding had been able to do. Coca-Cola were buying incomparable brand marketing, and have remained a sponsor of Fifa ever since, as have Adidas, although the prices they have paid to soak their brand into football's have dramatically increased.

Blatter told me that the project still needed to win over Fifa's own executive committee, and there was resistance to it from European representatives, particularly from Germany, who wanted to restrict it to one probationary year. It was only the intervention of a long-serving African representative, Rito Alcantara, a pharmacist from Senegal, who served on the executive committee for twenty years from 1968 to 1988, which made the difference, according to Blatter's account. He said that Alcantara had spoken up, to say he could not understand how such a development programme could be turned down, when the money was there and the sponsor signed up.

Consistent with his analysis of almost every episode over the whole course of his time at Fifa which we discussed, Blatter saw the reason for that initial resistance to the development programme as one of internal power politics and personal ambition. Nobody within the Fifa executive committee appears to have been troubled at this fateful sale of football's image and qualities to junk drink, which would lead to the largely unquestioned spectacle ever after of junk food cleansing its brands through sport. Blatter said the Europeans were not opposed because they believed it was wrong to take such coaching and support around the world to developing countries, but because they were against Havelange.

'They wanted Havelange out,' he said, in a tone which suggested this political motive was obvious. 'It wasn't because they didn't like to play football, it was a question that Havelange had to be stopped. They thought the development programme would help Havelange because he would have more alliances around the world, and he promised that, especially to Africa.'

If that was the fear of the Europeans, they read the impact of the programmes on Fifa's internal political dynamics absolutely correctly. Such was the appreciation of the African and developing countries' football associations for this sustained help they were now receiving that they did indeed always support Havelange, who remained unchallenged as president, becoming like an emperor of Fifa over twenty-four years. Blatter, itchily ambitious, very soon the secretary general of the organisation after Havelange brutally ousted Käser, observed the workings of that realpolitik, the electoral basis for the president's authority, supported by constituencies directly benefiting from the regime, and he understood it, to his bones.

At the time of the next World Cup, in Argentina in 1978, I was thirteen and remember, with all the football-obsessed boys around me, looking forward to it with a desperate longing. I confess that I experienced it as a carnival of football, entranced by the ticker tape snowing down from the vaulting stands of River Plate's vast stadium, and the flowing skill of Argentina's star player Mario Kempes, with his long, thick hair and socks louchely rolled down to his ankles. The impression broadcast to me as a kid, then, was exactly as Argentina's military junta intended it, when after their coup deposing Isabel Martínez de Péron two years earlier, on 24 March 1976, they concentrated on hosting a well-executed tournament as an advertisement for their regime.

Fifa cannot be accused of awarding the World Cup to a ruthless and murderous junta; Argentina was chosen as the host for the tournament ten years before the coup, in 1966, as Rous believed in giving countries plenty of time to prepare. But once the generals did take over and began kidnapping, murdering, torturing and disappearing tens of thousands of Argentinians deemed subversive, they viewed the great sporting event as sundry totalitarian regimes have through history: as an ideal vehicle for propaganda. There were protests and campaigns to boycott the tournament, although it seems there was no serious consideration by Fifa to move it: Rous' policy of steering a 'non-political' line endured, and, anyway, Havelange was a creature of the military dictatorship in his own, neighbouring country.

Documenting the boycott efforts, particularly in France, by members of Amnesty International, Professor Raanan Rein has written:

'In an attempt to silence both protests and fears [of violence against the regime during the tournament], the military spokespersons declared that Argentina was enjoying a period of social peace and that no violent incidents were anticipated. The junta launched an international campaign to improve its image and to discredit those accusing Argentina of systematic human rights violations.

'Seeking to reinforce the image of a peaceful Argentina, the regime spent the months before the World Cup redoubling its repressive efforts, and slum residents in the cities selected to host World Cup events were forced to leave their homes in order to demonstrate that poverty "no longer exists".'

The Estadio Monumental in Buenos Aires, where Argentina won the final in a ticker-tape wonderland and Kempes scored twice in the 3–1 victory over Holland, was just down the road from the Navy School of Mechanics, which was used by the junta as a place of torture. The generals hailed the national ecstasy which acclaimed the victory as a joyous vindication of Argentina and their fascist vision for the country. Rein quotes Hebe de Bonafini, one of the founders of the Mothers of Plaza de Mayo, who did not rest in publicly protesting the disappearances of their sons and daughters, saying: 'It was a party for the masses and a tragedy for the families of the *desaparecidos* [disappeared].'

Commercially, Patrick Nally recalls that Fifa had signed away the rights to the 1978 tournament to the host country, and that he had to negotiate with the junta to restore them to Fifa so that sponsorships and TV deals could be sold. Still working with Dassler, they brought in Canon, Gillette and the airline KLM for the billboards around the stadiums where this World Cup of glories and terrible darkness was held. They moved on to the 1982 World Cup in Spain – the first that my generation would watch for which England actually qualified – expanded by Havelange, true to his promise, to twenty-four countries. There were fourteen places for European countries; two, Algeria and Cameroon, from Africa; Kuwait from the Asian Football Confederation; Charlie Dempsey's New Zealand qualified from Oceania; El Salvador and Honduras from Concacaf; Argentina, Brazil, Chile and Peru from Conmebol.

The expansion meant that more money had to be raised to help Spain with the stadiums and other necessary preparations, and for Fifa itself; 45m CHF for both, according to Nally. Dassler had set up a company to raise the money, called Rofa, named after two of its other investors: Robert Schwan, the former general manager of Bayern Munich who became Beckenbauer's personal manager – and Beckenbauer himself.

Nally says that as Dassler needed money at the time, he had agreed to buy out Dassler's interest in their own joint marketing company, but then the Japanese advertising giant Dentsu offered Dassler huge money, $500m, to break the relationship with Nally and go into partnership with them. Nally said that Dassler told him he could keep the programme they were working on, but after that, his deals with Fifa would be via the new company Dassler formed with Dentsu in 1982: International Sport and Leisure, ISL.

'From being quite successful one minute,' Nally said, 'the next, I was utterly bereft.'

Blatter's take on that, when I met him, was brief. 'Nally had problems with Dassler and if Dassler isn't happy with somebody, he just kicked them out.'

ISL, according to Nally, was still going to be in position as a new company to acquire the rights to future World Cups from Fifa, because Dassler had 'manipulated control with his special relationships', including working on the ousting of Käser. ISL were finally exposed years later, after their monstrous financial collapse, for having kicked back bribes to Havelange and the South America football chiefs Ricardo Teixeira and Nicolás Leoz, among others, when paying Fifa for the marketing rights to the 2002 and 2006 World

Cups. But that wrongdoing was not perpetrated by Dassler himself. He died from cancer in 1987, aged only fifty-one. His is a legacy still unravelling from the insides of Fifa, having become more than a boot and sportswear entrepreneur of the Adidas three stripes, which seduced mine and other generations as the acme of sporting sophistication. Dassler took the sale of gear, and its endorsement by elite sports stars, to their unrestrained conclusions, involving himself, his influence and his protégés far into the politics, deep into the workings, of the modern sports governing bodies themselves.

At the World Cup in Mexico in 1986, Michel Platini crafted his place permanently in the legions of enduringly great players, captaining France to victory on penalties over Brazil in a monumental quarter-final. Platini, born in a small mining town, Joeuf, in the provincial east of France to a footballer father, had played his way up from the local club, to Nancy, St Étienne, then to bestriding European football as the number 10, worshipped by fans as *le roi*, at Juventus of Turin. At Juventus Platini had lifted the European Cup at Heysel the previous year, but in the horrific context of the thirty-nine deaths of Juve supporters in a crush caused by a collapsed wall following a charge by Liverpool hooligans. In 1982 he captained his French team's first announcement of its modern brilliance, to the semi-final of the World Cup, where an epic 3–3 draw and ultimate defeat to Germany on penalties was scarred by the terrible challenge of the Germany goalkeeper Harald Schumacher, who barged Patrick Battiston unconscious, broke his jaw and knocked out two of his teeth. In between, Platini lifted the 1984 European Championship for France, a classic victory for flowing, passing football and his particular art of deftly quick attacking midfield vision. After retiring from his stellar playing career, Platini would first become the national coach of the French team, then co-president of the national organising committee for the 1998 World Cup in his home country, which brought him into Blatter's intimate company.

At the 1990 World Cup in Italy, Cameroon, memorably led up front by Roger Milla, an experienced striker in Europe, delivered some fruits of Fifa's programmes and African football development, reaching the quarter-final where they gave England a genuine challenge before losing 3–2. My generation, which had seen England fail to qualify for two tournaments, watched disbelievingly as the team, managed by Bobby Robson and featuring Paul Gascoigne, Gary Lineker and Chris Waddle, actually improved as the tournament progressed and ought really to have beaten Germany in the semi-final. The tournament, Italia 90, rehabilitated football's broader appeal from the shame of hooliganism, the ban of English clubs from European competition after Heysel, and the horror of Hillsborough, where ninety-six Liverpool supporters were unlawfully killed by police mismanagement of a well-behaved crowed at the 1989 FA Cup semi-final against Nottingham Forest. The BBC's coverage of the World Cup just one year later, presenting the tournament as an involving operatic drama, with 'Nessun Dorma', sung by Luciano Pavarotti, as the theme tune, drew a nation back to football's essential beauty, and readied public sentiment for the excitement, marketing and payTV consumption of the Premier League era.

Germany won the World Cup again, beating Diego Maradona's Argentina team 1–0 in a dire match ruined by the Argentinians' widely criticised fouling and diving, which included the first ever sending off in a World Cup final, of Pedro Monzón for a foul on Jürgen Klinsmann. Germany's coach was Beckenbauer, looking older, upright and dignified in his jacket and tie, wearing glasses, his curly hair receded further back on his head, as he ran with his clenched fists raised to celebrate another ultimate triumph. He has the distinction of being the only person ever to captain as a player, then manage, his country to victory in a World Cup final, and the second man, after Brazil's Mário Zagallo, to win the tournament as both a player and a manager. The place of *der Kaiser* in the affections of the German public was raised to iconic status; he also always seemed thoughtful, decent and perceptive, and was liked as well as worshipped.

Four years later, Fifa successfully organised the first World Cup in the USA, part of long-term efforts to crack soccer in a potentially huge territory and market, where it had always struggled for recognition beneath the major US sports of football, baseball and basketball. That 1994 tournament marked its further expansion, as promised by Havelange – and first proposed by Rous – from twenty-four to thirty-two teams, with three African teams, Cameroon, Morocco and Nigeria, and two from the Asian Football Confederation, Saudi Arabia and South Korea. As part of the hosting arrangements, the US football authorities had to commit to forming a competitive domestic league, which they founded from scratch with the clubs as a centralised system of franchises which owners could buy: Major League Soccer. That initiative went along with more coaching and grass-roots programmes to have young people playing the game, which soccer entrepreneurs like Clive Toye, a former English journalist who ran the New York Cosmos in the 1970s, had always argued was the key. Despite the game's lesser profile and popularity in the US, a World Cup of generally tactical caution was watched by huge crowds in the great stadiums of the states, with 94,000 watching the final between Brazil and Italy at the Rose Bowl in Pasadena. The image of Roberto Baggio, Italy's star of the tournament, on his knees in despair having missed the crucial penalty in the shootout which ceded the trophy to Brazil, was the defining one of the tournament.

Havelange had presided at Fifa over this double expansion of the World Cup, a commercial and sponsorship packaging up of the tournament and greater broadcasting income, and years of development programmes which secured allegiance from the member FAs. There had been agitation from the European FAs and Uefa, complaining at too little transparency at Fifa about how the money was handled, and that information was kept tight among a trusted inner circle. The full scale of what had been happening through the Havelange years, that behind the hype, marketing and lionising of the president was an entrenched culture of corruption, would not be exposed for years yet. By the late 1990s, Havelange was ageing. Sepp Blatter had been at Fifa since 1975, working diligently for his regime, and as the secretary general since 1978. There was to be a sudden multiplication of income for Fifa, but this was not a result of João Havelange's business brilliance, rather a consequence of the TV rights hyper-inflation which Fifa reaped principally after the France World Cup in 1998.

The organisation of Fifa, its work and its political shape and intricacies had become Blatter's life, and he began to see that when Havelange finally stepped down he could become the president himself, after a lifetime of servicing them. He bolted too early, appearing at a Uefa executive committee meeting in 1996 seeking backing for a challenge to Havelange. Lars-Christer Olsson, the Swedish Uefa secretary general, who like many of the Scandinavian administrators is contemptuous of Blatter, seeing him as a hustler for self-advantage, nevertheless acknowledges him as an expert player of the politics. Olsson said the Uefa meeting, at which Blatter seemed to be 'challenging his own president, trying to throw him overboard', was too soon and irregular, and the executive committee dismissed him.

But Havelange did indicate his intention after that to retire two years later, in 1998. Lennart Johansson, the Swedish president of Uefa, determined to stand for the Fifa presidency, and introduce what he propounded were necessary European standards of governance and transparency, while still funding development programmes, particularly in Africa. At Uefa, Johansson had made much greater collaborative moves towards the other confederations and initiated the Meridian Project, an agreement with CAF which included providing development support from the rich European confederation to the African FAs struggling for resources. With those moves, Johansson and his European supporters believed they had a foundation for marshalling enough support in Africa and worldwide to succeed Havelange and restore a European model of administration.

Blatter took his time, to the consternation of his European opponents, and waited almost to the deadline, before finally declaring himself a candidate. He told me that, typically, he was motivated in part by preservation of his own role within Fifa, saying he might have been willing to stay on under Johansson as the secretary general, if that had been guaranteed.

'This would have been a possibility,' he said, 'but in Europe they approached me and they said: "We don't want only to get rid of the patriarch, we also want to get rid of you, the prophet."'

The Europeans supporting Johansson's Scandinavian vision for running Fifa were looking for a change of culture and cleaning of the stables after Havelange, and Blatter was seen as his long-term, eager lieutenant, the continuity candidate.

'I was approached by a member of Fifa from Italy, saying: "We don't want you." I said: "If you don't want me to go on with my job as secretary general, then maybe I will go as president." He was laughing.

I thought: OK. At the end, they tried to convince me not to go, but it was too late. This was the big risk I took in my life.'

When he finally declared his candidacy, on 30 March 1998, the secretary general showed he had learned the electoral lessons from Havelange, who had had the aura of Pelé bestowed on his campaign in 1974. Doing the same for Blatter, and also splitting the European football associations' vote, was another genuine star, a player, coach and icon of the world game, globally recognised and idolised: Michel Platini, suddenly at Blatter's side, supporting his campaign for the ultimate office.

CHAPTER 5

1998: President Blatter

There is a publicity picture taken for the 1998 election campaign, of Sepp Blatter with Michel Platini, each placing a hand on an Adidas football, promoting with fixed smiles Blatter's bid for the Fifa presidency. Blatter, going up in the world, looks in the pink of health, sleek, smart, savvy, knowing exactly where he is heading and how he is planning to get there. Platini looks boyish next to him, taller, with more hair, his smile brighter and more genuine, like a young guy being treated to a day out by his wealthy uncle. Blatter looks like he belongs in a suit, which fits him like a second skin, his silk tie perfect. Platini's jacket is ruffled up slightly on his shoulder, and his tie is askew to the right, like a freer spirit who has fished out the smart outfit he keeps for the odd stuffy occasion. Still, he looks pleased with the opportunity for advancement presented by hitching himself to Blatter's climb up the organisational ladder. Looking at the picture now, after the fall of both men together in December 2015, in a scandal which dates right back to this first entanglement, you wonder if Platini really had a clue what he was getting into.

Platini had come to know Blatter and work with him while he was the president of the organising committee for the 1998 World Cup in France, and Blatter clearly saw the advantage of having his support. That tournament, and the victory by a France team of diverse, multi-cultural backgrounds, led by its star and captain of Algerian descent, Zinedine Zidane, was felt in the ecstasy of celebration to have united modern France. Platini, the former playing legend, captain and coach, now a central figure at the tournament mingling with the other dignitaries at the new Stade de France, was admired in a new incarnation.

Their alliance was forged in January 1998, when Platini has said that Blatter approached him in his hotel room in Singapore and asked: 'Can you imagine being Fifa president?'

Platini had at that point held no official position at Uefa or Fifa, and took the blandishment to be flattery from Blatter – although forever after he did always appear to feel that he was set on the administrative path to be Fifa president when Blatter finally tore himself away, destiny for a guy who always reached the top. Platini's account is that he told Blatter he was not interested in running for Fifa president, and that Blatter said he would run, but he needed his support. Platini was at his side then, charming FAs on their travels and taking away from Johansson French and other European support, and when Blatter won he would give Platini a job as his international adviser. The terms they agreed, how much Platini would be paid by Fifa, and how they documented it, would become a timebomb quietly ticking in the filing cabinets of Fifa House, finally blowing both men up and out of football, seventeen years later.

Sunk in gloom at his ban from football, which has been his whole life, Platini barely appeared in public during 2016 and although I interviewed him twice while he was the Uefa president and saw him at events and press conferences, he declined to be interviewed for this book.

By 1998, the world governing body formed in the backroom on the rue St Honoré ninety-four years earlier by amateur gentlemen from seven European nations had grown to a federation of 200 countries' football associations, a historic phenomenon and an undeniably great achievement. The politics had never been changed from one country, one vote, for major policy decisions taken at the annual congress. This system of admirably equal, basic democracy has never been subjected to a sustained challenge despite, as some European FAs exasperatedly observe, a great football power like Germany, for example, with a population of eighty million, therefore having the same say as Trinidad, with a population of one million.

The national associations elect the president at a congress on the same one country, one vote basis. Hence the need for any candidate, as Blatter absolutely understood, to gain the support of as many countries, including developing nations, as possible. In 1998, the

Confederation of African Football had fifty-two voting countries, the Asian Football Confederation had forty-four. In Asia, they were scattered across a huge geographical area, and spread of political and economic circumstances, from Indonesia, its football association formed in 1972, to Qatar, the UAE and the other kingdoms of the gulf, to Uzbekistan and three other small former territories of the broken-up Soviet Union. Concacaf, of which the president was Jack Warner with Chuck Blazer long installed as his secretary general operating out of New York, had grown through the 1980s and 1990s, with the addition of some tiny islands, like Turks and Caicos, population just 33,000; Anguilla, with 15,000 people, and Montserrat, population 4,900, which joined Fifa in 1996 and had the same voting power as every other country. Warner always tried to lever maximum influence at Fifa by encouraging the Concacaf countries to vote as a block, and in particular his Caribbean Football Union grouping of islands, so wielding an influence way beyond their proportionate status. The vote for president invests the national associations with power, and they are entitled, indeed required by their football populations, to use it with a view to what a president will do for them, for development.

Blatter knew intimately how all this worked, having been engaged from the very beginning of Havelange's rule, when many African FAs did not have the money to send anybody to the congress to exercise their voting rights, or even to pay the $150 annual Fifa affiliation fee. Through running the Coca-Cola-sponsored programmes to developing countries he had come to know and help the presidents of associations across Africa and Asia. Warner was an ally, his votes necessary. Since that coaching and educational development programme had been developed from 1976, Fifa's income from TV rights and sponsorships had grown steadily but now, between the World Cups of 1998 and 2002, it was set to grow exponentially.

Fifa's financial figures show that in the four-year cycle, as Fifa accounts for its income, leading to 1998, Fifa's revenue from the World Cup was $308m, including $162m in TV rights. After that came the dramatic escalation of income, when ISL, which continued to be the marketing company tightly close to Fifa after Horst Dassler died in

1987, bought the future rights for both the 2002 and 2006 tournaments. ISL went bust in 2001 but Fifa managed to secure the rights and sell them on to one of the German Kirch media companies, which also subsequently went bust. Fifa itself sold the sponsorships for the 2002 World Cup to a now-familiar roster of corporate partners, including, of course, Adidas and Coca-Cola, who were said to have paid £9m each to burn their brands into the consciousness of the football-watching global village. The income recorded for the four-year cycle to 2002 was $1.5bn, a fivefold increase, including TV rights sales alone of almost $1bn.

Yet many African associations were still impoverished, according to Emmanuel Maradas, of *African Soccer*, who actively worked for Blatter in the 1998 presidential elections:

'For years, it was impossible to make even a phone call to the football associations; many of them had nothing. In my country, Chad, there was no money. Egypt's FA had a headquarters, but most countries did not, maybe a room underneath a local stadium, in a very poor way. Blatter understood this, and the need to promise that he would help the Africans.'

Johansson also understood that it was necessary, and a core part of Fifa's purpose, to use the money which it generated to help with development in countries which had no other access to funds. He had forged Uefa's alliance with CAF and its president, Issa Hayatou of Cameroon – still the president even now – and his commitment was that the development funds would go through the confederations to administer, for FAs which needed investment. His presidential credentials were, however, fundamentally undermined by references he made in an interview with the Swedish newspaper *Aftonbladet*, widely condemned as racist, for which he made a public apology. Following a trip to South Africa to discuss the country's then idea of bidding to host the World Cup in 2006, Johansson had said: 'The whole room was full of blackies and it's dark when they sit down together. What's more, it's no fun when they're angry. I thought if this lot get in a bad mood, it won't be so funny.'

Johanson said he could not remember speaking in those terms, but said: 'I am not a racist. I apologise to anyone who interpreted it as if I was one.'

Uefa sought to dismiss the fallout, claiming there had been 'some kind of misunderstanding', but, given the history of African football's battles and relationships with European administrators, including Rous, it was a dreadful episode, not wholly mended by Uefa's new engagements with CAF.

Blatter's initiative, later described by Fifa itself as his 'visionary proposal', was more direct, and appealing: simply to promise very big money to every Fifa member country's football association, directly. A 'financial assistance programme' would eventually provide $250,000 a year to each of them for running costs, including paying salaries to staff. In addition, there was what became the 'GOAL' programme, in which Platini was involved with Blatter from its conception, making $400,000 available to each association to build new facilities, including a headquarters. This was an offer to share Fifa's great mountain of dollars, amassed in Zurich from the proceeds of selling the rights every four years to the greatest televised sports show on earth, so substantially that it could transform the threadbare fortunes of member FAs around the world – and the lives of the people who ran them. The presidents of the associations, promised such transformational cash, were voters in the election.

Blatter, as he admits himself, did not stint on the campaign, having the use of a private jet to fly around the world, including to the minor football nations of Africa, to personally assure voters of the benefits his presidency would bring. It was said at the time that the plane and significant financial support came from Qatar, and from Mohamed bin Hammam, a construction magnate grown super-wealthy in the state's building boom, and a rising figure in football politics. Bin Hammam, a Qatari football enthusiast, had become a significant power in the Asian Football Confederation and, from there, a member of the Fifa executive committee from 1996. In this 1998 election he was a key supporter of Blatter's, but Blatter told me that bin Hammam did not provide the plane, although the Emir of Qatar gave him one ride in his:

'The only thing that was done – not by bin Hammam but by the state of Qatar – was that one day I could use their flight [by private plane], which was in Paris, to go, I think, to Senegal. But to come back I had to take my plane, because the other plane, from Qatar, was going further. This was the only one where I can say Qatar helped me directly,' he said. 'And I was not the only one on the plane.

'It is not true that Qatar flew me around; it was one flight. I had a personal sponsor who later offered me, from the airport of Paris, a bourgeois, he gave me a plane.'

Although it has been widely understood that his backer was a wealthy individual from the Gulf, Blatter said that he had never confirmed who his backer was. 'The people were not involved in football,' he said, 'but they were my sponsor, who knew somebody with a plane.'

Blatter said 'the state of Qatar was a supporter' and began to support him after 1995, when Qatar hosted the U20 World Cup. That was very shortly after the new Emir, Hamad bin Khalifa Al Thani, began to work towards the modernisation of the country. Blatter believes that the excitement generated by the U20 tournament in a country which had remained conservative and underdeveloped under the old Emir, prompted his understanding of sport's prestige and the germ of the idea to host an actual, grown-up World Cup.

'We were looking for a country who could [host the tournament]; it was hard to find a country,' Blatter told me. 'We were happy to play there, at the last minute. At the time it was not a well-developed country; not a lot of cars or rich people. The building had not even started; some hotels but I remember even the city [Doha] was a small city.

'I think at that time, the Emir was thinking: football could be good.'

In the vote for president of Fifa's nations at the Equinox Hall in Paris in June 1998, Joseph Blatter, who still, aged eighty, talks about having come from a small-town background in the obscurity of the Swiss Valais, ascended to the highest administrative role of the world's richest and most popular sport. He beat Johansson in the vote with the support of 111 countries to 80. The victory was then and has always afterwards been subject to accusations of bribery and vote-buying, again focused on African delegates, alleged to have received money the previous night in the Meridien Hotel, to switch their vote from Johansson to Blatter. Blatter denied it then, responding to the accusation of corruption at a press conference with the retort: 'The match is over. The players have already gone to the dressing room. I will not respond.'

In 2002, before his next election battle, Blatter obtained a court injunction to prevent Farah Addo, president of the FA in civil war-torn Somalia, repeating his allegations that votes were bought by Blatter's side in the election. Addo, who died on 19 November 2008, had told the journalist Andrew Jennings for his book *FOUL!* that he had been offered money by a middleman from the Gulf to vote for Blatter. Jennings put to bin Hammam the rumoured allegations that he was behind other instances of paying inducements, and bin Hammam, while acknowledging that he 'helped Mr Blatter immensely in his campaign in the 1998 election', denied there was any bribery.

In his interview with me, Blatter denied it completely again, while accepting it is a story which has always lingered, and throwing out some allegations of his own.

'No,' he said, 'you will never bring this thing away, but it is not true. I was never in the hotel. It was not bin Hammam – nobody from my group was going to pay anybody.'

And then the reason he gave was profoundly revealing of his approach towards the electoral politics of Fifa; he spread his hands and smiled: 'We had the votes.'

Blatter rejects the claims that Johansson had more votes pledged the night before the vote, which he recalled being made by Johansson's key ally, the president of the German football federation, Egidius Braun.

'We had the votes. When I was announced in the first round, I expected at least one hundred and ten. But then Braun said something is wrong; that we [Johansson's side] had one hundred and ten [votes guaranteed], but now Blatter has them, so [the allegations against Blatter started]: he paid. And they won't bring it away.'

Dr Paul Darby, a reader in the sociology of sport at the University of Ulster who has extensively researched and written about the politics and development of football in Africa, gave this assessment of the 1998 election win achieved by Blatter, with Havelange's backing:

'Whilst financial inducements may or may not have impacted upon the election, it is clear that Blatter and Havelange demonstrated considerable political astuteness throughout their campaign. Of particular significance was their skill in reading and ability to manipulate internal Confederation of African Football politics in order to convince at least half of the African voters that a policy of continuity represented a better option for safeguarding their interests within world football.'

That first election was the crucial victory won by Blatter; although, as he acknowledges himself, he was still perceived by many as the secretary general fixer figure rather than a man of presidential heft like Havelange. But then, with the vast new income from World Cup TV rights galactic compared to the pennies being earned when Havelange took over in 1974, he was able to make the money flow straight away. The financial assistance programme, already approved under Havelange, began immediately in 1998, and between then and 2014 when totals were published, Fifa says it distributed $778m to the 200-plus national FAs, $331m to confederations: $1.1bn altogether. The GOAL programme was started, fulfilling Blatter's election promise, in 1999, and by 2014, $284m had been spent on 668 projects around the world. Most, 191, were to build new FA headquarters and facilities in Africa; 158 were initiated in Asia. With other programmes, featuring dedicated support for FAs to improve their administration, education, women's football, and $120 million for special projects, mostly in Africa, including the installation of forty-five artificial turf pitches, Fifa stated that from 1999 to 2014 it had distributed more than $2bn to associations and confederations.

Platini was duly given a job straight after the election victory, as promised – football adviser to president Blatter, and he became the deputy chairman of the GOAL programme. Bin Hammam, promoted in importance by Blatter following his support with the election, was made the chairman, the wealthy Qatari dispensing Fifa's money to poor, grateful FAs around the world, and in the process building and extending his own political alliances.

Telling the story in the folksy way he likes, as if the implementation of a $2bn global development programme at the governing body of world football was like a neighbourhood park scheme worked up by friends over coffee in the Valais, Blatter said it was bin Hammam's idea to dedicate money to building headquarters.

'He is an entrepreneur in construction, he is one of the biggest constructors in his country. He said: "Why should we not build something?" And then the three together [Blatter, Platini and bin Hammam], we came out: yes, start first with the house of football.

'After me coming as president with this famous GOAL project, all national associations got a house of football. It was important, to instil the importance of football in every country. When I have visited a lot of these countries they had no house of football; they had an office or two offices perhaps, in a stadium but in an old stadium, no furniture, or offices in a business building. So it is a must: the importance of football; you must have a house of football.

'So in the first congress after '98, an extraordinary congress in Los Angeles, I said: "Give everybody a house."'

To critics of this whole machinery constructed at Fifa by Blatter, pouring money into the FAs which had a presidential vote, his perceived political devilry at surviving and repeatedly remaining in power on a majority of their votes, the GOAL and financial assistance programmes look like giant slush funds. There is also a suspicion, even an assumption, that the programmes are rife with corruption, with football officials in the recipient countries very often pocketing the dollars rather than investing them for development.

Mark Pieth, Professor of Criminal Law at Basel University, who, after the first erupting scandals in 2011, was asked by Blatter to helm a Fifa reform programme, turned into an arch critic of the way Blatter operated to cement his electoral favour. While recognising that the GOAL programme did produce 'houses of football' and other significant development around the world, Pieth says it did clearly act as a vehicle for ensuring support.

'It was a presidential programme,' Pieth observed, 'it operated under the auspices of the office of president. So you can understand how Sepp Blatter and Mohamed bin Hammam, acting as the bagman, were going round Africa buying votes with it.'

In an official interview with bin Hammam, by then the president of the Asian Football Confederation, posted on its own website by Fifa in April 2003, he confirmed the essential details set out by Blatter, that the proposed GOAL programme had been a promise of the 1998 presidential campaign.

'Up until 1999, I wasn't involved in the programme, but at the end of that year, the president asked me to chair the bureau, and I gave him the idea of building an infrastructure for national associations.'

He related his proposal to Blatter that they build countries a 'house of football' and he explained it as a strategy for ensuring they left permanent reminders of Fifa's help.

'I told him … we can have ongoing courses but after a year or two, people will forget what we have done. If, however, we start building headquarters or training centres, it is a structure that will remain.'

Asked about the memories he himself would have of a trip to Uganda, where he had just 'put scissors to ribbon' for the new, GOAL-funded headquarters in Kampala, bin Hammam said:

'I can't remember how many projects I have inaugurated, but I always receive a tremendous welcome. Uganda has been no exception and I feel they have opened the door to everybody. There could have been ten thousand people at the ceremony yesterday, and it is the same all over the world. The project was well received from top to bottom in Ugandan society, and this is particularly gratifying. I enjoyed the joy of the people and to say that, as a member of Fifa, you have been able to add something physical to the country.'

Fifa itself, even after bin Hammam's and Blatter's defenestrations, rejects strenuously the accusation that the development programmes were principally about buying presidential votes. The organisation points to the concrete facts of development having taken place as its most important purpose: pitches laid, headquarters built, all over the world, including in many of the world's most difficult countries. The development department points in particular to recent investment in Somalia, which had an artificial pitch funded by Fifa at the Banadir Stadium in Mogadishu that was severely damaged, along with other facilities, in the long and vicious civil war. In 2013 Fifa ran a development course in the country for the first time since a mission had last visited Mogadishu, before all the bloodshed, in 1986. The pitch at the Banadir Stadium has been refurbished, hosting matches in a Somali league of ten teams, and two further GOAL development projects are planned: a technical centre at Mogadishu's College University Stadium, and another artificial pitch.

In Afghanistan, over the course of a decade from 2003, despite the war-torn conditions in the country and continuing presence of the Taliban, Fifa says it has invested $1.5m in two standard GOAL projects in Kabul: a grass pitch at the Afghan football federation complex, and the building of the AFF's 'house of football'. The Afghan Premier League launched in 2011–12 with eight teams, all matches being played in Kabul for security reasons, almost 20,000 footballers were registered in the country, the national team has improved strongly in the Fifa rankings and there has, remarkably, even been progress in developing women's football, with twenty-three clubs open to women.

The Afghanistan women's national team captain, Zahra Mahmoodi, said: 'Our objective is to build a powerful women's national team to compete at an international level. We want to show the other face of Afghanistan to the world.'

The AFF president, Keramuddin Karim, did thank Fifa for making the investment in this development: 'Eight years ago, Afghan football was almost dead,' he said. 'However, through strategic planning in the area of infrastructure we have been able to set up the basis for the future. Fifa's first GOAL project was fundamental since it provided us with an artificial pitch we are currently using for our league matches in Kabul.'

Mark Gleeson, the authoritative South African journalist and broadcaster who has travelled through Africa covering football for thirty years, told me it had to be recognised that the Fifa investment had made a dramatic difference in the continent.

'You take a country like Lesotho,' he said, 'they literally do not have access to another source of money. They have to pay, rather than be paid, for their football to be shown on television. In general there are stories of corruption in Africa and some of the development money not going where it should, of course, but overall, there is a picture of development.'

Emmanuel Maradas says that Blatter clearly had political self-interest in distributing the cash to Africa, and did gain support and votes for having done so, but he is credited with a genuine understanding of the countries' needs, and, after he was voted in at that 1998 congress, for delivering:

'Some of the money might have disappeared into people's pockets,' Maradas says, believing there was too little accountability for it, particularly at first, 'but the bulk of the money is there in facilities, overall it helped Africa a lot; it is like night and day compared to where they were in the 1980s. You go to national associations now, they have headquarters, they are well organised – it is amazing.'

Francis Oti-Akenteng, the technical director at the Ghana FA, who has been involved in implementing GOAL and financial assistance programmes in the country, confirmed that assessment from his own experience:

'This Fifa money is very important to Africa, especially the west and east,' he said. 'From my travels I can personally deduce that. For Ghana without it, football development programmes would have suffered severely, especially the grass roots, youth football and women's football.'

Oti-Akenteng said that the Fifa funds are not as vulnerable to corruption as is commonly perceived: 'Fifa has been very strict with the financial assistance programme [FAP],' he said. 'Fifa auditors check every detail of expenditure, and there are itemised headings; you cannot even juggle them – if it is money for youth development, it must go there, not any other item. Failure to do that, you would be punished. You may lose the next instalment. I think it is not as easy to make use of the FAP money for your own pocket as people are thinking.'

Domenico Scala, the Swiss corporate executive who was recruited by Fifa in 2014 to head the governance reforms, and became chairman of the audit and compliance committee, told me that when he started people pointed to the development programmes as a hotbed for corruption and the basis for a stinking system. He said that he investigated, and they conducted audits, and did not find it to be the case.

'In fact there was not as much corruption as people thought,' Scala said. 'There is clearly a concrete record of development with the money, the evidence is there on the ground. But it was a system of patronage, by which the president distributed money to the electorate. Blatter was a master of playing the electorate, and the Fifa system.'

The development programmes do seem to have entrenched, perhaps inevitably, a culture at Fifa of less well-off countries, federations and their presidents asking the wealthy for money, to help them with development. And that culture clearly bought the loyalty of football associations and their presidents to Blatter throughout his seventeen-year tenure at the top, which was buttressed by his facility for allocating many comfortable and nicely paid committee posts. Later, bin Hammam, harbouring presidential ambitions himself, was found to have liberally indulged in largesse to Asian and African FA presidents asking for aid. As the investigations into the discredited bidding process for hosts of the 2018 and 2022 World Cups showed, this culture of patronage infested the executive committee, too. Presented as an objective process to responsibly choose the best country to host a tournament, the long and wastefully expensive beauty parade was exploited by some confederation representatives on the executive committee, Jack Warner, brazenly, foremost among them, to make demands of the countries bidding for their vote.

At the 2015 congress in Zurich, Mario Semedo, for sixteen years the president of the FA in the tiny islands of Cape Verde, off the west coast of Africa, delivered a set-piece speech which captured the flavour of the Fifa system hatched under Havelange, then Blatter. It combined a record of genuine, admirable development, with a toe-curling public vote of thanks to Blatter, and the then Fifa secretary general Jérôme Valcke – before he too was banned in 2016 for multiple financial offences. Semedo described dramatic progress, a leap up the Fifa rankings for Cape Verde from 179th place to 37th, becoming the sixth strongest football nation in Africa. In front of the assembled FAs gathered to vote for the president, he solemnly thanked and praised Blatter. Semedo said Cape Verde had had no grass pitches in 1998, and now had twenty-five, five of them funded by Fifa.

'Thanks to the impetus of the international federation, its financial assistance, the projects we have been allocated, plus the training and expertise – all under the leadership of president Blatter,' he told the assembly, with Blatter smiling humbly on the platform, 'we have been able to secure funding from the government and other bodies which would never have contributed to our development in the past. We have been able to invest in our youth, in all those young people who dream of being able to play football.'

Blatter himself pointed to the performances in the 2016 European Championships of Wales, who reached the semi-final, and Iceland, who strongly beat England, both of whose FAs gave credit to the investment for development they had received from Fifa. He said Fifa did audit the programmes – the rules were tightened gradually over the years.

'I was not giving them money,' Blatter said, a little strangely, 'I was giving them ideas to develop football. And what do you say now [that] they pay four times more than in my time?'

Gianni Infantino, the former Uefa secretary general under Platini's presidency, who won the Fifa presidential election in May 2016 held after Blatter and Platini were banned, stood on a promise to quadruple the money going to the FAs forming his electorate.

'I have done it because I have promised,' Blatter said, 'and then [the FAs] agreed that what I have done was good. The president of Iceland said the progress is only because of the development programmes we have made. Definitely this is too easy to say: Blatter, he gave the money to the national associations, that they would vote for him. So you have a politician, and he wants to be head of state or a region, and he says: "What I want to do now when I am elected, I will make better roads, more security and help you in educational programmes." They vote for him, and he does it, and so what: he has to be in the corruption, or what?

'You know in football, people are mad. Football makes people mad.'

After 1998, however, while Platini worked as the football adviser to the president from an office in Paris and flew on occasional official visits with Blatter, Johansson and the Europeans on the executive committee did not let up their opposition. Concerns that Blatter was secretive about Fifa's financial situation, and had formed a tight sub-bureau of the finance committee – peopled only by him, the Argentinian FA president Julio Grondona and Jack Warner – were deepened after the collapse of ISL in 2001, Horst Dassler's marketing company having spectacularly overpaid for other sports rights including the tennis ATP tour. The fallout from this insolvency would ultimately, years later and after a cover-up by Fifa, reveal the endemic corruption which had taken place throughout Havelange's time.

Blatter faced, then, in 2002, a seriously confrontational, elemental battle, his enemies rallying around a dossier worked up by a whistleblower at the very heart of the operation, the new secretary general, a Swiss lawyer, Michel Zen-Ruffinen. He alleged criminal mismanagement by Blatter, supported by a twenty-one-page dossier and 300 pages of internal documents. The charge sheet included that GOAL projects were prioritised for personal political advancement by Blatter, particularly to Concacaf, where Warner provided his crucial block of voting support. Zen-Ruffinen remade the claims that votes had been bought for Blatter in the 1998 election, and he also advanced evidence alleging that Blatter awarded TV deals for less than their commercial value. A whole section was reported to have been devoted to Warner, claiming that financial favours were given to Warner and his family, including overgenerous deals on World Cup TV rights for the Caribbean, and that a £6m loan was improperly written off.

At his own press conference, calling for a criminal investigation, Zen-Ruffinen said it was time for Fifa to 'clean its house'. He claimed: 'It wasn't a case of the president being bought, but it was a case of the president buying.'

David Will, the Scottish representative of the British associations on the executive committee, alleged that Fifa's loss from the ISL collapse had been £300m rather than the £37m claimed by Blatter, and that Fifa was effectively insolvent. He and his allies, European and African members of the executive committee, succeeded in forcing an internal audit committee report into Fifa's financial situation, but Blatter deftly managed to have it delayed until after the presidential election in May.

Blatter's opponents, prepared to fight to the political death with him, made a criminal complaint alleging fraud, corruption and mismanagement to the Zurich prosecutor's office. Eleven of the twenty-four-member executive committee joined the complaint, led by Johansson, Per Omdal of Norway, Will, and Issa Hayatou of Cameroon, who accused Blatter of 'illegal' and 'reprehensible' practices. Hayatou was the rival candidate in this election against Blatter, backed by Johansson and other European power brokers, who hoped that the candidacy of an African would play better in Africa than Johansson's own bid had, four years earlier.

Blatter retorted by denying any malpractice, and denouncing his critics. His backers and allies on the executive committee then included Warner, Nicolás Leoz of Paraguay, since found by Fifa to have received bribes from ISL, Grondona, who was accused of massive corruption in the US criminal indictment after his death in 2014, Ricardo Teixeira – Havelange's son-in-law – of Brazil, and Chuck Blazer.

The Zurich prosecutor, Urs Hubmann, announced in December 2002 that he was taking no action, saying that several of the allegations were about financial transactions which the executive committee had themselves approved, calling that 'reprehensible' and 'bordering on false accusation'. In *FOUL!*, Andrew Jennings quoted Hubmann saying that while dismissing all but two of the allegations, he discontinued those two for lack of sufficient evidence. In December 2015, after Blatter's ban, a spokeswoman for Hubmann declined to elaborate, citing 'professional confidentiality'.

Omdal and Johansson told me then that they believed the prosecutor had missed an opportunity to clean up Fifa in 2002, and that action at that time could have avoided more years of mismanagement.

'I feel we, Fifa and football were let down by the Swiss authorities,' Johansson said. 'They had evidence, we filed a complaint in court asking for an investigation, we had Swiss lawyers helping us to present the case, but we lost and Blatter somehow kept everything under control.'

In 2015, the Swiss attorney general, Michael Lauber, announced that he was investigating Blatter for potentially criminal wrongdoing in a 2m CHF payment to Platini, and for World Cup TV rights sold for one dollar to Warner. The written-off £6m loan alleged by Zen-Ruffinen was confirmed in 2013 in a devastating report for Concacaf, which concluded it was part of a massive fraud by Warner over his personal ownership of a training complex in Trinidad, funded by Fifa, and christened the Dr João Havelange Centre of Excellence.

Blatter argues that he did nothing improper when paying Platini, and that the TV contracts with Warner were favourable to Fifa because they included a clause that Fifa should receive 50 per cent of any profit made. When I talked to him, he was confident that he would not be charged with any criminal offence, despite the multiple investigations by the US and Swiss authorities, their possession of every financial and computer record, email and file, subjecting to microscopic scrutiny all his affairs at Fifa, over forty years.

In the teeth of that battle in 2002, with the Zen-Ruffinen file at the prosecutor's office and not yet dismissed by Hubmann, and eleven of his executive committee united so fiercely and accusingly against him personally, Blatter nevertheless comprehensively won a majority of the vote, 139 to 56, to continue as president. Clearly, whatever he had been doing, it was working for the vast majority of the world's national football associations. After surviving the attack and winning this second term of four more years from the wider football 'family' of Fifa, Blatter vowed to 'throw Zen-Ruffinen out of the door', pricelessly denouncing him to the Swiss newspaper *Blick* as 'Mr Clean'.

It was meant as a scathing insult.

CHAPTER 6

2010: 'And the Host of the 2022 World Cup Will Be ... Qatar!' (1)

Two senior football administrative figures, one a former Fifa executive committee member, have told me the same illuminating anecdote about the vote to send the 2018 World Cup to Russia, and the 2022 World Cup, still almost unbelievably, to the tiny Gulf state of Qatar. Neither of these men wanted to be named, because they were worried about any risk of jeopardising their current positions. Both, quite separately, told me that during the long and now most investigated and pored-over World Cup bidding process ever, they were told by Jérôme Valcke, Blatter's secretary general: 'If it is Russia and Qatar, we are finished.'

But then, on 2 December 2010, it was – and they are.

The executive committee, rather than all the national associations, had in 1964 been invested with the power to vote for the host of a World Cup, because it was thought then that this would ensure a more responsible, objective decision. Sir Stanley Rous had recommended the change because he said, as quoted in Alan Tomlinson's *Fifa: The Men, the Myths and the Money*, that having the decision made by the individual FAs was putting a 'strain on friendships' and the choice of hosts was being made 'on not wholly relevant issues'. After the executive committee's credibility-shredding vote to send the 2018 and 2022 tournaments to Russia and Qatar, amid allegations that, at the very least, some executive committee members had sought money and favours for themselves or their confederations, the hosting decision has now been given back to the national associations. The need for bidding countries to pitch to all of Fifa's now 211 countries is felt to be some kind of safeguard, diluting the favours which can be offered compared to the need to win the votes of just twenty-four people – but Rous' experience, even back in more amateurish days, had clearly led him to the opposite conclusion.

Before the vote, Sepp Blatter was in a supremely rarefied position, for which he had worked and schemed all hours, all his professional life. After beating off the tough challenge from Johansson in 1998, then the acrimonious confrontation with Zen-Ruffinen and almost half his executive committee in 2002, five years later none of his opponents could even muster a candidate to challenge him. He was seventy-one then, but still obsessively attached to the workload, pressure, status and acclaim which came with being the head of world football and the organisation he had inhabited for thirty-two years. He was evolving his rhetoric in public, the increasingly messianic claims for football's higher purpose. When he was confirmed in 2007 as the unchallenged president, he said football would 'acquire a more pronounced and extensive social role' in his third term. In his speech to the assembled national associations at the congress, he thanked 'the help and support of members of the global football family'.

There were always stories that Blatter was fixated on capping his life journey from the backwoods of the Valais to the heights of Fifa with a Nobel peace prize. I had thought this was mischievous gossip, but then Per Omdal, the former Norway FA chairman, told me that he did indeed receive suggestions from allies of Blatter that he recommend him for a prize to the Nobel committee, which is based in Norway.

'It was out of the question; we didn't progress it at all,' said Omdal, one of Blatter's vehement opponents on the executive committee and criminal complainants in 2002.

The same had happened with Havelange, Omdal said; Fifa's congress in the late 1980s actually decided that Fifa should formally promote the president for a Nobel peace prize. That, Omdal said, was 'completely out of order'.

Internally, after the career-ending threat posed by Zen-Ruffinen, having turned whistleblower from so privy and trusted a position, Blatter conducted a purge. Zen-Ruffinen has always maintained that he had planned to leave if Blatter was re-elected, and would stay on only to steer the operation of the 2002 World Cup in Japan and Korea. He has said he did that, then resigned, and received a settlement from Fifa. Blatter insists that Zen-Ruffinen was fired. Whichever way it was, Zen-Ruffinen left. People who had worked at Fifa and known Blatter for almost thirty years, since he joined as a smart marketeer on the way up, complained that he had turned ruthless in shoring up his position.

Valcke, who joined Fifa from the French broadcaster Canal+ as marketing director in September 2003, was himself fired in December 2006, after Fifa lost a legal action brought by MasterCard, the credit card giant which had been replaced as a World Cup sponsor by their rival Visa. Valcke was found by a judge in the US to have lied to both MasterCard and Visa when they were bidding to be a 'partner' sponsor for the 2010 and 2014 World Cups for a price of $180 million. Valcke himself subsequently explained in an interview in the *Independent*: 'I made the biggest mistake of my life by saying [in court] that in business we don't always say the truth, and you could describe that as a commercial lie.'

But he insisted his intentions were honest, that he had not been seeking to engage in a secret bidding war between the two corporations by talking to Visa despite MasterCard having first refusal; Valcke said he only wanted to ensure one of the companies would sign up. Then, in May 2007, the original damning judgement was set aside on appeal, and Fifa and MasterCard were reported to have settled, costing Fifa $90m. Very soon after that, Valcke was back at Fifa and promoted to secretary general, right-hand man to Blatter. In that interview in the *Independent*, he said to the journalist David Owen about his rehiring by Blatter: 'Our world is a very small world. We worked closely together for three years. Whatever Blatter asked me and what I committed to deliver when I joined Fifa, I did. So we have a strong relationship, Blatter and myself.'

During his initial three-year stint at Fifa, Valcke had streamlined the main sponsorships down to six: Adidas and Coca-Cola, as ever; Emirates, Hyundai, Sony and Visa, for 2007–14. Those corporations paid more than $1bn to have their names broadcast globally, wrapped around the World Cup. In the same interview, when asked about the widespread allegations that bribes or commissions were endemic in the awarding of sports rights, Valcke replied:

'I agree with you. The old world was the system of commission. Twenty years ago ... you were giving commissions to people in order to get market or to get product or whatever. Today the legal system has changed. I don't know if it's an improvement or not, I just say it has changed. You can't do it any more.'

He said, however, that he had never been offered a kickback for signing up a deal with a partner on Fifa's behalf, or to offer a beneficial deal on behalf of his Fifa masters. 'I have never been asked to use commercial rights to please someone from the executive committee. I have never been asked to sell [anything] for less than market value to one of the countries represented by an executive committee member. [I have] never been asked by Blatter or a Fifa member to make [their] political life easier by using our commercial assets.'

The World Cup was held in Germany in 2006 following a bid led by Franz Beckenbauer which is, at the time of writing, now the subject of criminal investigations in Germany and Switzerland. The tournament itself was at the time hailed as a wonderful success and experience. If the 1954 'miracle of Bern' had breathed greater confidence – helped by Adidas boots and screw-in studs – into the new country still wrestling with the aftershock of war and Nazism, and 1974 had strengthened West Germany's confidence in its modern capabilities, 2006 showed the world a fun side to the reunified Germany. The innovation of the open-air fan zones, where people could have a drink outside and watch the matches on giant screens, was an unexpectedly huge attraction; the fan zone in Berlin, originally expected to cater for 25,000, had eventually to be expanded to host a phenomenal 900,000, once fervour for the football caught on.

The young German squad, managed by US expatriate and former national team centre-forward Jürgen Klinsmann, presented an attractive vision of modern Germany, playing smart, entertaining, passing football. These were the first fruits of the German game's 'reboot', with its emphasis on sophisticated youth development, following dismal failure at the European Championships of 2000 when Germany finished bottom of their group. Klinsmann's team reached the semi-final, where they lost 2–0 to the eventual champions, Italy. But above all, the World Cup in Germany was a celebration, joyful, imbued with a sense of humour, surprising some who experienced it. A documentary about the enchanted month of football, shown in cinemas around Germany was entitled *Deutschland. Ein Sommermärchen* ('Germany: A Summer's Tale'). This was a playful reversal of the poet Heinrich Heine's famous work of 1844, in which he chronicled a visit to the country at a grim, repressive point in its history, entitled *Germany. A Winter's Tale*.

Fifa, basking in the *Sommermärchen*, boomed again, recovered from the collapse of ISL, making a record $3.3bn over the four-year financial cycle up to and including the 2006 World Cup. The TV rights for the World Cup alone accounted for half that, $1.6bn; the sponsorships, with sixteen official 'partners', reaped $700m. Almost a quarter, 23 per cent of this income, was spent in development, including $100m on the GOAL programme and $300m on the financial assistance programme, cash paid directly to the national FAs.

In his foreword to Fifa's 2006 financial statements, headed 'Dear members of the football family', Blatter pointed out 'the extremely positive way' Fifa had managed to recover from 'the turbulent events' of ISL's collapse, a 'rebirth' achieved partly by having taken out a loan advance on the expected massive marketing income. Despite the difficulties, he said Fifa had managed to pay all its commitments to the member associations – and move into its new, granite, bunker-like 240m CHF headquarters near the zoo, 'financed entirely from Fifa's own coffers'.

Looking ahead to further fortunes for the 2010 and 2014 tournaments, Blatter said: 'Football "made by Fifa" is a prized product that makes it possible to provide a house for everyone – as embodied by the Home of Fifa.'

Blatter had not wanted that World Cup to go to Germany; to be fair to him, as the president, he does seem to have wanted tournaments to be where strategically they would expand football territorially, but he had to try and manoeuvre the characters on the executive committee his way. Blatter supported the bid of South Africa to host the tournament for that year, wanting the landmark of a first World Cup in Africa, rather than in Germany again. He was deprived of being able to deliver a casting vote in the event of a 12–12 draw by the abstention of Oceania's Charlie Dempsey, still the subject of the allegation that Dempsey was paid $250,000 by ISL before the vote in 2000, which Dempsey always denied.

For the 2010 World Cup, Blatter got his wish: the first World Cup in Africa, hosted by the country liberated from apartheid, a landmark for Fifa, too, after having expelled South Africa in 1976 following Rous' tortuous tolerance. An ageing and ailing Nelson Mandela, father of the post-apartheid nation and one of the world's most respected and beloved heroes, had been pressed into lobbying work in the service of winning over the Fifa executive committee for the bid in 2004 – particularly Jack Warner. When a majority on the committee did vote for South Africa over Morocco, Mandela, then eighty-five, said he felt 'like a young man of fifteen'.

When the tournament came round six years later, he was weaker and older, but still managed to be a totem of the historic celebrations. After dire warnings about violence and high crime levels in South Africa, the tournament, played in a winter chill and to the wailing of the vuvuzela, was proclaimed a triumph, felt by the government to have broadcast to the world a more positive image of the country, and the continent of Africa itself. Of now six African countries with qualification places, Ghana went furthest, to the quarter-final, losing to the Uruguay of Edinson Cavani, Diego Forlán and Luis Suárez, who was sent off for a notorious handball which prevented a certain Ghana goal in the last minute of extra-time. Asamoah Gyan failed to score that penalty, then Ghana went out in the penalty shoot-out. Germany, now coached by Joachim Löw, reached the semi-final again, losing to the mesmeric passing of Spain, who won the World Cup for the first time in their history with a 1–0 victory over Holland. Mandela – Madiba – made it in person to the closing ceremony, days from his ninety-second birthday, and managed to wave to the crowd, although his grandson complained that Fifa had put Mandela under 'extreme pressure' to be there.

More than the World Cups played in the US or Europe, where stadiums were already built, severe doubts have since been expressed about whether the cost was worth it to South Africa, with its range of entrenched social problems and poverty. An official report released two and a half years later, in November 2012, stated that the government had spent $1.1bn on building and upgrading stadiums, some of which did not have a viable future after the few games played in the one month of 2010 were over. A further $1.7bn was spent on transport and ports of entry. But the government which had itself pressed Fifa so determinedly for the tournament, involving the president, Thabo Mbeki, having personal meetings with Blatter, insisted there was an 'intangible' legacy of pride and unity in the hosting of Africa's landmark great global sporting event.

Fifa made a booming $3.9bn in its 2007–10 cycle, including $2.4bn from the TV rights to the World Cup in South Africa, and cleared $1bn for the marketing rights from Valcke's streamlined six blue-chip partners. Of this, $794m, 22 per cent of the total income in Zurich, went to the member FAs in development cash. Blatter, in his presidential foreword to these financial statements, highlighted $550,000 given to every FA around the world in an 'extraordinary' payment from the Financial Assistance Programme, and $5m to each confederation. He had no worries about his own position, as he looked forward to standing again, contrary to hints he may have given, particularly to Mohamed bin Hammam, who believed he had a commitment from Blatter to succeed him in 2011. Beaming about the World Cup in South Africa which underlined, he said, 'the immense social and cultural power of our game', the development cash, and the long-term contracts with 'multinational companies [which] still seek to identify with football', Blatter added: 'All of this fills me with great optimism and confidence for the period that lies ahead.'

Six months after Madiba and his wife Graça Machel waved to the world from the Soccer City stadium at the emotional closing ceremony in Johannesburg, Blatter was opening a can of worms for Fifa. It was contained in an envelope in Zurich, which he withdrew, seeming to hold it at a distance from himself, before declaring with a rictus grin: 'And the host of the 2022 World Cup will be ... Qatar.'

The World Cup had grown so enormous as a global event, with the prestige and feelgood glow it bestowed on its hosts – even if it was very expensive and the actual legacy was often 'intangible' – that governments were more centrally involved in the bidding than ever. Bill Clinton was at the vote in Zurich, accompanying the USA bid to host the 2022 World Cup, and was said to have been furious when it lost to Qatar, in the final round, fourteen votes to eight. David Cameron, then British prime minister, went to lend his peculiar, Old Etonian breed of glad-handing to England's bid to host the 2018 tournament, with Prince William and David Beckham, cringingly dubbed the 'three lions'. Their efforts did not nudge England's vote above one; Blatter told me:

'There was no sympathy for England. There was no chance for England. I think because they have the best football, they are dominating club football, taking all the best players; there was no sympathy, not in Africa, nowhere.'

Throughout the process, Fifa's executive committee members had been flattered, visited, entertained, indulged, beseeched for their vote. The questions asked in the aftermath, in a more sustained way than ever before, given European and US bewilderment at the Qatar decision, was whether any of them were paid.

England had bid to host the 2006 tournament, losing in the second round with only two votes, but that experience of unsuccessfully engaging with Fifa's executive committee did not deter the FA, and the government, from seeking the reflected sheen of glory again. The bid, to mount a marketing campaign and travel around the world seeking the votes of Jack Warner, Nicolás Leoz, Ricardo Teixeira, Thailand's FA president Worawi Makudi, and all their colleagues, would cost £21m. Of that, £3m was public money, paid over by the twelve local authorities in which the proposed host stadiums would be based. Just as the global financial crisis hit, and the British government began to severely cut its funding to them, the local councils, whose job was to maintain public services for the impoverished populations of Manchester, Liverpool, Sunderland, Newcastle and elsewhere, were each persuaded to put in £250,000.

Headed by the former Manchester United commercial director Andy Anson, an engaging and optimistic character, the theme of England's bid was to showcase the country's deep football heritage, and the ready, refurbished stadiums and flourishing clubs of the Premier League era. The England bid rejected warnings that this was a waste of effort and a great deal of money, because the world thought English football had enough to be going on with, and Fifa's culture had long been suspected of corruption, or at least of favours. Instead, the FA proceeded as if their bid could win the executive committee over, by showcasing the evident qualities of a World Cup in England. They quickly found they were being asked, particularly by Warner, for services, benefits, which had nothing to do with the merits of a World Cup. One member of the England bid team confirmed to me, looking back, that Warner was relentlessly showering them with demands and requests, but that it was part of the strategy to seek his vote and those of the other Concacaf executive committee members.

High-profile public benefits for Warner, covered in the media at the time, included in the summer of 2009 the FA's England bid helping to host a training camp for Warner's Trinidad and Tobago U20 team. The England bid actually sponsored a gala dinner at the annual congress of the Caribbean Football Union, in February 2010 at the Hyatt Regency hotel in Trinidad, suggested by Warner using his leverage, which cost $55,000 (£45,000). In September 2010, David Beckham flew to Trinidad as an ambassador for England's 2018 bid, to launch a six-day football festival run by his academy. The Trinidad journalist Lasana Liburd, who has critically investigated and covered questions over Warner's activities for years, asked the England bid team at the press conference how much the festival was costing, but said he was given no answer.

These efforts for Warner were not greatly questioned at the time, but Warner himself shamelessly played the indignant victim when the British press did question gifts, of Mulberry handbags worth £230 each, presented by the bid to the wives of executive committee members, including Warner. The bags were comfortably within the limits Fifa allowed for gifts, whose giving and receiving had become embedded into the culture over the years. Members of the bid team say they had to think carefully about gifts, that they had to give them, and wanted items which would be interpreted neither as too meagre nor too lavish, so came up with the Mulberry bags, for a dinner in London. But after criticism was made of them, Warner, whose wife had accepted hers, sent it back, with a furious letter to the FA chairman, Lord David Triesman. It was a typically flowery and exaggerated protest, with Warner proclaiming his dignity and honour:

'Had [my wife] or I known then that the acceptance of what we all felt was a kind gesture would have resulted in the tainting of her character and mine together with the untold embarrassment to which we are still being subjected, none of us would have attended the dinner, nor would she have accepted what we thought was a gift in honour of her birthday,' Warner wrote. 'I have faced and continue to face all kinds of indignities from all manner of persons, but when these insults touch my wife, it represents an all time low.'

Then he attacked Triesman, accusing him of failing to defend the Warners adequately: 'Equally disappointing is the deafening silence from you and the FA and which seems to support these allegations. No one has sought to correct this betrayal in a way that would unequivocally remove any doubt or question not only in the global village at large but among my few peers where honour is valued and character is cherished.'

Warner then brazenly said: 'there is nothing that your FA can offer me to get my vote', saying that if England did get it, it would be 'because Concacaf and I sincerely believe that England is deserving of the honour'.

After this characteristic outburst at his integrity being impugned, in private Warner continued to relentlessly ask for favours. The England bid always said that they dealt with the culture of gifts and favours by clearing any proposed activities with Valcke in Zurich, to ensure they complied with the rules.

In the initial phase of the bid, England had employed as a consultant Peter Hargitay, a press and public affairs operator who had worked for Blatter within Fifa. Hargitay knew Warner well, and was also close to Mohamed bin Hammam. Triesman, when he was appointed FA chairman, was not keen on retaining Hargitay, and after the contracted six months' initial work, which had an option on both sides to continue, Hargitay was asked to reapply, which he says he refused to do. Shortly afterwards, he was hired to work as a consultant, also to use his contacts and knowledge of Fifa, and do media relations, for Australia's bid to host the 2022 tournament. Led by Frank Lowy, the Czech-born billionaire owner of the Westfield retail empire and chairman of the Australia FA (FFA), the bid would cost $43m of Australian government money, but ultimately gain only one vote. That was widely assumed to have been cast by Franz Beckenbauer, who now occupied a seat on Fifa's executive committee.

Triesman himself was forced to resign in May 2010 as the chairman of the bid, and of the FA itself, after he was taped in a restaurant by a friend, Melissa Jacobs, sounding off about Fifa. His gossip, published by the *Mail on Sunday*, included that Spain and Russia were plotting to bribe referees, which outraged both countries' bids and led to the FA having to issue hasty apologies.

Triesman said he was only commenting on 'speculation circulating about conspiracies around the world', and he complained: 'Entrapment, especially by a friend, is an unpleasant experience both for my family and me but it leaves me with no alternative but to resign.'

Geoff Thompson, the FA's former chairman, who had risen up the amateur FA ranks of administration and was actually on the Fifa executive committee, took over as the chairman of the bid. Thompson had been secretary of the Sheffield FA, for whom he rewrote the statutes – the rulebook – and he had done the same for Durham and Birmingham, before returning to Sheffield with the proviso that they make him the county's representative to the FA council. Thompson was a faithful server on Uefa and Fifa committees, quietly spoken, never quoted in the press in on-the-record interviews, largely unknown by English football supporters throughout his chairmanship. He went about the role as if serving Fifa in another age, perhaps that of Rous or Drewery, doing a dogged job of the necessary paperwork in his allocated committees, while never truly building the English FA an influence or removing the perception that he was a decent enough man out of his depth among the cast of characters at Fifa's heart.

For all the investigations and inquiries into the events and circumstances leading to a majority of the executive committee voting for Russia and Qatar, and the limited evidence of wrongdoing which they have uncovered, it is striking to recall how little emerged before the vote itself. The most powerful intervention was made by the *Sunday Times*, another undercover sting, in which reporters posed as lobbyists for the USA's bid to host the 2022 tournament. Among the large number of football officials and aspirant middlemen they recorded, they had secretly filmed two members of the executive committee,

Amos Adamu of Nigeria, and Reynald Temarii, the president of the Oceania Football Confederation, asking for development money.

Published on 17 October 2010, just six weeks before the vote, Adamu had been recorded asking for $800,000 to build four artificial pitches in Nigeria. He had asked for the money to be paid to him directly, rather than to the Nigerian football federation, and suggested, according to the newspaper, a relative's European trading company as a conduit. Adamu had, however, previously emailed the reporters reminding them that it was 'against Fifa code of ethics to solicit, directly or indirectly' anything that would influence the vote. Yet the paper did record him pledging to vote for the USA bid for the 2018 tournament, for which the country was at that point still bidding, and the second round of the 2022 vote.

Temarii had told the reporters he was looking for £1.5m to build an academy at Oceania's Auckland headquarters, and that when World Cup bid officials came to talk to him about casting his precious executive committee vote, he would usually ask them: 'OK, what will be the impact of your bid in my region?' He said: 'This is the basic approach when I talk with someone who wishes to get my vote.'

In the recorded meeting, and subsequently, Oceania clarified with the reporters, whom they believed were lobbyists for the USA bid, that any cash offers for development were not directly linked to how Temarii would vote. The *Sunday Times* wrote:

'His officials had become suspicious by the end of the meeting. Temarii said he would vote for the USA second [sic] because of the television revenues and in the latter part of the meeting said the financial assistance could not be linked to his vote.'

Following an investigation into this sting, a month later, Fifa's ethics committee banned Adamu from football for three years for breaches of the official code of conduct, including the rules against bribery. Temarii was suspended for a year, not found to have been soliciting bribes, but for breaching rules on loyalty and confidentiality as a Fifa official. Four other senior Fifa officials were caught in the sting, saying that bribes were being offered to executive committee members for their votes, and they were all banned, too. The ethics committee chairman, the former Swiss international striker Claudio

Sulser, criticised the *Sunday Times* coverage, however, as 'sensationalist', telling a press conference in Zurich:

'What I cannot tolerate is the fact that they changed the sentences, they changed the way they presented the truth. If footage is taken out of context that's twisting the facts. They showed footage that lasted four minutes; we have looked at audio and video footage of several hours.'

The paper stood by its coverage. Adamu and Temarii said they were innocent of any wrongdoing, and would appeal. Adamu said that he was: 'Profoundly disappointed with the ethics committee's findings and had honestly believed I would be exonerated of any charges by now.'

Temarii, from Tahiti, was himself a former professional footballer, who had played in France for FC Nantes in the 1980s and captained the national team. After retirement, he had worked for the government of French Polynesia as the minister for youth and sport, before becoming president of the OFC. He appears to have been dedicated all his career to developing football, and sport, in these distant and struggling islands of his birth. Now his career and life were suddenly blighted. According to one senior member of England's 2018 bid, Andy Anson sympathised with Temarii and gave him a good character reference to the ethics committee proceedings. Anson was clear that in all his dealings with Temarii – the English FA had a signed agreement in 2006 to do development work with Oceania, and the England bid had been discussing renewing it on improved terms – Temarii had never asked for anything personally, and was motivated only by securing better facilities for football in his region.

A week after the first exposé, the *Sunday Times* revealed that it had covertly filmed Michel Zen-Ruffinen, too, who was giving his insights into the executive committee eight years after losing his battle with Blatter. Zen-Ruffinen was recorded saying that some members of the committee would want money for their votes, one was 'the guy you can have with the ladies and not with money', and that another, not named by the paper at the time but understood now to be Jack Warner, was 'the biggest gangster you will find on earth'.

Zen-Ruffinen, who was back practising as a lawyer in Basel, offered to work for the bogus lobbyists for £210,000, making introductions.

When splashed by the *Sunday Times*, Zen-Ruffinen was revealed to have threatened the paper with an injunction to prevent the publication. He said he had been making 'exaggerated' comments to 'awaken' the lobbyists' interest, that he was only offering to make introductions for them, and was 'totally against' bribery. He was said to have been outraged that such stings, in which reporters masqueraded in different identities and published covert recordings of the meetings they were able to attract, were permitted by law in England.

So, Fifa dealt with this crisis by banning Adamu and suspending Temarii, one-twelfth of its highest decision-making body, the executive committee, and to simply press on with the vote on the hosts for the World Cups of 2018 and 2022. Jérôme Valcke said that the prompt action by the ethics committee had 'showed how important it is for us to keep things under control'.

Yet the wider culture of Fifa uncovered by this affair was not addressed. After the vote, when further revelations were made about how bids, including England's, had been conducted, it was clear that the process was used by some on the executive committee as an opportunity to profit from their voting power. The Adamu and Temarii stings have passed into memory as the two men soliciting money for themselves personally, which was not proved. In fact, both were talking in terms of cash for development. Often overlooked in the perception of Fifa, and these kinds of requests, as riddled with corruption, are the huge disparities in football, still, between the rich world and developing countries. For all the good work done in development with the $2bn flowing in projects after the GOAL programme was introduced in 1999, there were also individual agreements for development, like the ones England had with other confederations, including Temarii's Oceania. Some delegates from African FAs, Oceania and elsewhere have come habitually, and to see it as their duty, to seek development opportunities from the hugely wealthy football regions which can afford to do it.

But deciding which country should best host the next World Cup should be a strategic decision made by Fifa itself, for sound, considered reasons, discussed collectively. Rous recommended back in 1964 that the executive committee take the decision, rather than the congress, precisely because he perceived that the national FAs in the congress were deciding on what he termed, diplomatically, 'not wholly relevant issues'. Yet the teams bidding to host tournaments forty-six years later, with the World Cup burgeoned into a global, multi-billion-dollar prestige reflector for countries aggressively eager to have it, were finding some executive committee members had their hands out. This was not necessarily for crude personal bribes, as the Temarii example showed, but however unfortunate and well-intentioned he protested he was, he clearly saw the World Cup vote as a major opportunity to seek development money.

Stepping back from the detail, which came later, in the fallout, you could argue that the 2018 and 2022 World Cups went ultimately to the two countries which wanted them most. Neither is a true democracy, and both were prepared to spend essentially unlimited fortunes on winning the bid, then on building the necessary infrastructure. Qatar's official bid, led by Hassan Al Thawadi, a young lawyer educated in the US and England – first at college in Scunthorpe, of all places, then in Sheffield – had a budget of £100m. Backed fully by the Emir, they based their marketing pitch for the virtues of a World Cup in Qatar on picturing it as a sumptuously resourced catalyst for joy, unity and peace in the Middle East, a corrective to the wars, hostilities and terrorism dominating the world's perception of the region. They had the money to build however many new stadiums and all the linked infrastructure necessary, as part of the Qatar 2030 strategic plan, launched in 2008, to develop the country, broaden its cultural profile and diversify the economy from reliance on oil and gas. To weave the idea of a World Cup in a tiny, mostly undeveloped state in the Gulf into a vision of football, they enlisted some football legends, well paid as ever, to be ambassadors, including Zinedine Zidane, Ronald de Boer and Pep Guardiola, who had had a final lucrative stop in Qatar at the end of his playing career. Al Thawadi's official bid team had travelled the world, including to Angola for the 2010 CAF congress, at which they paid for exclusive access to the African FAs and three executive committee members by generously sponsoring the event. Mohamed bin Hammam was one of the twenty-two remaining executive committee members voting, and his role, not officially part of the bid, was unclear. Major rumours emerged of an alleged pact between the Qatari bid and its Asian supporters, and the Spain bid to host the 2018 tournament, to vote for each other, but Fifa held an internal inquiry which stated it had not established the evidence for such collusion, which would have been in breach of the rules.

Of Russia, even now, little detail is known, except that President Vladimir Putin wanted the 2018 tournament, and that the oligarch Roman Abramovich, Chelsea's owner, was actively involved. Abramovich was one of the handful of men who became overnight billionaires in notorious sweetheart auctions of state industries in the 1990s after the end of communist ownership, in return for support given to the then president, Boris Yeltsin. Vitaly Mutko, the Russian sports minister throughout the time his department was implicated by the World Anti-Doping Agency in an alleged Russian state doping programme of athletes, uncovered just before the 2016 Olympics, which he denied, was leading the bid, and was a member of the Fifa executive committee itself. The 2014 winter Olympics in Sochi, which Putin had also wanted as a proclamation of Russia's global presence and power, were hosted on a vast, purpose-built site, and the total cost, in a country of wincing inequalities, with a majority of the population still sunk in poverty, was a truly astonishing $51bn.

The men who would make the decision, to whom such geo-political power and vast money had to bend at the knee, still with their reputations and positions intact at that crucial point, included Chuck Blazer, Jack Warner, Ricardo Teixeira, Nicolás Leoz and Julio Grondona, all of whom would be accused within five years of massive alleged fraud and corruption by the US authorities. Mohamed bin Hammam, who within two years would be banned by Fifa for life for multiple violations of its ethics code, was assumed to have been a key influence at the time and serenely accepted the congratulations afterwards. Chung Mong-joon, later banned for six years by Fifa for allegedly linking a proposed lavish development fund to the South Korea bid to host the 2022 World Cup, which he denies, was a voter. As was Worawi Makudi, convicted in 2015 of forgery in his re-election campaign for the presidency of the Thailand FA. Adamu and Temarii were absent already, but their conduct and attitude towards the bidding process was not treated by Fifa as a signal that perhaps there was a problem at its core.

Blatter and Platini, of course, were voters. Platini's vote for Qatar, changing his mind from supporting the 2022 tournament being held in the USA, still infuriates Blatter, who finally revealed in 2016 that he had wanted Russia in 2018, then the USA, and had worked to secure a consensus in the executive committee. Platini later admitted that he changed his mind following a lunch at the Elysée Palace in Paris in November 2010 with his country's president, Nicolas Sarkozy, and the son of Qatar's Emir, Tamim bin Hamad Al Thani, who peacefully succeeded his father in 2013. At the lunch, Platini has acknowledged that Sarkozy made it clear he wanted him to vote for Qatar to host the 2022 tournament, and he also was seeking to persuade the Qataris to buy Paris Saint-Germain, the flagship Ligue 1 club then in financial difficulties. There were also very significant trade deals with Qatar which Sarkozy was endeavouring to secure for his country's economy, during the financial crisis which afflicted Europe and the west, when the Gulf countries' wealth increased in significance.

Platini has maintained that Sarkozy did not explicitly ask him to vote for Qatar, but accepted that he knew what the president of France wanted. The then Uefa president also said he did not change his mind due to that influence from the president of his country, but decided a World Cup across the Gulf, in winter, would be 'beautiful'. The vote was, in fact, for a World Cup only in Qatar, in the summer. After the vote, Qatar Sports Investments, a sovereign wealth fund, did buy Paris Saint-Germain, the club Sarkozy supports. QSI, and the Qatar Tourism Authority as a €200m a year sponsor, have since poured in fortunes to fuel star player purchases, PSG's capture of the Ligue 1 championship and routine participation in the European Champions League.

Qatari money for France did not stop at PSG, though; three weeks after buying Sarkozy's club, it furnished the whole of France's Ligue 1 with new riches. The broadcaster beIN Sports, part of Qatar-owned Al Jazeera, did a joint deal for the league's TV rights, paying a hugely increased €607m a year from 2012 to 2016. That was renewed in 2014, increasing to €726m a season from 2016 to 2020. The Qatari chairman both of PSG and QSI, Nasser al-Khelaifi, is also the chairman and chief executive of beIN Sports.

Most significantly for Sarkozy, the Qataris also completed major trade deals with France. These included Qatar Airways ordering fifty A320 neo-family planes made by Airbus at its base in Toulouse. The list price of one Airbus in 2010 was put by one industry journal at $375m. At that price, the total income from that one trade deal with Qatar to the French economy was $18.75bn.

Platini's son, Laurent, a lawyer, was given an executive role at a kit company, Burrda, owned by the Qatar Investment Authority, but Platini denied it had any connection to his having voted for Qatar. Blatter absolutely believes that Platini was influenced by political pressure, and says Platini told him so. He, the undisputed expert of Fifa and executive committee politics, is also convinced that Platini's vote, taking four European votes with him, was the crucial deciding factor giving Qatar its fateful majority.

The technical reports written by Fifa's representative, Harold Mayne-Nicholls, from Chile, had highlighted as risks the heat in Qatar, and that the tournament would effectively all take place in Qatar's only major city, Doha. Mayne-Nicholls was himself later banned from football for seven years, reduced on appeal to three years, by Fifa's ethics committee, which found he had sought favours for relatives, reported to have involved asking for internships and work experience positions in Qatar's Aspire Academy system for his son, nephew and brother-in-law. Mayne-Nicholls, who was well-respected and considering standing as a Fifa presidential candidate when the initial complaint was suddenly made, launched an appeal to the Court of Arbitration for Sport.

Just two days before the vote, true rottenness in the heart of Fifa was alleged with more conviction than ever before, in a programme researched and presented for the BBC's *Panorama* by Andrew Jennings. It was the culmination of years investigating Fifa, during which Jennings had long alleged that ISL had paid bribes to senior people when the company was buying up the World Cup TV rights in the 1990s. Now Jennings had documents, and figures, apparently from the ISL liquidation and Swiss court proceedings which followed. *Panorama* claimed that Teixeira, then still the president, since 1989, of the Brazil football federation (the CBF), had been paid a staggering $9.5m. Leoz, Jennings alleged, had been paid $730,000 personally, in five separate payments, including three lots of $200,000, between 1997 and 1998. Leoz later claimed he gave the money to a school in Paraguay, years later. The other name on Jennings' list was Issa Hayatou, secretary general of the Cameroon Football Association and president of CAF itself since 1987. He was found to have been paid 100,000 French francs, with the German word *Barzahlung* next to his name, meaning a cash payment. Hayatou has always claimed the money was not for him, but for an anniversary celebration of CAF. *Panorama* also had evidence of another alleged ticket scandal involving Jack Warner.

After the 2 December 2010 decision of the executive committee, when only Hayatou added his vote to Geoff Thompson's as England's return for £21m spent, English FA officials would profess outrage at Fifa, imply that several members of the executive committee were untrustworthy for not fulfilling promises of votes and protest that the vote must have been corrupt. Yet before the vote, the FA had tried to have the *Panorama* programme pulled, writing an obsequious letter to the executive committee members themselves, to distance the FA and bid from the BBC's allegations. The letter, read now in the light of all that has happened at Fifa, and all that is known about the recipients, does not get any less shameful than it was at the time:

'It has been a difficult time for Fifa and *as a member of the football family we naturally feel solidarity with you and your colleagues*,' the FA's letter said (my italics).

Pleading with Leoz, Teixeira, Grondona, Warner and all the others to bestow a vote on England, the letter, signed by Thompson and the former Arsenal major shareholder David Dein, who had been recruited to lobby for the bid, said the BBC's programme was 'raking over allegations' and:

'We hope England's bid will not be judged negatively due to the activities of individual media organisations, regardless of one's view of their conduct. We hope you appreciate that we have no control over the British media.'

On the night the programme aired, a statement from the bid, sent by text, derided the *Panorama* allegations of serious, long-term corruption by four voting members of the executive committee, claiming three took bribes from ISL, as 'an embarrassment to the BBC'.

My colleague at the *Guardian* Owen Gibson always recalls as his abiding memory of the vote the sight of Chuck Blazer, sprawled on a chaise longue in the lobby of the Baur au Lac hotel the night before, like an overindulged emperor run to decadence, receiving the tributes of his subjects. Blazer was an abiding sight, as ever, in the row of executive committee members as they watched the final presentations, listened to world stars and world leaders, heard the promises of a development legacy from most countries including England, then went off to vote.

Blatter himself is bitterly convinced that the US authorities only began their investigations, and set out to bring Fifa down, because their bid lost out in the dire voting process of that winter's day in Zurich. The Department of Justice will not confirm when exactly the inquiries began or what prompted them, but it is not clear that they did actively spring from that 2022 hosting disappointment. The fall of Fifa which followed has a clear chronology. It began substantially six months after Blatter drew the name out of that envelope, and forced himself to say, with a jaw-straining smile: 'Qatar.' The voting process has been intensively investigated, with some illuminating results, and a criminal investigation continues by the Swiss prosecuting authority, searching for evidence of criminal wrongdoing.

The real trouble for Fifa, and Blatter, sprang from what happened next: the challenge to Blatter's presidency by Mohamed bin Hammam, in the election for the president due to be held in June 2011, and piles of dollar bills being handed out, on Jack Warner's orders, in a hotel room in Trinidad.

CHAPTER 7

'Crisis? What is a Crisis?'

Six months after the earthquake of Fifa's World Cup votes for Russia and Qatar, at the end of May 2011, Sepp Blatter was facing a challenge in the presidential election to his quest of sailing on for four more years. The challenger was his billionaire former supporter from Qatar, Mohamed bin Hammam. I was sent by the *Guardian* to a grey, drizzly Zurich to cover the congress and election – and the mad, volatile dramas which would unfold at an organisation which seemed to have lost its anchor.

Nobody really understood quite how the alliance between Blatter and bin Hammam, his long-term fixer, had disintegrated to the point of this challenge, the ultimate falling-out in a political culture based on personal loyalties. The bond between the two men had been sealed in the almost forgotten past of 1998, when bin Hammam, an obscure figure in Europe then but already an AFC representative on the executive committee, had been at Blatter's side on the private jet tour to beat Johansson to the Havelange succession. In an email to Jack Warner, which Warner subsequently leaked, Jérôme Valcke had casually predicted that bin Hammam had no chance of winning the necessary votes, and was standing only to 'show how much he hates SB [Sepp Blatter]'. Why he hated him, bin Hammam, the softly spoken kind of construction billionaire and Fifa intriguer, never said explicitly. But it was clear enough that he believed Blatter had given indications, through the years of bin Hammam supporting him, that he would step down and allow bin Hammam to succeed. Michel Platini, cutting an increasingly weary, often grumpy figure as Uefa president by the banks of Lake Geneva, seemed to have the same belief, that he was on a promise which Blatter was increasingly unlikely to fulfil. Bin Hammam had worked unceasingly on the steady elevation of his profile and influence, travelling the world cutting ribbons of GOAL projects whose money dispensary he chaired. He ascended to the AFC presidency in 2002 and, as would later emerge, generously entertained and privately donated money to a crowd of African FA presidents.

He had introduced himself to the English media, inviting several journalists, including me, to a round table with him in London in October 2008. Peter Hargitay, the Hungarian-Swiss media relations consultant hired by Blatter for Fifa six years earlier, was working for bin Hammam on his profile raising, and organised the event. It was at Claridge's Hotel, another in the list of plush, discreet, painfully expensive hotels routinely accommodating football's high-ups in the different world they inhabit. My only experiences of such places – the Dolder Grand, up on a hill in Zurich with a fleet of black Mercedes purring at the front, the Baur au Lac; in London the Dorchester and Claridge's – have been in connection with the regulars of these places who run the people's game. In London I'd always find myself late, on the tube, half running through streets crowded with ambling tourists, then arriving at the front of these palaces to be greeted by the calm authority of a doorman in a top hat, allowing access through a revolving door.

At Claridge's, we walked on carpets of impossible depth, through hallways lined with gilt-edged mirrors, to an upstairs room where bin Hammam was charm and humility personified. He had a wide and gleaming smile, a gentle manner, and his message was only that he wanted more international cooperation in football, and more recognition for Asia. Hargitay had billed bin Hammam as 'one of world football's relevant personalities, a member of the Fifa executive committee and chairman of the GOAL programme, as well as several Fifa committees'. Looking back, of course, it was a stage in bin Hammam's campaign to advance towards the pinnacle which Blatter had first claimed with his significant help.

He had had discussions with Platini, a long-term ally and deputy chairman of the GOAL projects, but Platini, having in 2007 become president of Uefa, also with Blatter's backing, had decided not to run for Fifa president so soon, and not against Blatter. Bin

Hammam began to give strong hints, then finally declared himself as a candidate in March 2011, aggressively late, as Blatter did in 1998. There was talk of the English FA supporting him, as the anyone-but-Blatter candidate.

The aftershocks of the December vote had rumbled on in the succeeding months, with suspicion relentlessly focusing on how Qatar managed to win over sufficient members of the executive committee for a World Cup in a tiny desert state in the sweltering summer. The official Qatar bid team furiously resented the assumption that corruption had to have been involved, believing it sprang recognisably from a prejudiced view of wealthy Arabs. They justifiably pointed to the lack of stories emerging about Russia's victory, in the same vote of the same Fifa men, after a campaign commanded by Vladimir Putin, whose country was described in US diplomatic cables released by WikiLeaks as a 'virtual mafia state'. Russian officials categorically denied wrongdoing, too, with the sports minister and Fifa executive committee member, Vitaly Mutko, pointing out that the World Cup had never been held before in the former communist east of Europe.

On 10 May 2011, the British parliamentary committee for culture, media and sport held an inquiry into the World Cup vote, which featured some more explosive claims. British law enables anybody to say anything in parliament, free from the libel law protecting people from suffering damaging claims against them, which cannot be proven. Under this parliamentary privilege, the committee published a letter from the *Sunday Times* journalists Jonathan Calvert and Claire Newell, featuring allegations the paper had not printed, and heard from the FA chairman, Lord Triesman, about his experiences as head of England's 2018 bid before his loose talk cost him his position.

The letter included claims that in 2004 the bid by Morocco, challenging South Africa for the right to host the 2010 World Cup, had paid bribes to executive committee members, including $1m to Jack Warner. The paper also said that its undercover reporters had been told by Zen-Ruffinen and two African Fifa officials that the current African members of the executive committee were being offered bribes by Qatar, including, one said, for 'projects'. The Qatar bid had described these allegations as 'entirely false', the paper said. The African executive committee members all denied throughout that they had taken or solicited bribes for their votes.

'It was a difficult story for the *Sunday Times* to publish as none of the three people who made the allegations against Qatar was ever likely to be willing to appear as a witness,' Calvert and Newell wrote.

Another story sent in by the *Sunday Times*, which the committee also published with parliamentary privilege, was more specific and explosively damaging to Qatar. The journalists said that a 'whistleblower who had worked with the Qatar bid' – she was later to be identified as the former head of international media relations, an Arab-American woman, Phaedra Almajid – claimed Qatar had paid bribes to the three African executive committee members. The *Sunday Times* said that they had previously published the 'whistleblower's claims' in December, 'in an article which did not name the bidder or the members involved'.

In their written submissions, the paper revealed that the bidder was Qatar, and the committee published the story. The letter said that the whistleblower claimed that Qatar paid $1.5m to two of the Fifa executive committee members with a vote, Issa Hayatou, the CAF president, of Cameroon, and Jacques Anouma, of the Ivory Coast. The letter said that a similar deal had been made with Amos Adamu, before he was banned by Fifa after the *Sunday Times* recorded him making the requests for money to build artificial football pitches in Nigeria.

The paper told the committee, 'The whistleblower said that the cash was to go to the three members' football federations but there would be no questions asked about how the money was used. "It was said in such a way that 'we are giving it to you.' It was going to their federation. Basically, if they took it into their pocket, we don't give a jack."'

From having been claims which could not be published, this was now a story the whole world could run, again and again, with protection from being sued. The *Sunday Times* told the committee they were dismayed that Fifa had not taken seriously and 'effectively swept under the carpet', the recorded comments that the World Cup bidding process paid bribes to the African delegates and that, in particular, Qatar paid bribes.

The Qatar bid again reacted furiously, staggered that in a democracy parliament could be used effectively as a publishing vehicle for allegations which could not be proved sufficiently to be made outside the Palace of Westminster. The Qatar FA responded by saying they 'categorically deny' the *Sunday Times*' and 'whistleblower's' claims.

'As the *Sunday Times* states, these accusations "were and remain" unproven. They will remain unproven, because they are false,' it said in a statement.

Triesman's account was more wide-ranging, not focused on Qatar, but on the Fifa executive committee members themselves, Jack Warner, Nicolás Leoz, Ricardo Teixeira and Worawi Makudi, whom he claimed made corrupt demands of the England bid in return for their votes. The former FA chairman had come prepared to tell these stories, fully aware, as a member of the House of Lords, that privilege protected him from being sued.

He claimed that Jack Warner had asked him and the chairman of the Premier League, Sir Dave Richards, for the FA to build 'an education facility' in Trinidad. Triesman said that Warner had asked that the money to build such an academy should 'be channelled' through him. In a Westminster committee room suddenly hushed with the excitement of stories being told publicly which might otherwise only be whispered, Triesman moved on to Leoz. He said that at a meeting on 3 November 2009, while England were lobbying for his vote, Leoz had personally asked Triesman for a knighthood, as recognition for his services to world football. Triesman said it was put to him that, as a former minister in the British Foreign Office in Tony Blair's Labour government, Triesman must know how such things were organised.

Of Teixeira, the president of the Brazil FA, Triesman said he had a meeting with him on 14 November 2009 in Qatar, when the English FA was bidding for Teixeira's vote. Triesman said he told Teixeira he was grateful for the support of Brazil's then president Lula, for England's bid. He claimed that Teixeira then said to him: 'Lula is nothing, you come and tell me what you have for me.' Triesman said he found this 'a surprising way of putting it and, in its way, a shocking way of putting it, because of how it was likely to be interpreted.'

Finally, Triesman, sitting on a cushioned wooden chair in front of the semi-circle of committee members, relayed his story about

Makudi, the president of the Thailand FA. The English FA and 2018 bid team were, without question, discussing with Makudi the prospect of the England team playing a friendly against Thailand, in Thailand. Triesman claimed that Makudi had been insisting that if the match were played, the money from the TV rights would go to Makudi personally, rather than to the Thai FA.

Makudi would deny this claim so vehemently that he mounted a sustained effort through the English courts to sue Triesman, despite parliamentary privilege, setting precedents in English law. His lawyers argued that statements Triesman made afterwards, in which he was trying to be painfully sure not to repeat his account outside of parliament, but in which he referred to what he had said to the committee, now meant that parliamentary privilege did not protect him. The English Court of Appeal ultimately found against Makudi, maintaining Triesman's protection. However, the former FA chairman's story given in parliament was not corroborated by other members of the England bid team, nor by an inquiry the FA commissioned a lawyer, James Dingemans QC, to undertake. In fact what Dingemans found reflected worse on the English FA than Triesman's account: they appeared to be preparing to grant a more generous than usual deal over the TV rights for the match – to the Thai FA, not Makudi personally – while they were bidding for Makudi's vote to host the 2018 World Cup.

Parliamentary privilege, allowing all these stories to be immediately broadcast and reported, blew new heat into the widespread belief that members of Fifa's executive committee were corrupt, and had used the World Cup bidding process to ask for favours or cash. The committee hearing was just three weeks before the Fifa congress at which Blatter was facing bin Hammam for election of the president. The atmosphere, as Fifa and the national FA delegates gathered in Zurich, was on the border between febrile and hysterical. In this environment, Blatter was viewed by much of the British and European media, certainly, as the incumbent who had sanctioned, and benefited from, a rotten culture, and the challenge to him was very welcome. As the opponent, bin Hammam was viewed as somehow fresh and modern; his own record, long history with Blatter and motives were not subjected to the same scrutiny.

Looking back, knowing what we would find out about bin Hammam, it is clear that in everything he said to support his candidacy there was not much to reveal any higher motivation than personal ambition. Principally, he confirmed that he believed Blatter had pledged to step down in 2006, then again in 2011, as bin Hammam was painstakingly, and expensively, building up his electability at Fifa.

'I was a supporter of Blatter and I have never regretted anything about that – he has contributed a lot for the development of the game,' bin Hammam had pronounced. 'But he has been there a long time in that position. There must be the question: Mr President – when is it enough? … Mr Blatter came wanting eight years, two mandates, then twelve years and three mandates, and now four mandates and actually nothing is changing in the last three or four years.'

When you recall now bin Hammam's professed idea of change, and his attitude to the corruption allegations rocking the foundations at the House of Fifa, he does not look like a reformer. His view, and appeal to the national associations, was similar to Blatter's: that in fact Fifa was being assailed by unfair criticism, and the president should repel it. His pitch to the world's FAs was similar to that made by the English FA to Fifa's executive committee before the BBC's *Panorama* programme: I am one of you. At the congress itself, Blatter would talk of 'devils' besetting Fifa, in a mammoth performance to keep a tidal wave of pressure from overwhelming him.

'I am not saying I am the Godfather of football,' bin Hammam said to one interviewer, in an unfortunate phrase, 'but I don't see anything moving, anything changing. Most of what we are seeing and hearing is criticism from outside towards Fifa and most of the time I don't think it's fair. This is what is driving me.'

Of Amos Adamu and Reynald Temarii, bin Hammam sent the signal to the world that he defended them:

'My opinion is that my two colleagues have been trapped,' he told the Press Association. 'Frankly speaking, I would like to give them the benefit of the doubt. Neither of them has asked for money for themselves, both has asked [sic] for the help of those promoters for their confederations, their countries; they personally were not going to benefit financially.'

Of the criticisms being levelled at Fifa's culture, the doubts over the integrity of those responsible for governing world football, bin Hammam said dismissively: 'Fifa is always under the focus for anything; people will attack Fifa a thousand times more than any organisation.'

Nevertheless, his candidacy made use of a familiar word, as a promise, which looks almost laughably empty now: transparency. At the time, it was irresistible drama; Blatter, emperor of Fifa grown bloated and suspect, facing a genuine challenge, from a lesser known figure who carried himself in public with a certain charm.

The action, beyond what we could have imagined, began as soon as we all arrived in Zurich. Three days before the election at which he would stake his claim before the world, bin Hammam suddenly withdrew. For an organisation scrambling to hoist up its credibility, the circumstances were quite resoundingly seedy. Jack Warner, the Concacaf president so long accused of serially corrupt activities, was at the heart of it. The two men had, according to Fifa itself, been exposed allegedly paying cash to delegates at a Caribbean Football Union meeting on 10 and 11 May, which had been called to give bin Hammam a platform to set out his credentials as a candidate for Fifa president. It is difficult to recall now who the whistleblower – one of them – was without laughing, and still wondering about his motive: Chuck Blazer. Warner's partner for years in the Concacaf and Fifa trough was now, extraordinarily, reporting him for involvement in corrupt activity.

The allegation, compiled in a report by an attorney, John Collins, instructed by Blazer, was that bin Hammam had taken cash to the meeting, at the Hyatt Regency Hotel in Trinidad, and $40,000 had been given to each to the CFU delegates, all of whose FAs had a vote in the presidential election. Warner had called the meeting, the Collins report alleged, and had been involved in the cash being handed out. A photograph of the money itself emerged and was reported worldwide: an actual brown envelope, with piles of dollars in it, apparently given on behalf of Mohamed bin Hammam as a casual bribe for a vote in a Fifa presidential election. After all the years of denial.

Fifa's ethics committee, first formed in 2006, which took proceedings on the initiative of the president's office at that time, was investigating, but Blatter, too, was sucked in. Bin Hammam claimed Warner's account was that he had told Blatter in advance that the cash would be handed out, and Blatter had raised no objection.

On the Saturday evening, 28 May 2011, Mohamed bin Hammam, who had spent a lifetime working, glad-handing, spending his way towards the presidency of Fifa, abruptly announced he was standing down from the election. He was facing the ethics committee hearing the following day, but claimed it was nothing to do with the allegations of cash being handed out, and that he would be cleared of any wrongdoing. It was because, he said, he had suddenly realised, unconnected to the scandal enveloping him and Warner, he should not be engaging in a contest after all:

'I cannot allow the game that I love to be dragged more and more in the mud because of competition between two individuals,' bin Hammam explained. 'The game itself and the people who love it around the world must come first. It is for this reason that I announce my withdrawal from the presidential election.'

Giving this literally unbelievable explanation, bin Hammam then actually said:

'I look forward to working closely with my colleagues to restore Fifa's reputation to what it should be – a protector of the game that has credibility through honesty, transparency and accountability.'

In fact, the opposite would happen: the events in the Trinidad hotel would prompt the crumbling of many of his colleagues' reputations, the concerted investigation by US authorities who had seen their dollars become the currency of Fifa corruption, and the fall of the House of Fifa.

Warner, whom bin Hammam thanked as a friend and colleague for 'his unlimited support', was facing a rapidly assembled ethics committee inquiry into the handing out of the cash. With characteristic fury, late in the night, Warner promised the Trinidadian press that he would in retaliation unleash a 'tsunami' of damning detail against Blatter – which sounded promising.

With a crowd of other journalists I went down to the Baur au Lac hotel where bin Hammam and other Fifa executive committee men were put up when they were in Zurich, transported there by limousine from their first-class flights and fast-track airport departures. Bin Hammam was there, still casting an air of serenity around him, but now he was not talking or explaining. All he did was smile, walk into the lobby, press his hands to his chest, and tell us: 'I am heartbroken.'

The following day, 29 May 2011, after the hearings separately of bin Hammam, Warner and Blatter, Fifa held a press conference in its headquarters at the bunker on the hill. Valcke introduced the deputy chairman of the ethics committee, a Namibian judge, Petrus Damaseb. He told us in a solemn voice that the ethics committee had decided to 'provisionally ban' both bin Hammam and Jack Warner from any football-related activities, due to the evidence signalling that they had apparently been involved in corruption activities. So, very neatly, Blatter was in the clear, now unchallenged by any alternative candidate, free to cruise through a non-election, the only name on the ballot paper, for four more years.

It seemed far too convenient for Blatter to be valid: how, I wondered, had he managed to trigger an ejector seat under his first opponent in nine years, just four days before the election?

Warner unleashed the first waves in his promised tsunami then, claiming that Blatter had given $1 million in cash to Concacaf, and laptops and computers to thirteen Caribbean associations, implying that it was in return for their votes. He also leaked a conversational email Valcke had sent him months earlier. That was the one in which Valcke pondered about bin Hammam standing even though he had no chance, wondering if it was to show how much he 'hated' Blatter – or, Valcke mused, was it because bin Hammam 'thinks he can buy Fifa, like Qatar bought the World Cup?'

That was truly incendiary, from the secretary general of the organisation which had up to then rejected all allegations of corruption in the bidding process. Valcke was forced to explain himself, at the beginning of a press conference called at Fifa House so that he and Blatter could reassure the world. We filed into the main building from an annexe outside in the gardens, to take our places in the conference room. You walk into the forbidding, black Fifa House, and it opens into a huge, vaulting, granite and marble lobby, with a reception desk dwarfed to the side. The effect is not to welcome visitors warmly into the home of the people's game; this entry chamber is a statement of corporate presence and power. We were guided to the left, up some stairs, to a large room set up like a lecture theatre, a platform in front, faced by banks of pull-down seats.

When the president and secretary general of Fifa arrived to face the media, Valcke opened with a clarification of his leaked Qatar allegation, to get it out of the way. 'What I wanted to say,' he told us, 'is that the winning bid used their financial strength to lobby for support. I have at no time made, or was intending to make, any reference to any purchase of votes or similar unethical behaviour.'

And no more, really, has ever been said about the casual assertion of the Fifa secretary general about the bidding process, that Qatar 'bought the World Cup'.

Blatter explained that the $1m to Concacaf alleged by Warner hadn't been any sort of bung at all in return for votes; it was for two extra GOAL projects. That amounted to Blatter admitting that he had it in his presidential gift to hand the money out to regions, shortly before he was standing for election, but it was presented as evidence of Fifa's probity. Blatter and Valcke were flailing at the rising tide of corruption allegations – if true, the Warner–bin Hammam vote-buying accusations surely unveiled a disturbing culture, not some isolated aberration. So they decided to show us all how straight Fifa was, by releasing a summary of the report James Dingemans QC had compiled into the allegations Triesman had made.

'We were happy that there are no elements of this report which would prompt any proceedings,' Blatter beamed. Valcke said the report showed the four Fifa executive committee members named by Triesman to have been 'completely clean'.

A sense settled in that room that we were trapped in a granite headquarters of delusion and bluster. The only candidate to oppose Blatter on the ballot paper had been shot out of the race with an obscure and unconvincing story about cash in a hotel in Trinidad, which, if true, denoted corruption, yet we were being told that their processes were flawless and clean. Blatter did promise reforms to Fifa's governance and compliance at the congress, and held up a thin brochure for the cameras.

'This is our ethics code,' he said archly. 'I am not sure everybody in the Fifa family has read it.'

Asked what he was going to do about this crisis, Blatter famously asked, in a voice which had a quiver in it:

'Crisis? What is a crisis? Football is not in a crisis. We are only in some difficulties, and the difficulties will be solved within the football family.'

My colleague at the *Guardian*, Matt Scott, was furiously challenging Blatter to answer more questions, without waiting for the microphone. That meant, apparently, that his protests were only just audible as agitated squeaks on the live stream, which Fifa's representatives kept product-placing, on fifa.com. Trying to hush him, and under unimaginable pressure, Blatter admonished:

'Listen, gentlemen. I accepted to have a press conference with you alone here. I respect you. Please respect me, and please respect the procedure of the press conference ... Don't intervene. We are not in a bazaar here, we are in Fifa House and we are in front of a very important congress – so please.'

At the end, as Blatter left, somebody in front scoffed at the whole performance, and Blatter produced this enduringly marvellous rebuke: 'Yes, you can laugh,' he retorted. 'That's also an attitude. Elegance is also an attitude. Respect is also an attitude.'

And then he was gone. Back in the annexe, helpful and attentive Fifa staff helped the cadre of journalists with wifi or other niggles, there were coffee and pastries, to help keep the media fuelled as they wrote reports condemning Fifa, lacerating its president. Somebody googled and reckoned they had found that 'Elegance is an attitude' had been a long-ago advertising slogan of Longines. They concluded that, faced with so daunting a challenge, Sepp Blatter's subconscious had come up with a line from one of his former lives.

Later, I had a look at the extracts of the FA's Dingemans report, which Blatter and Valcke had smugly told us ticked the organisation as 'completely clean'. It told a different story, in fact, and it did not look great for the English FA either. Dingemans had found that Sir Dave Richards, the Premier League chairman, supported Triesman's recollection that at a meeting in the Wyndham Grand Hotel, a plush affair, naturally, in London's redeveloped Chelsea Harbour, Jack Warner had indeed asked the FA to build an education block in Trinidad and Tobago. Richards did not, however, recall Warner asking for the money to be channelled through him, as Triesman had said.

Nobody else involved with the England bid confirmed that Nicolás Leoz asked for a knighthood, as Triesman claimed. However, Andy Anson did recall that people who worked for Leoz, including a Conmebol staffer, Alberto Almirall, did show them a book full of honours bestowed on their boss, and 'hinted that it would be nice if England were to recognise Dr Leoz in some way and it would be nice if he would get to meet the Queen'.

Almirall had, the report said, sent an email to a consultant to the England bid, Les Dickens, listing a clutch of countries which had honoured Leoz, including a *Légion d'honneur* from France, and said: 'Confidentially, I know that he would love to have a decoration from the British Crown or government.' Into 2010, Dingemans found that the England bid team were actually looking at ways they could satisfy this yearning.

'Internal discussions ... were taking place within England 2018 about what honour might properly be given to Dr Leoz.'

They had learned that Leoz had vigorously promoted the development of disability football, and been previously honoured for it.

'It is apparent that there was some discussion about creating a FA Disability Cup, and some consideration about whether that might be named after Dr Leoz.' The report continued, however: 'there were different views in England 2018 about whether the proposal was a good idea and the matter was not pursued.'

Triesman's allegation against Teixeira was not corroborated by anybody in the bid team, and left dangling. Considering Teixeira's propensity for real, multi-million-dollar corruption, it was a fairly thin incident, and open to an innocent interpretation, that Teixeira had only been saying it was his opinion of the World Cup bids which counted, not his country's president.

The Makudi allegation, which was to prove so painful for Triesman, who had to fund his own costs to defend the repeated legal actions, was difficult both for him and the FA. Dingemans found that nobody in the bid team agreed that Makudi was looking to have the television rights to the friendly himself. However, the report stated that 'often', when playing a friendly match overseas, the FA retains the UK and worldwide rights, leaving the host FA only the rights in their own country, which would have been Thailand. In this case, by a letter dated 24 November 2010, just a week before the vote, a senior official in the FA's England team structure wrote to Makudi about the TV rights.

'It is apparent there were proposals being discussed whereby the Football Association of Thailand retained not only domestic TV rights, but also rest of the world TV rights except for the UK,' the report concluded.

So, the FA had been discussing giving an honour to Nicolás Leoz, the Paraguayan president of Conmebol, whose vote they wanted, following the suggestions of his own staff. They had given Warner short shrift on the academy suggestion, and the Teixeira comment was inconclusive. But the English FA was discussing a more generous than usual TV rights arrangement with the Thai FA, a week before the World Cup 2018 decision at which they wanted the vote of its president. After England lost, and Makudi was found not to have voted for England, the FA cancelled the discussions about the friendly, which strongly suggests a match with the England team was being used as a sweetener for the World Cup vote. Three years later, when further allegations and unceasing pressure had led the ethics committee to mount an investigation into the World Cup bidding process, it would conclude:

'According to the report, three of the four Fifa executive committee members made improper requests for support or favours towards the England 2018 bid team and/or the FA during the bidding process. With regard to at least two of these Committee members, England 2018 accommodated, or at least attempted to satisfy, the improper requests made by these executive committee members, thereby jeopardising the integrity of the bidding process.'

And yet, at the time, Valcke told the world's media, exhibiting the report for emphasis, that it showed they were all 'completely clean'. It was clear that was nonsense just by actually reading the extracts of the report Valcke had made available. I laid out some of the detail in an article for the *Guardian* the following day, and my colleagues wrote as the headline: 'Sepp Blatter and Fifa reach for the whitewash over FA's report'.

That night, the congress formally opened, with a gala event in the concrete bowl of the Zurich Hallenstadion, an arena which is home to the city's ice hockey team, the ZSC Lions. The highlight was Grace Jones, billed as 'one of the most iconic figures of the 1980s', still on remarkably arresting form, sitting on Leoz's knee in the front row and asking the ageing delegates: 'Are you ready to party?' There was a 'medley of Swiss and international artists' on the programme, between speeches about corruption including from the president of Switzerland, Micheline Calmy-Rey. She clearly felt she had to tell the assembly: 'Where there are concerns about corruption and transparency, it is necessary to listen and reform your governance.'

She was followed by a juggler, Alan Sulc, and a seven-piece breakdancing group, Flying Steps, and the congress, hosted by Melanie Winiger, described as a former Miss Switzerland, was formally open.

The following day, of the election itself, there was a rumbling grey sky, and mizzle outside the Hallenstadion. As the black Mercedes limousines unloaded their FA presidents, there was a demonstration, too. They were young people, shouting something about Blatter, so I asked one of them about it. He said they were the young Green Party of Switzerland, and were protesting Fifa's privileged, tax-free status in the country, which applied to non-profit amateur sports associations, when Fifa made $4bn and its senior figures helped themselves to huge money. I asked him what they were chanting, and he said it was: 'Sepp Blatter: Fuck Off.'

The congress itself was not preparing to do the same. Before the main event, the English FA chairman who had succeeded Triesman, David Bernstein, formerly the chairman of Manchester City, had decided to have his say. He walked to the podium in the capacious arena, the representatives of the then 208 worldwide football associations spread out in front of him. Bernstein called for the election to be postponed, given the envelopes of cash which had apparently disqualified bin Hammam, and asked that time be given for another candidate to be mustered.

'We are subject to universal criticism from governments, sponsors, media and the wider public,' Bernstein told them. 'A coronation without an opponent provides a flawed mandate. I ask for a postponement for an additional candidate or candidates to stand in an open and fair process.'

He then had a very long walk back, across the floor of the arena, picking his way around the tables and chairs, wading through an icy silence. The ferocity of the response was quite shocking at the time. There were prepared speeches, from the Haiti, Congo and Fiji delegates, condemning Bernstein, and lavishing praise on Blatter. The Benin FA president, Moucharafou Anjorin, made a rallying call to the hall: 'We must be proud to belong to Fifa,' he shouted. 'We must massively express our support to President Blatter. Please applaud!' And they actually, mostly, did.

The English media took some hits from speakers including Costakis Koutsokoumnis, the Cyprus FA president, then from Julio Grondona himself, who had a day earlier said he would have voted England for 2018 if the government had given the Falkland Islands back to Argentina. He also said he voted for Qatar to host the 2022 World Cup, because to vote for the USA would have been like voting for hated England.

'We always have attacks from England,' Grondona, the chairman of the finance committee, said, on the podium of Fifa at the sixty-first congress. 'Mostly with lies, and the support of a journalism which is more busy lying than telling the truth. Please leave the Fifa family alone!'

This demonstration was such an extreme outburst of non-transparency, political sycophancy and diversion tactics it was funny, of course. But it was chilling, too, disturbing – and, if you love football, extremely depressing. Towards Grondona, who became the president of the Argentina FA in 1979, and was an associate of the murderous generals who ruled the country and disappeared opponents while ruthlessly laying on a World Cup, I felt an instinctive repulsion. Listening to him, there was the inescapable impression that Grondona gave off an air of fascism.

Bernstein lost his vote for a postponement almost completely: 172 votes to 17. Talking to him now, for this book, he said he felt 'brilliant' about doing it, that he had protested and stood up against a Blatter coronation. But when you reflect on his futile stance, it was also a signal of how absent the FA, football's original founding governing body, was from any international influence at Fifa. The FA, which the founders of Fifa had almost begged to join in 1904, which flounced out twice in the 1920s, was led back in by Rous after the war and played a central, constructive, generally respected role after that. It is astonishing to think that a classic English FA administrator and ex-schoolmaster had been the president of this organisation for thirteen years until as recently as 1974. Now, the English FA was nowhere, and Fifa seemed like a totalitarian world of patronage and dependence, in which journalists were denounced as liars for writing the truth about a corruption scandal.

Blatter talked about the 'devils' and 'threats' swarming around Fifa, and he sank into a muddled, extended maritime vision, in which he was the captain of Fifa's *'bateau'*, steering it to calmer waters. 'Not only is the pyramid shaking,' he said, 'but our ship has drawn some water.' At that congress, he did promise reforms, the one which said the World Cup hosts would be selected by the congress of FAs from now on, not the executive committee; that there would be a governance committee, and the ethics committee strengthened. Looking back, you can see that he had actually taken some proper advice, and some of these decent reforms did happen.

They went through the whole demonstration of showcasing their democracy. Valcke, now wearing the hat of electoral returning officer, one in his multiplicity of roles fixing for Blatter, explained the procedure proudly and long-windedly, that the delegates would all go to a booth and vote in secret. Then he began to call them out in alphabetical order, beginning with Afghanistan. It took almost three hours to reach Zimbabwe, and all the voting FA delegates were filmed and live-streamed for fifa.com, filing dutifully into the booths, deciding where to mark a cross on a ballot paper with only one candidate.

Still, they did not have to vote for Blatter, and it turned out that, again, seventeen had not. Of 203 votes cast, 186 were for Blatter. This was 92 per cent, at a time of unprecedented scandal, when two more of the executive committee, the presidents of two confederations, the AFC and Concacaf, including a candidate for president, had just been suspended for handing cash to delegates, apparently as bribes for votes. As the music rolled and Blatter was handed a bouquet, promising to steer Fifa's 'ship' to 'clear, transparent waters', I remember him throwing out names of people who might serve on his reform committee. 'Placido Domingo!' he cried. 'Henry Kissinger!' Then I am sure he said: 'We will have a woman!'

He sounded like the captain of a ship who had been marooned in the ocean on it alone, clinging to whatever he could say, pleading to be allowed back. The delegates, their job done, having re-elected the president who kept the money coming, filed out for the limousines and the hotels. It all, still, seemed too neat, that bin Hammam had been ousted so completely, with a neatly packaged scandal of $40,000 bills, at just the right time. And yet, as the detail emerged in inquiries and hearings, it turned out, remarkably, to be all true. Here was bin Hammam, all these years after the first allegations of him paying money to delegates in the service of Blatter in 1998, which Blatter vehemently denied, apparently caught doing so to grease his own presidential challenge. Blatter emerged storm-lashed and windswept, still the skipper of the *bateau* at the age of seventy-five, sailing on for four more years. But in truth, this affair of the $100 bills in Trinidad had holed his liner below the waterline, rendered it too leaky for even his remarkable wiles to fix, and cast him off, without the means to reach the next port before its traumatic sinking would begin.

CHAPTER 8

Straight Citizens

For lovers of football, who do not want to believe that the men in charge of the world game are mired in corruption, or that they become involuntarily greedy once a grinning captain ushers them into his ship of plenty, there is some heart to be taken from the scandal which began to sink it. After all the many years of furious denial, it was really the first actual, publicly accepted instance of proven corruption at this high level in Fifa. That the first member of the executive committee to be exposed in this way was Blatter's challenger for an election four days later was so convenient, it still leaves a lingering trail of discomfort. Whichever way you look at it, though, it turned out that it was no fit-up of Mohamed bin Hammam and Jack Warner. They really did go to that hotel in Trinidad, bin Hammam pitched for the votes of delegates from the small island FAs in the Caribbean Football Union, who were then offered $40,000 in cash, in actual brown envelopes. Warner said it was 'a gift', that it could be used for football development – so casually was this most important work of Fifa used as a label for money washing around.

And yet, in the fall of Fifa which inexorably resulted from it, this concrete, blatant episode of corruption can be clung to as a restorer of faith in people, in football people: it was undone because there were some honest souls in the room. The story, which had dropped bewilderingly among us in the already feverish gathering of Blatter's re-election congress, was illuminated more clearly in the years which have followed. Bin Hammam was banned from football for life by Fifa's ethics committee, which he appealed to the Court of Arbitration for Sport (CAS). There were hearings, public decisions, including the reasoning of the ethics committee chaired by the Namibian judge Petrus Damaseb when suspending Warner and bin Hammam before the election. Evidence and documents spilled out from various sources, revealing what had happened almost in full. They exposed the insides of Fifa's business beyond the ground covered in the preceding decades, providing a chronicled account of those far-reaching days in May.

Looking back, it is remarkable that bin Hammam and Warner risked this, so brazenly, in front of so many people, so soon before an election. The only possible explanation for this is that they believed everybody in the room would eagerly accept $40,000 in cash. That suggests that handing out cash was a feature of the culture of Fifa, not an outlandish thing to happen, as Warner would later assert. But, clearly, some people assembled at the hotel did not accept that it was.

The facts, as they emerged in the hearings and were accepted by the lawyers presiding over the judgement at CAS, began with bin Hammam indeed going to Trinidad, to talk to the delegates from the member associations of the CFU, on 10 May 2011. The meeting was held at the Hyatt Regency in the capital of Warner's island, Port of Spain. It is, of course, a plush establishment, commanding views of the ocean, of a uniform standard with the international chain hotels in which Fifa business is routinely conducted, a level below the independent world-class heights of the Baur au Lac in Zurich. It describes itself as 'a stunning Trinidad hotel and conference center', offering 'unprecedented luxuries in a breathtaking Caribbean destination'.

Bin Hammam had said that he could not obtain a visa to the US, and so could not go to the congress of the whole confederation of the Americas, Concacaf, which took place in Miami on 3 May. Warner, who had always marshalled the Caribbean countries as a block vote within his Concacaf presidency, had called a special meeting of the CFU on 10–11 May, at which bin Hammam would present his virtues as a candidate. Warner had told bin Hammam he would have to pay all the expenses, including hiring the Hyatt, and paying the substantial costs of travel and accommodation for the delegates, who otherwise had no reason to go. Bin Hammam was both exceptionally wealthy, through his Kemco construction company which had worked at the heart of Qatar's building boom after oil and gas were discovered, and used to paying out money to smooth his Fifa journey. He duly wired $360,000 to the CFU for expenses, and subsequently handed over a further $50,000 for additional expenses which might be incurred.

That $410,000 was not the money which was even the subject of the corruption claims; it was just a routine bit of expenditure for bin Hammam to hold a day and an overnight of Fifa meetings for some voters in the Fifa presidential election. It even emerged that Warner's own travel company, Simpaul, in Trinidad, had booked the tickets. Blazer, it was revealed later, had not wanted this to happen; he had told Warner there were 'ethical problems' with holding such a special meeting, which bin Hammam was paying for in order to present his candidacy to just the CFU voting associations. But Warner did not listen, which was said to have riled Blazer for a start. Bin Hammam flew in to Port of Spain on 9 May 2011, the day before the scheduled special meeting. He was with Fifa and AFC associates, including Worawi Makudi, the president of the Thailand FA.

Angenie Kanhai, the secretary general of the CFU, told the CAS hearing that as Warner was the minister of transport in Trinidad and Tobago at the time, his government ministry's protocol officer met bin Hammam at the airport. So the government of the Caribbean island was used in the service of a candidate for the Fifa election.

For all the time and expense of travelling such a distance to this meeting, bin Hammam only spoke about his candidacy for around forty-five minutes, humbly asking for the assembly's vote in the election against Blatter. After that, according to witnesses, Warner announced that there were 'gifts' for the delegates, and they should go up to one of the hotel rooms, which was being used by the CFU as a boardroom, to pick the gifts up, one by one, between 3 and 5 p.m.

The CAS judgement, issued in July 2012, recited what happened next:

'In the afternoon of May 10 2011 ... Ms Angenie Kanhai went to Mr Warner's office to collect a locked suitcase, which she then took back to the Hyatt and handed over to her assistants, Mr Jason Sylvester and Ms Debbie Minguell. The suitcase contained a number of unmarked envelopes, each containing $40,000.'

Kanhai, who did give evidence to CAS, provided this description: 'The suitcase was a very good quality one, orange and black,' she told the hearing, 'and it was not the kind of suitcase that Mr Warner normally uses.'

In his report about the affair compiled for Blazer, the lawyer John Collins wrote that there was in total $1m cash in the suitcase. After Warner announced there were gifts for the delegates, they began to go separately into the boardroom. There, they were each handed one of the envelopes, with $40,000 inside it.

'Some of the delegates were told at the time that the cash was a gift from the CFU to their national association for the development of football,' the CAS judgement narrated.

One of the delegates at the meeting, whose account of what happened was subsequently a central part of the evidence, was Frederick Lunn. He was the executive vice president of the Bahamas FA, there as its representative among the other FAs of the Caribbean. Lunn said that he went up to the boardroom at around 3 p.m., and there were other CFU representatives sitting around in the lobby area. He said the boardroom door was locked when he first knocked, he was asked to wait, then, after a few minutes, another delegate to the meeting, whom he didn't know, left the room and he was invited to go in. He said he entered, that Debbie Minguell was sitting at the boardroom table at the back of the room, she asked him to sign and print his name on a form, then a man, whom he did not know (later confirmed to be Jason Sylvester, the CFU staffer), handed him an envelope, stapled shut, with the word 'Bahamas' handwritten on the cover.

'I opened the envelope and dumped the contents on the board room table. I observed US currency, four stacks of $100 bills fall out of the envelope and onto the conference table,' Lunn later affirmed in his statement of evidence.

'I asked Ms Minguell and the male what this was for, and was told that it was $40,000 in cash, and that it was a gift from the CFU,' Lunn stated. 'Ms Minguell asked me to count the cash, and I declined. Ms Minguell also stated that I should not discuss the cash with anyone else, and that I should conceal it so that others would not know I had received the money.'

Lunn said that he told Debbie Minguell he was not authorised to accept the money, 'and that I could not take the cash through the

United States when travelling back to the Bahamas. Ms Minguell responded that I should mail the money back to the Bahamas.'

Lunn said that he decided to hold on to the money and contact the president of the Bahamas FA, Anton Sealey, about it. He took his jacket off and covered the envelope with it, so that when he left the room, nobody waiting outside would see he was carrying it. He texted Anton Sealey at 3.18 p.m. asking him to call urgently. Sealey's recollection, given in an affidavit of evidence, was:

'I promptly called Mr Lunn who told me that he had just been handed a package containing US$40,000 in cash as a "gift" for attending the special bin Hammam CFU meeting. He asked me if I knew anything about this cash gift. I told him that I did not and that under no circumstances would the BFA [the Bahamas FA] accept such a cash gift. I told Mr Lunn to return the cash and make sure that the individuals in the conference room change the sign-in sheet to make it clear that he had returned the money.'

At 3.33 p.m., Lunn took a picture of the cash and envelope with his Sony camera – the photograph which would go round the world as an indelible image of Fifa corruption: dollar bills, in a brown envelope. Then he went to give it back. He stuffed the envelope, with the cash in it, 'in the waist of my pants', so that it wouldn't be seen. He said that he told Debbie Minguell and the man whom he did not know, that the Bahamas FA would not be accepting the gift; they said it was no problem, and took the money back.

The texts between Lunn and Sealey became part of the evidence. This crudest form of corruption, which had always been denied at Fifa – paying stacks of cash, for votes – was being played out while, remarkably, the televisions in the hotel were broadcasting reports of the parliamentary committee in London which had that morning heard from Triesman and the allegations of bribes paid by the Qatar bid.

Lunn's text at 4.23 p.m. read: 'Sealey a lot of the boys taking the cash this is sad given the breaking news on the tv CNN right as I type the note. I'm truly surprise [sic] it's happening at this conference.'

Sealey replied: 'I am disappointed but not surprised. It is important that we maintain our integrity when the story is told. That money will not make or break our association. You can leave with your head high.'

Lunn then asked: 'Should I save the photo for you to see?'

'Of course,' Sealey replied. 'I have never seen that amount of money. I need to see what it looks like. LOL.'

'It hurt to give it back,' Lunn texted, 'what bill it could pay. But it was the right decision. They said no problem.'

At 5 p.m., still at the Hyatt, Fred Lunn called David Sabir, the secretary general of another Caribbean FA at the bin Hammam gathering: Bermuda. Sabir's experience had been identical; he had been invited into the boardroom, given the envelope with $40,000 in cash, but had not accepted it, and called Larry Mussenden, his FA president. Mussenden is a senior member of the legal establishment in Bermuda, having qualified as a barrister in 1995; he also served as a major in the Bermuda regiment for sixteen years. He had been appointed a senator in 2003, from 2004 to 2006 he was the attorney general and minister of justice, offices which made him the chief legal adviser to the Bermuda government. At the time Fred Lunn was in Trinidad with the brown envelope of cash down his trousers, Mussenden had his own law firm, was president of the Bermuda FA and chairman of Fifa's own appeals committee. In March 2016 he was appointed director of public prosecutions in Bermuda. When he took the call from Sabir, Mussenden does not appear to have wanted to jeopardise all of that career and reputation for $40,000 dished out by Mohamed bin Hammam and Jack Warner in a brown envelope.

In the account of Mussenden's reaction related by Damaseb's ethics committee judgement: 'Mr Mussenden had advised [David Sabir] that the Bermuda Football Association would not accept any cash gifts and that if any contribution was to be made to the Bermuda Football Association it would have to be accompanied by the proper letters authorising such contribution and it would need to be wire transferred.'

Another delegate at the meeting who refused to accept the money and later spoke about it was Sonia Bien-Aime. She was secretary general of the Turks and Caicos Islands Football Association, the archipelago of coral islands, still a British Overseas Territory, with a total population of 33,000, near the Bahamas. She confirmed to Collins that she had been offered $40,000 in cash, had called her FA president, Christopher Bryan, and he had said she should not accept it.

What happened next turned into the firing of the torpedo into the hull of the Fifa *bateau*: Anton Sealey called Chuck Blazer. Sealey told him about the money, that at this meeting called by Warner to hear bin Hammam's presidential credentials, $40,000 in cash had been handed out as a cash 'gift'. Sealey asked him if this money had possibly come from the CFU, as stated, and Blazer told him the CFU did not have access to anything like that sort of money.

Blazer, in his evidence, given to Damaseb's hastily convened ethics committee inquiry, revealed that he had not wanted Warner to hold this meeting and had said bin Hammam should speak at the Concacaf congress. He said that Sealey had called him, told him that Fred Lunn had been offered the $40,000 in cash, and this was 'a very unusual, and what he felt, uncomfortable situation'. Blazer, oddly, did not call Warner then, but said he emailed him, at four o'clock the following morning, 11 May 2011. He said Warner replied that he would call him at 8 a.m.; in fact Warner did not call Blazer until 2 p.m.

Warner, after receiving the email from Blazer, brought forward the next day's morning meeting from its scheduled start at 10 a.m., to 8.30. At it, he hectored the attendees in characteristically florid tones and, this time, language which damned him. Fred Lunn said that Warner told them he had already received calls from both Fifa and Concacaf about the 'cash gift' and that Warner pronounced himself: 'Disappointed with some of the attendees who told Concacaf about the money contrary to the CFU's instructions.'

A film of Warner's speech was later leaked, and it was a fine and strident lecture in the requirements of omertà, delivered in Warner's unique style:

'There are some people here who believe they are more pious than thou,' Warner told them. 'If you are pious, open a church, friend. But the fact is, that our business is our business. You can come in here to cuss and disagree and rave and rant but when we leave here, our business is our business. And that is what solidarity is about.'

He moved on to give an explanation, which confirmed that bin Hammam had been the source of the $1m, explaining that a suitcase of cash was nothing out of the ordinary; he had brought it to save him carting actual gifts halfway across the world to the meeting:

'It was given to you because he said he could not bring the silver tray and some silver trinkets and so on. So I said forget all of that, put a value on it and give it to the countries. And the gift you get is for you to determine how best you want to use it for development of football in your country.'

Warner said it could be used for 'grass roots programmes', or whatever they wanted.

'But it is not a gift that I told him to give to you, because … I didn't want him to appear that he is buying votes.'

Warner said: 'If there is anybody here who has a conscience, and wishes to send back the money, I am willing to take it and give it back to him at any moment. Or conversely, you think you don't want it, then give it to somebody else who you think is in need.'

Warner looked around the room and suggested some of the other FAs to which the money could be given, mischievously naming his own, Trinidad and Tobago. Then he repeated his warning: 'But don't go and talk about it outside, and believe that you are pious and you are holy, and you are better than anybody else. I hope that is very clear.'

They all sat and listened to this blatant, casually delivered threat to keep the episode in-house, but it was too late for that. Sealey had already called Blazer, the secrets were out, and Blazer was sweating extremely worriedly on the implications. Blazer's account was that when Warner finally called him back at 2 p.m. that second day, 11 May, Warner was relaxed about it all, saying: 'bin Hammam was going to be giving out money and he didn't want it to come from him [bin Hammam].'

'I said to him, I said: "Listen,"' Blazer told the ethics committee when he gave evidence in person, 'I said: "I'm getting calls that people are complaining that there's money being given out. What sort of response am I able to give them? Where is this, what is this about?"'

Warner, Blazer said, replied that the money was instead of gifts, and that 'even the president', meaning Blatter, 'knows about it and I've got his okay'.

Both Blazer and bin Hammam gave this evidence, that Warner had said Blatter had known about it and given the OK. Warner was ultimately to deny having said that.

Afterwards, Blazer was hailed as a whistleblower, a figure who had stood up for ethics at Fifa, and for a brief time, while he was still free to, Blazer revelled in that saintly status. At the time, I fished out the card he had given me at the Emirates Palace Hotel in Abu Dhabi and called him, and he told me he had reported Warner because: 'I believe it was the right thing to do.'

Now, when the world knows that Blazer had been taking kickbacks and embezzling money, and not paying tax, for years, it is clear it was not that straightforward. There are theories about why, really, he turned whistleblower, called Jérôme Valcke and set in train the whole ethics committee procedure which would blow bin Hammam out of the presidential race and also send Warner spiralling out of football. But actually and probably unwittingly, Blazer gave away a persuasive explanation for why he did it, in his own evidence to the ethics committee. After Warner blithely told him the cash gifts were fine and Blatter had sanctioned them, Blazer said he replied:

'Jack, listen, this is not an answer that I can give anybody. There is absolutely no justification of what you're telling me. There's nothing that I can say in what you're telling me that I could even expect anybody else to understand.'

Blazer put his predicament, then, in terms of needing an explanation from Warner for the honest people, how he could reassure them that nothing corrupt was going on – which might lead to further difficult questions. Blazer appears to have been instinctively alarmed, that this episode was reckless, much too public and uncomfortably close to home.

Damaseb's five-man committee asked Blazer about Warner and their relationship. In Concacaf, they went back as far as 1983, Blazer said. Within a couple of years from meeting then, they had realised 'the opportunity was there to consolidate the votes of the Caribbean', uniting the islands to cast their votes as a block of thirty-one among Concacaf's forty-one countries. That would ensure a president could be elected from that relatively provincial part of the Americas, rather than Mexico or the other bigger football countries, and enable Warner to wield influence there, and at Fifa. Blazer soon suggested to Warner he should go for it. He said that the very day after Trinidad and Tobago missed out on qualifying for the 1990 World Cup, losing

1–0 at home to the USA in that notorious match, Blazer had gone round to his house and suggested Warner stand for president.

'It was a discussion that he and I had had in 1986 when we looked at the old men that were sitting up in front of the room at that time and … said: "One day, you know, it'll be us."'

Warner won the election on the vote of the numerically superior smaller associations of the Caribbean, and he then immediately elevated Blazer from his role in the US FA to become secretary general of Concacaf. Blazer boasted a little about what a good job they had done together since taking over; the confederation had had only $50,000 in the bank, he said, but now it had 'a good marketing programme, good competitions, good support … good staff, good people'. And they had been able to stay in control for twenty years – Warner, he said, had been able to keep 'the base of the votes, the core votes, together in the Caribbean'.

But Warner had in more recent times become erratic and more difficult to deal with, Blazer said; there was 'a major change in his whole attitude'. He had become involved in real politics at home – he was actually an MP and a government minister – and had been stepping back from his Concacaf activities.

'There are times when he thinks he's above it all,' Blazer said. 'And that's certainly the attitude that I found in this case when I dealt with him and spoke with him about it, as if: "I can do whatever I want."'

The next passage of explanation is acutely revealing of the culture they had shaped and protected, and how Blazer saw it. It is only so clear now because the world knows about the financial takings Blazer and Warner were helping themselves to in all the years at Concacaf, when their business was their business and nobody more pious than them knew about it:

'It's one thing if [Warner] wants to harm himself,' Blazer said, referring to the 2006 ticketing scam which was at that point the only decided case of misconduct against Warner. 'If he sells a World Cup ticket at a profit and he … gets his knuckles rapped on it, that's one thing.

'But when he starts to turn around and put packages of money together to give to our member associations, many of whom are *unsuspecting*, many of whom *don't know* [my italics]; and many of whom, like Anton Sealey who is – you know he's a member of his national bank. He's – this is a guy who is a straight citizen.

'When you start putting people like that in jeopardy it crosses the line … It wasn't a personal issue, I just had to stop that from being the case and I had to report it. It was my obligation to do so.'

It is difficult to read this explanation for why Chuck Blazer reported his partner of twenty years at Concacaf, without seeing it as expressing a need to stop Warner from further breaching the omertà. Perhaps the opportunity to deal a fatal blow to bin Hammam played into Blazer's decision as well; perhaps he believed Blatter would usefully owe him for removing his presidential opponent. But actually, like Valcke, nobody within Fifa seems to have believed bin Hammam stood a chance of beating Blatter for votes, and even after all this, Warner might have wielded the Caribbean block vote for Blatter. Blazer's motives seem much closer to his own interests than those political calculations. He appears to have been greatly concerned, flustered, that Warner, by engaging in an episode as reckless as cash in brown envelopes, handed to all the associations, was doing exactly what Warner cautioned the Caribbean FAs not to do: showing the world their 'business'. By conducting business like this, outside of their closed doors, involving 'a straight citizen' like Anton Sealey who would need a convincing answer that all was above board, Warner was becoming a liability. If Blazer had no 'answer he could give' to a straight citizen like Anton Sealey, but did nothing about reporting the incident either, perhaps the straight citizens would start to wonder about him. And so, Blazer had to report Warner. He was not being more pious than thou; he was doing necessary business.

At 8.30 on the morning of 12 May, Blazer called Valcke. 'I said: "We have to deal with this and we need to deal with this in some quick fashion,"' Blazer told the ethics committee.

It then happened extremely quickly – the election was barely more than two weeks away. Blazer contacted John Collins, the attorney, on 15 May, to carry out a full inquiry, and Collins talked to Lunn, Sealey, Sabir and Mussenden, and gathered evidence from them. He said he talked at length to Sonia Bien-Aime but that although she confirmed what had happened, she did not want to go on record and swear an affidavit of evidence. Collins told the ethics committee: 'She was concerned that the Caribbean is a series of small islands and there could be retribution if something happened in the case.'

Blazer himself also told the committee that Bien-Aime 'felt in jeopardy', and 'intimidated', about giving her evidence, after the members had been told not to provide information.

I did ask her, Lunn, Sealey, Sabir and Mussenden to talk about their experiences, telling all of them it appeared to be heartening that they stood out in the fall of Fifa as honest people who did what was right. None was prepared to do so. Bien-Aime did not reply, nor did Lunn or Sealey, to repeated requests. Mussenden's office in the ministry of legal affairs of the Bermuda government responded to say: 'Please be advised that Mr Mussenden declines the invitation for an interview.'

Sabir also declined, but his reply was a little fuller: 'While my position on the issue of good governance and integrity, in particular, the fight against corruption in football is unwavering I respectfully decline your request for such an interview at this time.'

I got the impression that for these people, too, standing up so publicly, through a tremendous, globally exposing process which saw many of their long-term colleagues at other FAs disciplined, banned or lose their jobs, had not been easy. And that the Caribbean is indeed a small place for all of this to happen.

John Collins was forthright in his report and evidence and he concluded that the money was provided by bin Hammam in 'a campaign to buy the voting needed to win the election'. Collins believed that was the reason bin Hammam had not gone to the Concacaf congress in Miami, and deliberately went to Trinidad instead – in a private plane, Blazer said – because he would not be subjected to the same level of scrutiny and questions about arriving with a suitcase full of dollars. CAS did not rule on that point; in fact their judgement accepted as a fact that bin Hammam was denied a visa to the US.

Collins' report concluded: 'Mr bin Hammam and Mr Warner caused cash payments totalling approximately $1m to be paid or attempted to be paid to officials … Mr bin Hammam and Mr Warner organised this special meeting of CFU officials for the express purpose of allowing Mr bin Hammam to represent his candidacy to these Fifa voting members, ask for their vote, and present his $40,000 cash "gift" to each one. This gift was in addition to paying all the travel costs for these officials to attend this "special meeting" in Trinidad.'

The politics of Fifa did, surely, influence the speed with which the pair was dispatched by the ethics committee and bin Hammam ejected from the presidential election. At that time, the ethics committee was not independent – that, to be fair to Blatter, was introduced as part of the reforms after he won his one-man election. In effect, the president asked the ethics committee to investigate possible breaches, a very handy power for Blatter. Collins' report was only completed and sent to Valcke on 24 May, one week before the election was to be held. Valcke immediately asked the ethics committee to investigate and they found the time to do so straight away.

The ethics committee wrote to bin Hammam the next day, 25 May, telling him he was under investigation for multiple breaches of the Fifa code, including possible bribery, and inviting him to attend a hearing in Zurich on 29 May. On 28 May, with so many Fifa delegates and the world's media gathered in Zurich for the congress, he announced he was stepping down from the presidential race. On 29 May itself, the ethics committee provisionally banned bin Hammam and Warner from all football activities, and Damaseb was giving his unconvincing performance in the press conference, which I attended, announcing the bans to the world. That was five days from the arrival of Collins' report in Valcke's inbox, to Blatter having an unopposed election for another term as president.

Blatter's evidence to the committee, a transcript of which has also been leaked, was a masterclass in presidential grandstanding and exposition of his ease with the levers of Fifa power. Blatter was, after all, accused of serious ethics breaches, of having sanctioned the payments: David Sabir and Blazer both said that Warner told them he had cleared the 'gifts' in advance with Blatter. When he sat down in front of the committee, Blatter was greeted by Damaseb, the interrogator in chief, like this: 'Welcome, President Blatter.'

Blatter proceeded to give his account of the episode: he recalled he had indeed had a conversation with Warner before the meeting, and he had told Warner he should not organise such a meeting of the CFU, which was not a full meeting of Concacaf.

'And when he was speaking about the aspect of money,' Blatter said, 'I told him again: "Don't speak about that."'

This was Blatter's evidence, that when Warner talked to him about the meeting and said they might give money, Blatter had told him 'to not speak about the money'.

Clearly relaxed, Blatter argued that he was accused of not having reported a breach of the Fifa ethics code he knew about, but he said he had no knowledge of any such breach, because this was a conversation before a meeting, which he told Warner not to hold. Asked if he wanted to say anything in his defence, Blatter told them it was 'a sad day to be here', but he was happy to defend himself. Then he recalled that at the 2006 congress in Munich he himself had had 'the initiative' to set up the ethics committee on which they were sitting. At the time, as bin Hammam and his lawyers would point out in their appeal to CAS, the Fifa executive committee, over which Blatter smoothly reigned, appointed the members of the ethics committee and fixed their fees for the work. Irrelevant to the facts of what he knew in advance about the suitcase of cash at the hotel in Trinidad, it seemed to be a little reminder to his inquisitors that they owed their positions, and fees, to him. He promised that he was committed to 'zero tolerance', and he thanked them all 'for your dedication for the good of the game … I congratulate you.'

'Thank you very much, President Blatter,' Damaseb replied, before asking Blatter where he would be for them to communicate their decision.

'I am in my office, I am working,' Blatter said.

When he received the communication, it was to tell him that he was cleared of any charge, and therefore free to walk through the election to his fourth term as the president.

But although it had all felt at the time, in the heated, claustrophobic, paranoid cocoon in Zurich, like the whole scandal was too good for Blatter to be true, it was all pretty much as stated. Damaseb's committee's report, although produced in suspiciously record time, nevertheless recited the key elements of this crude episode, and concluded: 'It appears rather compelling to consider that the actions of Mr Bin Hammam constitute prima facie an act of bribery, or at least an attempt to commit bribery.'

Of Warner, the committee concluded, the fact that he planned to say the money came from the CFU itself: 'Makes it seem quite likely that the accused contributed himself to the relevant actions, thereby acting as an accessory to corruption.'

Not holding back on the force with which they were suddenly pursuing out of Fifa bin Hammam and Warner, two long-term fixtures at the heart of the executive committee, the ethics committee commissioned a heavyweight investigator: Louis Freeh, a former director of the FBI and US federal judge. His Freeh Group produced its report on 29 June 2011, with Blatter off on the winds of his new term already. The report concluded, like the ethics committee:

'There is compelling circumstantial evidence ... to suggest that the money did originate with Mr Bin Hammam and was distributed by Mr Warner's subordinates as a means of demonstrating Mr Warner's largesse.'

While bin Hammam was at the Baur au Lac touching his hands to his chest, telling us he was heartbroken, and saying no more, Warner was rattling with fury and saying a lot. That first night, he dropped Valcke's email about Qatar having bought the World Cup, and he was threatening his 'tsunami' of revelations from his many years in the executive committee, during which he had been a confirmed ally of Blatter. Then, on 20 June 2011, when he was still provisionally suspended and facing a final hearing, Warner suddenly announced he was resigning from all positions in football, thus putting himself beyond reach of Fifa. Warner, similarly to bin Hammam's explanation for standing down as a presidential candidate, maintained he was innocent but was resigning to spare Fifa, Concacaf and the CFU 'further acrimony and divisiveness'.

In his statement, Warner said: 'I am convinced, and I am advised by counsel, that since my actions did not extend beyond facilitating the meeting that gave Mr Bin Hammam an opportunity to pursue his aborted bid for the Fifa presidency I would be fully exonerated by any objective arbiter.'

He reserved some scorn for Blazer, saying: 'I have lost my enthusiasm to continue. The secretary general that I had employed, who worked with me for twenty-one years, with the assistance of elements of Fifa has sought to undermine me in ways that are unimaginable.'

Considering that the ethics committee had found compelling evidence that Warner had been an accessory to corruption, and had said corruption 'affects the very core of sports and is to be considered as nothing less than life-threatening for sports', Fifa issued a startlingly eulogising statement of farewell to Warner.

'Fifa regrets the turn of events that have led to Mr Warner's decision,' Fifa said in its statement, bewilderingly. 'Mr Warner is leaving Fifa by his own volition after nearly 30 years of service, having chosen to focus on his important work on behalf of the people and government of Trinidad and Tobago as a cabinet minister and as the chairman of the United National Congress, the major party in his country's coalition government.

'The Fifa executive committee, the Fifa president and the Fifa management thank Mr Warner for his services to Caribbean, Concacaf and international football over his many years devoted to football at both regional and international level, and wish him well for the future.'

He could hardly have had a more congratulatory leaving statement if he was retiring at the height of his career. Fifa went out of its way to emphasise he was not guilty of anything, even though he had been suspended.

'As a consequence of Mr Warner's self-determined resignation, all ethics committee procedures against him have been closed, and the presumption of innocence is maintained.'

Warner also said, about the cash being handed out to CFU delegates at the meeting, that it was part of the culture of Fifa:

'It's not unusual for such things to happen and gifts have been around throughout the history of Fifa,' Warner said. 'What's happening now is for me hypocrisy … This is giving the impression that Fifa is sanitising itself.'

It remains a puzzle, still, why Warner, who pronounced his innocence and all-round rightness with such extreme rhetoric, would suddenly step down without fighting the charges. And why Fifa, with a case against him so blatant and all but proven, would shower him with praise. It would emerge later, from a forensic audit of the AFC's accounts, that bin Hammam had paid Warner $1.2m for what the two men had said were legal costs – Warner had some trouble persuading any bank to accept the money – but that does not explain it. Some have said that Warner had agreed to calm his 'tsunami' and certainly, from that point, his allegations against Blatter and Fifa did abate until the major storm of the indictments blew in.

On 18 August 2011, the Fifa ethics committee announced its final decision on bin Hammam: guilty of breaching the world football governing body's code on bribery, giving gifts and other offences. After so many years constructing a career and political empire in football, lending support to Blatter in 1998 and 2002 in ways which have still never been fully revealed, Mohamed bin Hammam was banned from football by Blatter's Fifa, for life. Bin Hammam did not accept that, and he appealed to CAS. Their panel of three senior lawyers, including the noted human rights barrister Philippe Sands QC, were not at all impressed by Fifa's conduct of the case, nor, in particular, by the total exoneration of Warner. They did not accept that Fifa's ethics committee should have stopped its investigation into Warner despite his resignation, arguing Fifa 'disabled itself' from a thorough examination of what had happened.

Blatter gave evidence to CAS but, the judgement said: 'Mr Blatter declined to answer its questions concerning the circumstances of Mr Warner's resignation and the termination of disciplinary proceedings against him, as well as the relationship between these two events.'

CAS did not in fact uphold the life ban on bin Hammam, finding, perhaps surprisingly, that Fifa and its ethics committee had not proved that the cash in the suitcase definitely came from him. Blatter had made contradictory statements: in the first, a written one the day before his tour de force performance at the ethics committee, he had said that Warner did tell him in advance that CFU members would receive money from bin Hammam. But then in the hearing itself, Blatter said: 'But we didn't speak about that the [sic] money is coming there – from who the money is coming.'

Angenie Kanhai, the secretary general of the CFU at the time of the scandal, also gave contradictory statements, CAS found. In July 2011, soon after the events, she had given her version in a note to the CFU executive. In that, she said Warner had told her there would be gifts for delegates at the Hyatt, but not that he'd said bin Hammam was the source of the gifts. She made her second statement on 27

February 2012. The CAS proceedings were far advanced by then, with bin Hammam arguing that the Fifa ethics committee had been biased, partly pointing to the fact that its members were appointed by the executive committee, 'chaired by Mr Blatter, and composed of his close associates, who deal with the compensation of the committee members and its staff'. Bin Hammam was also arguing that he was not the source of the cash in the suitcase at the Hyatt, and that the ethics committee had no definitive proof that he was. Fifa was adamantly defending its ban of bin Hammam and the ethics committee process, and arguing that it had sufficient evidence, including from statements Warner had made, that the money came from bin Hammam, who was the only person with 'a motive to provide gifts'. At the time Angenie Kanhai made her second statement, Fifa was compiling its response to some of these challenges by bin Hammam. Kanhai, the CAS judgement says, was unemployed at the time – following the scandal, she had resigned as CFU secretary general in December 2011. In this second statement, made two months later, she did tie bin Hammam in as the definitive source of the money, differing from her earlier statement by saying that before the 10 May meeting: 'Mr Warner told me that the gifts were token gifts from Mr Bin Hammam.'

Two days after making that second statement, the CAS judgement records, Fifa gave Kanhai a job, as a development officer. CAS were not very impressed.

'It may be that the timing is entirely coincidental,' the judgement states, 'but given the significance of the addition to the statement, and her failure to provide a compelling (or any real) explanation for it, the panel is bound to treat the evidence with some degree of caution.'

I asked Angenie Kanhai, via her LinkedIn profile and Fifa's own press office, for her response to this questioning of her credibility; Fifa replied on behalf of their employee that she did not want to comment, and later she confirmed that herself.

With these flaws in the Fifa process against bin Hammam and its baffling exoneration of Warner after he stepped down, CAS pronounced the case against bin Hammam not proven for an offence so serious as bribery. However, it was an empty victory for bin Hammam in his striving to prove he was actually innocent. The CAS panel were clear that they did believe it was 'more likely than not that Mr Bin Hammam was the source of the monies that were brought into Trinidad and Tobago and eventually distributed at the meeting by Mr Warner'.

The judgement emphasised that, in applying the law, the panel 'is not making any sort of affirmative finding of innocence in relation to Mr Bin Hammam ... It is a situation of "case not proven," coupled with concern on the part of the panel that the Fifa investigation was not complete or comprehensive enough to fill the gaps in the record.'

This result of the cash being handed out in brown envelopes at the Hyatt Regency in Trinidad was, on the surface, that bin Hammam's ban was overturned, but without clearing his reputation of the smell of bribery, and Warner had resigned from football with his record intact despite his central involvement. Blazer was hailed as a man who did the right thing by football. Blatter was in the clear as president. But the respite for all of them was brief. These men were all conducting themselves as if nobody could see into their privileged, luxurious bubble of Fifa politics. But this was, after all, basic and very public corruption, in the US's backyard, using US currency, which some of the delegates sought clearance to take through US airports – there is a limit of $10,000 by law.

Then, in August 2011, Warner launched another broadside at Blazer, saying in an open letter:

'I began to be concerned with Blazer several years ago when I became aware of the large sums he was earning in commissions. He refused to respond fully to my questions in regard to them ... Up to this point in time [since 2004], neither he nor his company has any valid contract with Concacaf.'

Warner did not seem to realise how damning for him, as well as Blazer, his ranting allegations were, and that serious questions were mounting very publicly indeed now, about the money and running of Concacaf by Warner and Blazer, and of the AFC by bin Hammam. Soon, there would be some very serious people, not just Fifa and its looking-glass world of political manipulators, seeking proper answers.

In Kuala Lumpur, headquarters of the Asian Football Confederation where bin Hammam had been the president for nine years, reformers took the opportunity of his suspension by Fifa to have a look at the books. Led by Prince Ali bin Al Hussein, a member of the royal family in Jordan yet an unlikely battler for openness and democracy in football, the AFC instructed forensic accountants PricewaterhouseCoopers (PWC) to conduct an examination. Their report was published on 13 July 2012, after CAS had heard all the evidence on the Trinidad shamelessness, and just four days before its panel was due to deliver its 'most likely guilty, but case not proven' verdict.

The PWC report itemised multi-millions of dollars being paid, unexplained, into and out of a private account kept for bin Hammam at the AFC. It highlighted $14m paid into that account, for bin Hammam personally, in 2008, and connected that payment to the AFC's sale of its TV rights, although the report said there was no 'direct evidence to confirm a link'. Then, listed over nine pages, was $2m of payments going out to individuals and FAs, some unexplained, others with a range of reasons adding up to a strange tombola of apparently random patronage from bin Hammam. The report said that the AFC made these payments on bin Hammam's personal instruction over several years, with 2008 being the most active year.

One of the direct beneficiaries was Jack Warner himself, in March 2008 $250,000 being sent to a Concacaf account in Trinidad, with a confirmation which noted: 'payment to Jack A Warner on behalf of AFC president'.

A name from the past, Elias Zaccour, the agent who supported João Havelange's efforts to win the 1974 election and paid the overdue fees of several African FAs, was handsomely paid by the AFC under bin Hammam thirty-three years later. Described by PWC, based on reports, as 'a racehorse owner and purported Fifa lobbyist', Zaccour was paid $139,100 to his account in a Luxembourg bank, described as being 'on behalf of AFC president', but with no further explanation PWC could see.

Mostly in 2009 and 2010, bin Hammam had the AFC pay significant amounts to fifteen Asian FAs, largely in poorer countries, stated to be for various football-related needs, including $90,000 to North

Korea's FA to build a pitch for the mini-soccer game, futsal, and for fencing. Bin Hammam was also paying off fines and fees charged by the AFC to some FAs, which the report said 'appears highly unusual', and subsidising some countries' fees to participate in AFC championships. In July 2009, bin Hammam had the AFC pay Fifa just under $8,000 to settle fines imposed against Myong Chol Kim, a coach for the North Korea FA, for offensive behaviour during a match.

'We do not know why the AFC president would pay a Fifa imposed fine on behalf of the offending party,' PWC said. 'This may be seen by some as a clear conflict of interest.'

Bin Hammam was found to have had the AFC pay more than $700,000 in travel and 'allowances' for Confederation of African Football delegates to go to Kuala Lumpur on trips in 2008, for which the expenses included 'city tours, shuttle services, shopping and entertainment within Malaysia'. The AFC also bought a Nissan pickup truck costing $26,820 for the Gambian FA, whose president explained that it was so that talent scouts could get around the country to watch players. It was not explained why the Asian Football Confederation should be making such direct payments to delegates and FAs in Africa.

Some of the payments appeared to amount to personal generosity to people in football, including $20,000 to the secretary general of the Bangladesh FA, who was undergoing treatment for cancer, and paying the hospital bills for the president of the Philippines FA.

In amongst it all was some largesse to Sepp Blatter, too, in February 2008: $1,983 spent by the AFC, on bin Hammam's instruction, on fourteen shirts made for the Fifa president by the Lord's Tailor, apparently a renowned and expensive outfitters in Kuala Lumpur. In September 2008 Issa Hayatou, the president of CAF, was bestowed a similar gift: suits, from the Lord's Tailor, costing $4,950, paid for by bin Hammam's AFC. There were gifts for Warner, too, a Canon camera costing $490, and a Samsonite, presumably a suitcase, costing $367 from a department store in Malaysia.

Bin Hammam also put his own personal and family expenses through the AFC books, including having cash advances of $1m between 2002 and 2011, for which he gave no reason or receipt, the report said. There were hotels, meals, a car was bought for $12,840 in October 2010 – 'the recipient of this car was not stated' – $232,370 for three privately chartered flights; many payments to the Lord's Tailor to buy suits for bin Hammam; cosmetic dentistry for his daughter ($4,748); evening dresses; $100,000 to bin Hammam's wife, Naheed Rabaiah, with no reason given; and $2,114 for bin Hammam's son's honeymoon.

The forensic accountants' advice to the AFC was that the vast money paid in for bin Hammam's personal benefit looked 'highly unusual', and 'there does not appear to be any rationale or AFC business purpose' to the pack of payments made on his behalf to FAs and individuals. The conclusion of this investigation, after all the effort bin Hammam had put in to be exonerated over the Trinidad cash, was distinctly damaging:

'In view of the recent allegations that have surrounded Mr Hammam [sic],' PWC wrote, 'it is our view that there is significant risk that:

The AFC may have been used as a vehicle to launder funds and that the funds have been credited to the former president for an improper purpose (Money Laundering risk),

The AFC may have been used as a vehicle to launder the receipt and payment of bribes.'

Of the array of payments and mingling of his own private life with that of the football confederation, the report said: 'There remains a risk that potentially inappropriate expenditure has been incurred by the AFC in relation to the President, his family, friends, business contacts and other third party individuals such as member associations and related individuals.'

PWC also believed the AFC might even have breached international sanctions, by making dollar payments to people and the FAs in Iran and North Korea, which were subject to sanctions regimes.

The journalist James M. Dorsey, who covered the PWC investigation in regular blogs and in his book *The Turbulent World of Middle East Soccer*, reported that bin Hammam did instruct accountants of his own in an effort to justify all expenditure set out in the PWC report. Bin Hammam denied wrongdoing and there are not understood to have been any criminal or other legal proceedings based on the report. However, while CAS said the report had come too late to be taken into account for its judgement into the Trinidad payments, and anyway was not directly relevant, Fifa's ethics committee seized on it. On 17 December 2012 bin Hammam, who two years earlier had basked in the triumph of his country, Qatar, being awarded the 2022 World Cup, then mounted a challenge to Blatter for the Fifa presidency, resigned from all his roles in football and committed never to be active in football again. But additions to the ethics committee's powers had given it the authority to still discipline individuals even after they have resigned and so it banned bin Hammam for life from football anyway.

The announcement of their decision stated that bin Hammam's ban was for 'repeated violations' of the rules against having conflicts of interest, while bin Hammam had been AFC president and a member of the Fifa executive committee, in the years from 2008 to 2011, 'which justified a lifelong ban from all football related activity'.

From the refusal of some honest people not to take what was alleged to be bin Hammam's money, offered in brown envelopes in a Trinidad hotel in an almost ostentatiously public procession, light was being shone for the first time into the fiefdoms of Fifa. And some long-time chiefs, former supporters and allies of Sepp Blatter, were beginning to fall, very hard indeed.

CHAPTER 9

The Dr João Havelange Centre of Excellence

Chuck Blazer was still glowing under the halo of his claimed reinvention as a whistleblower, the ethical exposer of Jack Warner and Mohamed bin Hammam, shocked by corruption in football, when, on 6 October 2011 he suddenly resigned as secretary general of Concacaf. His resignation statements are another set of Fifa-related baloney difficult to read, now the world knows what it knows about him, without laughing. After the alarming – to Blazer – public disaster organised by Warner in Trinidad, which led Blazer to the high-stakes gamble of finishing his thirty-year partner, a crowd of the Caribbean football officials who took the money were subject to disciplinary proceedings, and Concacaf was engulfed in infighting.

Lisle Austin, president of the Barbados FA, who replaced Warner as interim president, immediately fired Blazer, apparently for having hired John Collins to mount the investigation into Warner and the envelopes of cash. Austin nevertheless launched an investigation of his own, an audit of the Concacaf finances, but when he turned up to the Concacaf offices in Trump Tower, 725 Fifth Avenue, New York, Blazer's den for years, Blazer did not let him in. The Concacaf executive committee then suspended Austin for exceeding his own authority in the removal of Blazer, pointing out that the statutes invested only the executive committee with the power to sack the secretary general. Austin challenged his removal by taking legal action in the Bahamas, to which the Concacaf executive committee responded by complaining to Fifa, whose statutes require people with disputes over 'football matters' to settle by arbitration at CAS, not in full public view in the courts. In August 2011 Fifa suspended

Austin for a year, and Concacaf replaced him with another care-taker president: Alfredo Hawit, a fifty-nine-year-old lawyer and former professional player, from Honduras.

Yet when, after this titanic battle to keep him, Blazer abruptly stepped down, in a period of total, unprecedented scandal and upheaval at Concacaf, his public explanation was to say: 'We've been through a little bit of a stagnation period.'

Chewing on ideas for his future plans, Blazer pondered: 'I want to do something entrepreneurial.'

In reality, he was in very deep trouble. The risk he took that reporting Warner would haul their business back from the plain sight of 'straight citizens' had had the opposite impact. The cash in the Trinidad Hyatt Regency was the most naked of corruption scandals, and the whole world, and the US law enforcement authorities on whose patch it had taken place, were now keenly interested. The investigations initiated by Austin also continued, and in August 2011 the journalist Andrew Jennings reported in the *Independent* that the FBI was investigating offshore accounts operated by Blazer in the Cayman Islands and the Bahamas. Jennings reported that three payments had been made to these accounts in 2010 by the CFU, whose president was still Warner at that time: $250,000, then $205,000, then $57,750, a total of $512,750. As Blazer was employed by Concacaf, and did not work for the CFU, Jennings wrote that the FBI wanted to understand why the money was paid.

Blazer, still revelling in his new reputation as a battler against corruption, had insisted in response: 'All of my transactions have been legally and properly done, in compliance with the various laws of the applicable jurisdictions based on the nature of the transaction.'

In hindsight, it is clear Blazer knew the exposure of these payments was potentially lethal. He told Jennings first that the $250,000 payment, in March 2010, was 'repayment of a personal loan' he had made to Warner. Then, desperately in retrospect, he changed his story, alleging Warner may have 'misused CFU funds' and that he, Blazer, would be prepared to pay the money back if that was the case.

That drew another fire-and-brimstone response from Jack Warner, on 31 August 2011, which now looks, as Blazer feared Warner was becoming, astonishingly reckless. Given in a statement reported by Richard Conway, then of Sky News, later an award-winning reporter of Fifa affairs for the BBC, Warner denied making any personal loan to Blazer, but dug both of them a much deeper hole. Warner said he had in fact paid Blazer three amounts of $250,000, a total of $750,000, 'from the Caribbean Football Union's account *with funds received from Fifa* [my italics]. I do not know why Blazer is pretending otherwise.'

Warner added that Blazer was asking for a further $250,000, to take the payment up to $1m, but Warner had refused to pay it unless Blazer 'provided me with a complete accounting of his Concacaf earnings'.

Warner threw in a further public allegation that Blazer had not had a valid contract with Concacaf since 2004 and was earning 'large sums' from commissions. Warner claimed that when he refused to pay the further $250,000, Blazer's 'attitude significantly deteriorated' and, clearly referring to the Trinidad scandal, that: 'Instead of providing the accounting, Blazer treacherously planned and coordinated an attack on myself and the CFU.'

It would be four more years before Blazer would tell his side of the $1m story, and the remaining $250,000 Warner had not paid him, and it would turn out to be arguably the most brazen, rotten Fifa scandal of all, an ultimate betrayal of football.

In *American Huckster,* Papenfuss and Thompson reported that it was less than two months after his resignation, on 30 November 2011, when Blazer first felt the hand of the FBI on his shoulder, as he rode his mobility scooter along 56th Street to another Manhattan dinner. They happened upon the story a couple of years later in the summer of 2014, because, Papenfuss would reveal, she had known Blazer's partner, Mary Lynn Blanks, personally years earlier when they were 'young moms' with children at the same elementary school. After Blazer had been collared, Blanks had impulsively sought Papenfuss out, and told her larger than life story. They first reported that Blazer had agreed to wear a wire for the FBI on 2 November 2014. Before that, the world was unaware that Blazer had accepted from 2011 that he was facing years in jail, very likely the rest of his life, unless he cooperated with the FBI and agreed to try and covertly incriminate his former colleagues.

Through 2011, further damaging stories continued to emerge from the falling out of Warner and Blazer, including that Concacaf had failed to file tax returns and owed millions of dollars in unpaid tax. In early June 2012, Warner would allege in the media that Blazer had paid the rent on his plush apartment in Trump Tower with money from Concacaf. Most extraordinarily, it was claimed that the Concacaf centre of excellence in Trinidad, built with millions of dollars from Fifa itself and named after the former Fifa president João Havelange, was not in fact owned by the football confederation at all, but by Warner himself.

The men left standing at Concacaf were struggling to rally their confederation amid these scandals raining down on it, and they decided to mount a substantial investigation of their own. It was established by the new president, Jeff Webb, who was elected on 23 May 2012, to succeed Alfredo Hawit's interim stint. Webb, then forty-seven, a banker in the tax haven of the Cayman Islands, had been president of the FA there since 1991. He was considered a capable, well-off character, rising in stature in football, and due to his election to the Concacaf presidency he immediately became a member of the Fifa executive committee. Within Fifa, Webb had already served for nine years as the deputy chairman of the audit committee, and was a member of the transparency and compliance committee. Now, on his elevation to the executive committee, he became chairman of the audit committee, and his expertise was also dispensed on the finance committee, the Fifa organising committee for the 2014 World Cup in Brazil, the development and strategic committees and the task force against racism and discrimination, in which role he travelled the world promoting anti-racism projects.

Webb had stood for election to be president of Concacaf on a platform promising 'Transparency, accountability and reform ... and to take necessary steps to preserve integrity in the sport of football.'

Upon Webb's election, at the Concacaf congress in Budapest – in a five-star hotel complex, naturally – reported by the Trinidadian journalist Lasana Liburd, Sepp Blatter was in attendance, and had been delighted, saying: 'The credibility of Concacaf is back.'

Webb himself said in his victory speech that he wanted to get back to a focus on football, away from 'politics and economics' at Concacaf: 'We must move the clouds and allow the sunshine in,' he said.

But Liburd also reported a warning given by one of the Concacaf member countries' delegates, the Cuba FA president, Luís Hernández, who said:

'In all our countries corruption and shady use of resources has a clear name: robbery and theft … There are robbers with guns and there are robbers with white collars – and I don't want us to be represented by a thief with a white collar in Fifa.'

Jeff Webb immediately set about implementing reforms, announcing the setting up of new committees focused on transparency and reform of the confederation, including an 'integrity committee'. Then, in July 2012, Webb and the Concacaf executive committee recruited their replacement for Blazer as secretary general. The new man to fulfil that central operating role was Enrique Sanz, a Colombian-American sports executive in his thirties. Sanz came to Concacaf from the US arm of the TV rights and marketing company Traffic, which bought the rights to many of the Concacaf and Conmebol tournaments and sold them for broadcasting and sponsorship. Sanz was billed as a supporter of the reform efforts initiated by Webb, and the right man to steer them to fruition. Webb introduced him as 'a professional with competence and integrity'.

Ted Howard, who had been acting as secretary general, stepped back to his previous position of deputy secretary general. Jill Fracisco, latterly acting as the deputy secretary general, who had worked at Concacaf since 1994, starting the competitions department then becoming director of competitions and events as the Gold Cup grew in prestige and profile, was passed over for any promotion by Webb.

The new integrity committee was launched on 14 September 2012. Webb and his colleagues had, true to their promises, not held back from appointing people of substance, who would properly investigate the deluge of allegations now swamping Warner and Blazer. This would be no whitewash or cover-up.

Its chairman was David Simmons, a former attorney general and chief justice of Barbados, and for twenty-five years a member of parliament on the island; Ricardo Urbina, a US judge for thirty-one years, and Ernesto Hempe, retired partner in charge of risk management and ethics at PricewaterhouseCoopers, based in Central America.

Jeff Webb introduced this threesome as a formidable team to do the necessary work of truth and honesty: 'We have invited the most qualified and reputable individuals in their fields to assist us in the fulfilment of our vision,' he said, 'building a powerful structure of integrity, transparency and accountability to allow our region to grow.'

The lawyers and ethics consultant on the committee had plenty to go at, and in their report, a 112-page wallop of a document produced on 18 April 2013, they did not hold back. Warner and Blazer had dominated Concacaf, and the business of football itself, right across the Americas, a huge geographical region, for two decades. They had lorded it as Fifa executive committee members in Zurich, London, Abu Dhabi and around the world, wielding the power of their turf's votes, allies of Sepp Blatter in his battles with the reformist Europeans. After the years of ferocious denials by Warner of any wrongdoing alleged to him, and Blazer's brief, ludicrous honeymoon as a feted whistleblower, this report crushed them both.

Before burying the men, the Concacaf integrity committee took a moment to praise them. Warner, elected president with the caucus of the Caribbean votes in 1990, and Blazer, whom he immediately appointed secretary general, had taken over a 'languishing confeder-ation'. Back then, soccer in the USA was still scrabbling for a foothold in the attention span of a nation obsessed with its own mega-sports; the World Cup had not been held there yet. Major League Soccer, MLS, the professional franchise which the US bid promised to set up if Fifa granted the country the World Cup, started in 1996. No US investors had yet shown an interest in buying Premier League football clubs, where the TV money and global profile was not yet vast enough to attract them. In Mexico and Central America, football always was passionately played in cultures with Spanish roots, but the Caribbean was a generally impoverished island region, the game struggling there. Blazer and Warner had always said Concacaf had no money when they took it over, there was threadbare TV rights income for the competitions, and 'little or no sponsorships'.

Over the next twenty-one years, the report said: 'Warner and Blazer together led Concacaf through an extended period of development and prosperity in which sanctioned football-related activities increased steadily and Concacaf grew substantially.'

Blazer had straight away, in 1990, set up new Concacaf head-quarters in Trump Tower apartments, so setting himself up, a hustler from Queens, as a made man in one of the most ostentatious addresses in Manhattan. Eventually he would spread across a whole floor of apartments, although, as reported in *American Huckster*, one, paid for with Concacaf money, ended up as the sole province of his cats, which peed all over the floor and made the place stink. People who came to work for Concacaf included Jill Fracisco and the English veteran Clive Toye, the former journalist who began his career on the *Exeter Express and Star* covering the local lower division professional club, Exeter City. Toye later ghosted a column in the *Daily Express* for Sir Stanley Rous 'a charming old man,' Toye remembers, 'a wonderful gentleman' – before moving into management in US soccer in the late 1960s. While running the New York Cosmos franchise in the North American Soccer League, in 1975 he managed to sign Pelé and Franz Beckenbauer for their final, razzmatazz-showered paydays.

They say that at Concacaf Blazer did the marketing and business, with Fracisco working all hours to organise and improve the status of the competitions, although Toye, who did PR, says Blazer was no kind of manager: 'The place was a shambles,' he says.

Blazer addressed the flagging competitions, immediately renaming the Concacaf Championship as the Gold Cup. He sought more lucrative TV deals for broadcasting the competition, and proper sponsorships. From 1996, they drummed up greater public and TV interest by inviting guest teams into the Gold Cup, beginning that year with Brazil, which had won the World Cup two years earlier in the USA, and sent their U23 team to compete in the Gold Cup. This was, of course, a tremendous boost to the status of Warner and Blazer and the Concacaf finances, from the country of the Fifa president, Havelange, who was stepping down two years after that and wanted votes for his chosen successor, Blatter, against Europe's Johansson.

Warner, given his own office in Trinidad, did the politics, exactly as he and Blazer planned back in the 1980s when Blazer first suggested Warner could be the Concacaf president. The campaign to consolidate power, within Concacaf and then at Fifa, was achieved by relentlessly coalescing the Caribbean islands as a block vote. Through the 1990s, Warner's influence as a president-maker grew with the addition of eight new associations into Concacaf, some of them tiny Caribbean islands – each with a vote he would add to the CFU's unanimity of numbers. The Cayman Islands FA, and St Kitts and Nevis, joined Concacaf in 1992, Dominica followed in 1994; Anguilla, the British Virgin Islands and Montserrat, in 1996, Turks and Caicos Islands and the US Virgin Islands in 1998. Warner was already on the Fifa executive committee, as one of the Concacaf representatives, as early as 1983, a confirmed ally of Havelange, then, later, a backer of Blatter.

Wielding the influence eventually of thirty-one Caribbean votes in the congress and three Concacaf votes out of twenty-four in the executive committee, often a decisive wedge, Warner passed up no opportunity to extract benefits in return. Gradually, huge money and lavish attention were paid to Trinidad by the greatest football empires on earth. Warner became widely admired in the country where, by his own account, he himself grew up poor, one of six children born to a father, Wilton, who was a heavy drinker, and mother, Stella, who took on cleaning work to feed and clothe her children. He laid out the bones of his remarkable rise in an authorised biography he had written with Valentino Singh, sports editor of the *Trinidad and Tobago Express*, in 1998, the year Warner became a Fifa vice president. Its title was *Upwards Through the Night*, with Warner, who began his professional life as a college history lecturer, borrowing from famous lines written by the American poet Henry Wadsworth Longfellow in his poem 'The Ladder of St Augustine':

> The heights by great men reached and kept
> Were not attained by sudden flight,
> But they, while their companions slept,
> Were toiling upward in the night.

The poem is actually a homage to the lifelong challenge of being good, and moral, rather than just tirelessly getting on while other men sleep. The passage is based on St Augustine's image of building a ladder to the skies by treading 'beneath our feet every deed of shame'. Warner, toiling upwards through the night, began to conduct his deeds of shame increasingly in public view.

Forceful, clever, influential and soon renowned on the world stage, Warner became celebrated on his island, and widely considered a Robin Hood figure, seizing from the rich in football and providing for the poor in Trinidad and the Caribbean: facilities, coaching, development programmes. Standing out among the spoils he brought home, a monument to Warner and Fifa itself, was securing millions of dollars from Zurich for the construction of the Concacaf centre of excellence. Driven on by Warner himself, this was presented as a training and academy complex which would be a classic project in the best tradition of Fifa development: 'to help raise the quality of Concacaf soccer'.

The Concacaf region consists mostly of the continental landmass and vast populations of Canada, the USA, Mexico and Central America, but Warner called for the centre of excellence to be constructed on a small island: his, Trinidad. He even had in mind the land where it would be built, in Macoya, in the ward of Tacarigua, on the east of the island. This was approved by the Concacaf executive committee, which Warner, as the president, dominated. The initial cost as stated in the integrity committee's report of their investigations, was projected to be $7.5m.

At the Concacaf congress held in Guadalajara in April 1996, the one at which Anguilla, the BVI and Montserrat were welcomed into the family, Blazer was able to inform delegates: '[Fifa's] support for the centre of excellence will enable Concacaf to have an ongoing facility for coaching and player development.' João Havelange himself, contemplating his retirement in 1998 and how to secure his legacy, was there and in his speech he confirmed Fifa's support for the project, and congratulated Warner: 'For his vision in building the Concacaf centre of excellence in Trinidad.'

The agreement was that Fifa would lend Concacaf the money directly, and that Fifa would be repaid by withholding some of the money due to the confederation over the years, from World Cup proceeds and the financial assistance programme. That year, 1996,

Fifa made the first interest-free loans to Concacaf for the centre of excellence project: $3.95m in six separate payments. A year later, Warner had approval from the Concacaf executive committee to raise a further $7.5m in total for the centre of excellence, on top of the original projected $7.5m which was going to come from Fifa loans – doubling the cost, after only eighteen months, to $15m. Fifa provided $6m in loans in 1998 and 1999, the money subsequently reimbursed by keeping back funds which were due to Concacaf.

Warner gained approval in March 1997 to separately borrow $6m of this $15m total not from Fifa, but from the Swiss bank UBS, agreeing to repay the loan directly at $2m a year. The following year came the Fifa election for president, Havelange finally stepping down after his era-dominating twenty-four years, and favouring Blatter to succeed him rather than Johansson, who was promising improved accounting and transparency. Warner wielded the Caribbean and Concacaf vote for Blatter who, supported by bin Hammam, won in that bitter and forever contested last-night chaos of the Paris congress. The following year, December 1999, Fifa repaid on behalf of Concacaf the full $6m due to UBS on the loan for the centre of excellence. When the complex was built, it was named for all the world to see after the outgoing president whose munificence had made it possible: the Dr João Havelange Centre of Excellence.

In 2002, when Blatter won the presidency once more, beating Issa Hayatou, Warner supported Blatter again, with the Caribbean vote unanimous. A year later, in May 2003, Fifa's finance committee, chaired by Julio Grondona, Blatter's stalwart Argentinian supporter, agreed to completely write off the $6m Concacaf owed.

Fifa paid a further $10m towards development of the complex, which was repaid by retaining $2.5m from the financial assistance programme each of the four years from 2003 to 2006. When it was finally completed, the money provided by Fifa for the Dr João Havelange Centre of Excellence, built on Jack Warner's island of Trinidad, population one million, was at least $25.95m. It consists of a football stadium, adjoining football pitches, conference and banquet halls, offices, a hotel and a swimming-pool complex. Clive Toye told me the first time he had suspicions about what was happening at Concacaf under Blazer and Warner was when he first went to the complex in Trinidad and did not find much football going on there; instead there were some political meetings in progress.

The integrity committee found in its investigations that, between 1996 and 2011, Concacaf itself provided nearly $11m in 'routine monthly payments to support operations at the centre of excellence and the president's [Warner's] office in Trinidad and Tobago'. The payments 'were usually made in round numbers'. In addition, Concacaf paid nearly $5.6m for further works at the centre of excellence between 2000 and Warner's resignation in 2011.

In May 2012, suspicions about this lavish complex and the money-making activities taking place there – weddings, dinners, shows – became public, with allegations that Concacaf did not even own it. Built with so much Fifa money, including that $6m gift, and stuffed with so many more millions from Concacaf in funds which would otherwise have been available for football projects and development throughout its geographical region, it was alleged that in fact the Dr João Havelange Centre of Excellence was owned by Warner himself.

The integrity committee looked into that, and, in a nutshell, they found that it was true. The three parcels of land in Macoya on which the complex was built were owned by companies belonging to Jack Warner and his wife, Maureen. The land was bought in 1996, 1997 and 1998, after the building of a centre of excellence in Trinidad was given the go-ahead and financial support committed by Fifa. One of the companies is called Renraw – Warner spelt backwards.

The integrity committee said the evidence 'strongly suggests' that Concacaf's own money from Fifa was used to buy the land for the Warners in the first place; they produced a chart and timeline showing the land was bought by the Warners after the huge dollars started flowing from Fifa in January 1996. The committee also found that the money paid by Fifa did not go to Concacaf, but bank accounts which Warner himself and his companies controlled. The accounts were, the committee believed, controlled via a partnership owned by the Warners, which was initially called 'Concacaf Centre of Excellence', then had its name changed on 18 January 1999, after Blatter won the Fifa presidency, to 'Dr João Havelange Centre of Excellence'.

The integrity committee report also found that the Australia FA, whose president was the billionaire businessman Frank Lowy, had paid $462,500 (this equated to Aus$500,000 at the time) to Warner's centre of excellence. It was paid on 23 September 2010, just ten weeks before Warner would be swinging the Concacaf vote for the hosts of the 2018 and 2022 World Cups. The report was clear that the money paid was connected to Australia's 2022 World Cup bid campaign: 'These funds were provided through Australia's international football development programme in connection with its 2022 Fifa World Cup bid,' the report stated, basing that conclusion on Concacaf and FFA documents it had examined.

The money was for an upgrade to the stadium at the centre of excellence, which the report said FFA representatives had visited in August 2010 to assess the scope of the project. The FFA sent the money to Concacaf one month after that visit. The report found that the money was, however, not accounted for in Concacaf accounts, and that Warner 'committed fraud' and 'misappropriated' that money.

But the committee did not interview anybody from the FFA and it was beyond its remit to ask why Australia, when bidding to host a World Cup, using government public money, was paying $462,500 to upgrade a stadium in Trinidad, home of the Fifa executive committee member, Warner, whose World Cup vote the FFA was seeking.

It is difficult to think of an internal investigation report related to football issues more forthright than the one into Warner and Blazer produced by this Concacaf integrity committee. Normally, however damning the evidence, the authors of such reports cannot seem to help but retain an insider wariness, a cosiness, a kind of there-but-for-the-grace-of-God reluctance to express a firm judgement. The senior lawyers and PWC ethics consultant in charge of this one felt no such restraint. Their conclusion on Warner and the Dr João Havelange Centre of Excellence in Trinidad, was that he owned it, secured millions of dollars from Fifa and Concacaf to build it and keep running it, and that he misled both Concacaf and Fifa into believing it was owned by Concacaf.

'In connection with the centre of excellence and Concacaf operations in Trinidad and Tobago [Warner's office],' the report stated uncompromisingly: 'Warner committed fraud against Concacaf and Fifa.'

The report noted that 'Warner's fraudulent conduct' took money from Concacaf which Fifa provided for the development of football in the region.

'In the end, as a result of his fraudulent conduct, Warner divested Concacaf and Fifa of approximately $26m, and Warner obtained title to the centre of excellence property, which rightfully belongs to Concacaf.'

Questioned about the ownership of the complex after the first stories emerged, Warner at first actually said he didn't own it. Later, according to Sanz, Warner claimed to have a letter from Havelange, in which he said Havelange had given the centre of excellence, as a gift, to the Caribbean Football Union and Warner's family. After the integrity committee reported the details of his ownership, based on land registry records and bank accounts, Warner was asked again about it, in April 2013. This time he explicitly said that Havelange had supported the centre of excellence, and given him the $6m loan which was later converted into a 'grant', in return for Warner bringing the votes for Blatter in the 1998 election. Warner's account was not the kindest, describing Blatter as 'the most hated Fifa official', for whom, he said, he wielded the Concacaf votes in a block, in the election Blatter won 111 to 80 – a margin of exactly 31 votes.

'Blatter was Havelange's candidate to succeed him for the Fifa presidency,' Warner explained. 'Blatter had been at the time the most hated Fifa official by both the European and African confederations and without my Concacaf support at the Fifa elections, Blatter would never have seen the light of day as president of Fifa. I told Havelange that, through him, Blatter will get Concacaf's total support.'

He claimed again that the centre of excellence had been 'a gift for the Caribbean and Jack Warner', and was never an asset of Concacaf.

'So there was no ambiguity,' Warner said. 'There was no uncertainty. There was no secret in my dealings towards Dr Havelange and the centre of excellence. So the centre of excellence was built, first by a loan that was given to Jack Warner that was converted into a grant, and by further assistance from Dr Havelange after whom I named the centre.'

According to Warner, then, he was actually admitting that the worst suspicions harboured by the world of football about Fifa were terribly true: millions of dollars were handed over to him personally, authorised by the Fifa president, in return for votes at the congress to elect the next president. And this fraud and money-making, on a massive scale, was masqueraded as Fifa's and football's highest purpose: development in a poor island region. Symbolic of all that it represented, the entity built by this corrupt shabbiness bore the name of the former Fifa president himself.

Turning their attention to Blazer's twenty-one years as the unchallenged, sprawling secretary general of Concacaf, the committee was to the point again, saying bluntly: 'Blazer misappropriated Concacaf funds.' The hustler who had claimed to be standing up for what was right when he blew the whistle on Warner over the cash in brown envelopes in Trinidad had not stinted on the amounts he took. The committee found he had misappropriated 'at least $15m' from Concacaf. While Concacaf was paying some of the eyewatering rent on the Trump Tower apartments as business expenses, the confederation also paid the rent, from 1996 until Blazer's resignation in 2011, on three separate apartments he, his girlfriend or his cats lived in. The rent for the forty-ninth-floor apartment, the committee found, was $18,000 a month. In total the committee found Blazer improperly spent $837,000 in rent.

They also found that some of Warner's complaints about Blazer in the bitter aftermath of the Trinidad scandal had, as always, a ring of uncomfortable truth. Blazer had from the beginning at Concacaf indeed been paid in commission. Rather than a salary as an employee, he had in 1990 agreed a contract, signed by Warner with Blazer's company, Sportvertising, to earn 10 per cent commission 'on all sponsorships and TV rights from all sources received by Concacaf or for Concacaf programs/tournaments'. In 1994, when this was renewed, his Sportvertising company which was paid the money was now registered in the Cayman Islands. In Blazer's time, the Concacaf sponsorships did greatly increase, from just over $1m in 1991 to over $35m in the Gold Cup year of 2009, and so did the money which was paid to him.

The second Sportvertising contract ran out in 1998, the committee found, and in fact Blazer had no contract at all with Concacaf after that, as Warner had blurted out publicly. But Blazer was nevertheless extravagantly running the organisation from his outsized empire, and he made sure he was still being paid the commissions – $11m, the committee found. Altogether, from 1996 to 2011, Blazer was paid $15.3m in commissions, $4.5m in fees, and the $837,000 rent, a total of more than $20m. He even took a 10 per cent commission, $300,000, on a $3m grant given by Fifa to build a TV studio in the Trump Tower offices.

Blazer was also found to have 'misappropriated Concacaf assets by using Concacaf funds to finance his personal lifestyle'. Anybody who knew or had even seen Blazer knew his personal lifestyle was an agglomeration of gargantuan appetites; the items the committee highlighted were the Trump Tower residences, the purchase of apartments for his personal use in a luxury hotel in Miami, a deposit paid on apartments on a resort in the Bahamas, the purchase of a Hummer car costing $48,554 with three years of Manhattan garage fees at $600 a month, and various insurances for him and his girlfriend.

The report said that Blazer 'actively concealed' his payments by paying himself through Sportvertising and other companies, and never raised with the executive committee the fact he actually didn't have a contract after 1998. He and Warner arranged for the audits of Concacaf finances to be conducted by an accountant who was not independent as he also worked for both men personally, and he did not carry out a proper audit, the committee stated.

The committee did not have the authority to investigate whether Blazer had personally paid his taxes – we know now that he had not, and this had led to the tap on his shoulder from the authorities in 2011 and the end of all his fun and misappropriation. However, the committee found that he did not file US tax returns or pay tax on behalf of Concacaf between 2006 and 2010, and for one of the Concacaf companies, CMTV, from 2004 to 2010, which, they said, was 'wilful'.

'Blazer went out of his way to avoid engaging the Internal Revenue Service at any level, at great expense to Concacaf,' the report said.

Of the financial statements made by Concacaf, required by law during their time in charge, the committee found that Warner and Blazer consistently provided false information on several issues, including the centre of excellence.

'Warner and Blazer committed fraud against Concacaf' was the verdict.

It was all devastating. The report was solemnly handed over by the chairman, Sir David Simmons QC, the job thunderously completed, to Jeff Webb, the new president of Concacaf, who was committed to transparency, integrity and reform. Enrique Sanz, the new secretary general, had been busily involved in and fully committed to the forensic investigation and exposure of his predecessor's wrongdoing. Sanz had told the committee that in September 2012 he had gone to Trinidad and Tobago to discuss some of the issues with Warner, who had taken him to the old Concacaf office where 'document shredding was taking place'.

Warner was already finished with Fifa, having resigned then been eulogised in 2011, and he was fully involved in politics in Trinidad. By the time the report was presented he was minister of security, but after its accusations were published he resigned. All of this, illicit personal enrichment exposed on a vast, extended scale over so many years, by men who talked publicly of ethics and honour, should have been the most profound scandal ever to sully football. It even bore the name of Havelange to help frame an understanding of it all. Yet it was not; this alleged fraud of millions of US dollars and failure to file tax returns, a grievous offence in the US, only amounted to more ammunition for the US law enforcement authorities, who were now fully engaged. There was a great deal more for them to uncover yet.

CHAPTER 10

Bribery in Switzerland is not a Crime

In this historic tumbling out of corruption denied for decades, the sudden naming, shaming and naked comeuppance for formerly unimpeachable football barons, there was at times a kind of poetic neatness. On the very same day that the thumping report was delivered into the frauds and alleged vote-buying which had constructed the $26m monument to himself in Trinidad, Dr João Havelange resigned. He had been the honorary president of Fifa, having been elevated to that sainted status after the election of his anointed successor, Blatter, in 1998. Yet fifteen years into this honorarium, on 18 April 2013, aged ninety-seven, the fearsome old ruler stepped down from the pedestal.

It was the same day as, but unrelated to, the revelations in Trinidad. Havelange's resignation came days before the public verdict in a completely different scandal, which definitively revealed endemic corruption by Havelange himself. It was even more far-reaching than the frauds exposed in the Americas, because this had been rooted in the heart of Fifa in Zurich. The revelations would finally taint Havelange's own record, and his and Blatter's entire forty-year era in control.

After years of resistance by Fifa under Blatter's presidency, a court document was finally to be published, which was reputation-shredding. It disclosed that Havelange had indeed taken bribes from the marketing company ISL throughout the 1990s, in return for him selling to ISL Fifa's TV and marketing rights for World Cups. The document had finally been exposed to daylight in July 2012 after applications, including by the BBC, that it should no longer be kept secret, as Fifa had adamantly argued it should. It was an order made by the prosecutor's office in the central Swiss canton of Zug, south of Zurich, when it stopped criminal proceedings against Fifa itself, as well as against Havelange and Ricardo Teixeira personally, in May 2010.

There has been some misunderstanding over the years of what this court order signified. It was not the settlement, repayment by Havelange and Teixeira to the liquidator of ISL, of the bribes they took. In fact it showed that the Zug prosecutor had been considering a criminal prosecution of those men – and of Fifa itself – for 'disloyal management'. The document detailed the closing of that action by agreement, after Fifa paid significant money to the court. The prosecution was being considered because Fifa, with Blatter as president, had not sought repayment of these bribes trousered by Havelange and Teixeira from ISL, despite learning these millions were paid when they sold Fifa's TV and marketing rights. Instead, Fifa had actually been involved in Teixeira settling any further liability to the ISL liquidator by paying just 2.5m CHF, and Fifa itself secured from the liquidator an agreement not to take any further action. Apparently robbed of fortunes over years by president Havelange, and Teixeira, a trustee on the executive committee, Blatter's Fifa had actually worked hard, in February 2004, to make the affair go away, settle it and avoid any publicity of the bribery.

The court order also highlighted that Blatter himself knew about one of the payments from ISL: 1.5m CHF for Havelange in 1997. It had been mistakenly sent to a Fifa account and was brought to Blatter's attention when he was still the secretary general. Without making any further inquiries, he had it sent back to ISL. The document states that this, among other things, proved that 'Fifa had knowledge of the bribery payments to persons within its organs'. Blatter, though, has always said he did not know it was a bribe.

The document published in 2012 which exposed all this revealed that the Zug prosecutor did believe that Havelange and Teixeira were guilty of criminal conduct in taking the bribes, and that Fifa was criminally guilty of sanctioning it by settling with the liquidator. But due to various factors, including the length of time which had passed, Havelange's age and the assumption that Fifa would reform, the prosecutor himself agreed to discontinue the action and did not proceed with criminal charges. Fifa had to pay 2.5m CHF to settle the proposed prosecution, as did Teixeira; Havelange, now ninety-four and pleading relative poverty, had to pay 500,000 CHF.

There are multiple layers of shame in what was exposed. The first and most basic is that Dr João Havelange – lauded, praised, sanctified by Fifa since his supplanting of Sir Stanley Rous in 1974 – was indeed corrupt. The document confirmed that it was really true: at the moment in the 1990s when the TV market ballooned in value, Havelange had sold the rights for the 2002 and 2006 World Cups to this company, originally founded by the Adidas owner Horst Dassler, with long tentacles wormed into Fifa and football. Havelange and Teixeira, his former son-in-law who had taken over as president of the Brazil FA, the CBF, and was a member of the Fifa executive committee from 1994, were paid bribes in return, of 41m CHF. The payments, itemised in a list with many round figures, were made to them by ISL throughout the nineties, from 1992 to 2000.

'João Havelange pocketed these commissions that he received due to his position in Fifa,' the court order says, 'and he refrained from disclosing or giving them to Fifa. The payments were aimed at using the influence of João Havelange as president of Fifa with respect to the contracts ultimately concluded between Fifa and ISL ... João Havelange was enriched to the extent of the commissions he received and failed, contrary to his duty, to pass on; Fifa suffered an equivalent loss.'

The prosecutor's document continues: 'There is nothing different about the conduct of Ricardo Teixeira, whose influence in Fifa was also of fundamental importance due to his close relationship (son-in-law) to João Havelange.'

Bribes had also been paid to Nicolás Leoz of Paraguay, who was later named in the report into the ISL bribes by the Fifa ethics committee. Issa Hayatou of Cameroon was another beneficiary, receiving a much smaller figure, 100,000 French francs, which he always claimed was for anniversary celebrations of the Confederation of African Football, not a bribe to him personally.

Yet there are many more awful, stinking truths trailing out of what happened, which have to be sifted and uncovered, from a forty-two-page document of Swiss-German legalese translated into clunky English. The revelations come in stages, general, then specific, exposing the underlying rottenness of the culture which Havelange grew in his years of unchallenged domination. Before laying out what was stolen, fixed, then covered up in the offices of Fifa House on the hill of Hitzigweg, the prosecutor's document sets out what Fifa's own statutes say about its sporting mission:

'The purpose of Fifa is to improve football continuously and to broadcast it globally, whereby the binding effect on nations – as well as the educational, cultural and humanitarian status of football – has to be taken in consideration … According to the statutes of Fifa, it is a non-profit organisation.'

Allowing for the awkward translation, it is clear that the prosecutor meant that the world governing body's central, expressed role is to bind nations together, and have an educational, cultural and human-itarian benefit around the world, through football. But, the order stated, this pure ideal of sport had been corrupted by paying bribes to influential decision-makers at governing bodies, as suspected, since the 1970s, 'when sports became an important factor in the economy'. The court had been told this by a previous ISL chairman, unnamed, who said that after he was appointed as a director in the early 1990s, he had been told that ISL 'had been using such practices since its foundation' by Horst Dassler in 1982. That pinned the bribery of people in governing bodies to Dassler of Adidas himself, who was so industriously involved in the backroom political manoeuvrings at Fifa in the early 1970s, initially having been very close to Rous, then gravitating to Havelange.

'The investigation revealed that the commission payments made by [ISL] could be traced back to the 1980s,' the document, damningly, notes.

The previous ISL chairman, the order said, had told the court: 'When he repeatedly insisted on stopping such favouritism, [the chairman's] successor made clear to him that these personal relations had led to further existing commitments.'

The chief financial officer of ISL had bluntly stated that payments had to be made, on top of the buying of the actual rights to the sporting events, 'to individuals who had helped conclude the contract'.

By the late 1990s, when the money for broadcasting dwarfed the sums which had obsessed Dassler, ISL had formed a fund in

Liechtenstein, a secretive, offshore banking haven in the heart of Europe, and stuffed it with 36m CHF for the payment of bribes. Havelange asigned to ISL all of Fifa's marketing rights – the right to sell its name and the irresistible appeal of football, to the familiar roster of blue-chip and junk food sponsors – in 1997 for 200m CHF. Then he signed over the 2002 and 2006 World Cup rights, ISL paying Fifa $1.4bn in total. This latter contract was signed 'on behalf of Fifa by João Havelange' on 26 May 1998, just days before the Brazilian stepped down as the president able to sign contracts for Fifa, and Blatter took over.

The multi-million-dollar bribes paid to Havelange and Teixeira in return for granting these contracts came to light not long after, when ISL went bust in 2001. Yet here came the next layer of shame: Fifa, with Blatter as president by then, Havelange honorary president, and Teixeira, Leoz and Hayatou all still on the executive committee, covered up the bribery, sealed it in a settlement. Fifa did not legally pursue the senior figures who had betrayed trust and enriched themselves, but sought to close down the whole affair and ensure it would never be raised again. The Zug court order states that this was done because, Fifa's own lawyers had said, it did not want to suffer bad publicity: 'Fifa expressed an interest, according to its own statement, not to be involved in speculations in connection with the bribery payments.'

So this was the thrust of the criminal proceedings: the Zug prosecutor was indeed accusing Havelange and Teixeira of 'embezzlement, possibly disloyal management'. But he had also been accusing Fifa itself of covering up for the pair. Fifa, the order states, actually sacrificed huge money to which it was entitled, which Havelange and Teixeira had pocketed, and instead settled and looked after them.

'Fifa refrained from enforcing its claim for surrender against João Havelange and Ricardo Teixeira who were, on the basis of their positions, obliged to surrender the assets [the money they took in bribes] to Fifa,' the order recorded. 'As a result, Fifa was damaged to the extent of its omission, which was in breach of its duty, while Ricardo Teixeira and João Havelange were thereby enriched to the same extent.'

The sequence of events began with the liquidator of the ISL collapse, when he discovered the 36m CHF slush fund for the payment of bribes, trying to get the money back as was right and natural. On 27 February 2004, Teixeira and Havelange agreed to repay some of it. The settlement does not look like a great achievement, requiring only 2.5m CHF from Teixeira; the court order does not explain why they were released from further action for so little. However, the Zug prosecutor became involved when his office saw that Fifa itself appeared to have paid this money on behalf of Teixeira. In return for the payment to the ISL liquidator, Fifa had sought a commitment that Havelange and Teixeira 'will not be made subject to any further actions'. Fifa's lawyer, who was not named, explained that football's world governing body paid this settlement, on behalf of people who had effectively stolen from it, because it did not want to be subject to bad publicity about the bribery having happened.

'That's why Fifa intercedes to help bring about settlements where foreign football functionaries have received commission.'

This is as bald an admission as can be that Fifa accepted that 'foreign football functionaries' were regularly bribed, but that instead of taking the necessary action against them, clean up the game and stop it happening again, Fifa 'intercedes' to tolerate it and hush it up. That is why the prosecutor had become involved – he was accusing Fifa under Blatter of acting against its own interests, sporting purposes and mission, therefore 'disloyally', because its main objective in the scandal was to protect 'certain of its members' and their 'personal, pecuniary advantages', rather than 'the alleged promotion of football'.

Fifa's lawyer presented a list of reasons protesting that this was not the case, arguing that in fact it had been legitimate not to claim the money back from Teixeira and Havelange, and instead to settle the bribery claim on their behalf and keep the whole affair quiet. One of the reasons advanced is quite shocking, even amid all the other squalor of this exposed culture. The lawyer argued that if Fifa had decided to try and reclaim the money from the people who had pocketed the bribes, it would 'barely have been possible' to recover any of it. This, he argued, was because:

'A claim made by Fifa in South America and Africa would hardly have been enforceable because bribery payments belong to the usual salary of the majority of the population.'

This bombshell is dropped, one sentence on page 32 of a dreadful document of record, and it is quite difficult to take in the full extent of its implications. Here was Fifa, in a court of law in its native Switzerland, stating, plain as day, that it believed bribery was part of the routine facts of life in South America and Africa. Fifa, which enjoys charitable and non-tax privileges in Switzerland, was partly controlled by the votes of its many African and South American football association delegates; it sends many millions of dollars to those continents every year for development, and in public always denied there was any corruption. Yet in court negotiations it never thought would be exposed, Fifa was actually mounting as a formal argument, a justification for not seeking repayment of Havelange and Teixeira's kickbacks, that bribes are simply regarded as part of a person's salary in those parts of the world.

The prosecutor did not engage with that argument. Instead the document dryly notes that Havelange and other members of the executive committee proven to have taken bribes did a significant part of their work in Switzerland, and so Fifa could have sued them in Switzerland.

The prosecutor, however, himself agreed that if they paid compensation to the court, there was no further public interest in mounting a prosecution against them. Fifa settled for paying 2.5m CHF; Teixeira agreed to pay the same, and Havelange the 500,000 CHF. They paid the money quite eagerly, 2.5m CHF from Fifa landing with the prosecutor's office on 18 March 2010, and the proceedings were stopped; Fifa was not prosecuted for sanctioning and covering up bribery. The costs of reaching this settlement, to avoid prosecution, were paid by Fifa: 92,000 CHF.

The date of the deal was 11 May 2010. The BBC's *Panorama* broadcast its programme, naming Teixeira, Leoz and Hayatou as alleged recipients of bribes, on the eve of the World Cup vote in December 2010, but the document was still not published until July 2012. I wrote about it for the *Guardian* on the day it was all laid bare. Sylvia Schenk, senior adviser on sport for Transparency International, the globally respected anti-corruption campaign, who had initially worked with Blatter on reform proposals, said his position was untenable.

'If the president of Fifa for years did not act on the knowledge that these payments had been made for senior executives' personal gain, and tried to hide it for as long as possible, then it is difficult to trust him as the person to reform Fifa in the future,' she said.

Blatter, though, did not accept he had done anything wrong, publicly pointing out, as Fifa always has, the remarkable fact that paying and taking bribes were not in themselves criminal offences in Swiss law.

'You can't judge the past on the basis of today's standards,' he said, 'otherwise it would end up with moral justice.'

That contradicted what the document itself revealed, that the prosecutor in Zug did believe the trousering of bribes by Teixeira and Havelange was criminal, 'disloyal' and 'embezzlement', and that Fifa, under the presidency of Blatter, was criminally 'disloyal' to its own sporting purposes in not having pursued repayment. Fifa and Teixeira denied criminal conduct; Havelange did not comment on the accusation of criminality.

This public confirmation that Horst Dassler's ISL had for twenty years corrupted Fifa and its monumental former president, which was covered up by his protégé and successor, came to be considered by the new ethics committee structure agreed as part of the reforms. After his 2011 congress, when he had stood on the burning deck throwing out names and promises of reform into the winds of change in Zurich, Blatter did indeed follow some through. He had appointed Mark Pieth, a professor of criminal law at the Basel Institute, to look at Fifa's structures and recommend improvements. We in the media had been suspicious, that a Swiss appointee might give Blatter's house a superficial makeover, but Pieth turned out to be genuine, with a distinguished record of anti-corruption work and no interest in having a Fifa whitewash on his record.

One of Pieth's recommendations, glaringly obvious to him, and accepted by Fifa, was that the ethics committee had to be more independent. The prosecution, judge and jury body acting on reports from the president's office, which had dispatched his challenger, Mohamed bin Hammam, within days of receiving reports of the Trinidad cash, was no more. The ethics process was split, to use the chosen language, into two 'chambers'. One was an 'investigatory chamber', which, as the name suggests, carried out the inquiries. It reported its findings to the 'adjudicatory chamber', which then decided how strong the evidence looked, and whether disciplinary action should be taken, pursued it if it was, and, if a person were found guilty, decided on the punishment.

The investigatory chamber was to be chaired by Michael Garcia, a former US prosecutor and lawyer based in New York. The adjudicatory chamber chairman was Hans-Joachim Eckert, a German judge with a long career of prosecuting organised and other serious financial crimes, in Munich. From 1999 to 2003, Eckert had led a department pursuing economic crimes, including from the Nazi era. From 2003, he had been presiding judge of the penal court in Munich, hearing cases of corruption and tax fraud.

This ISL settlement was the first major test of the newly constituted semi-independent ethics committee structure. Eckert looked at the bribes taken by Havelange and Teixeira, the extent of Blatter's knowledge, Fifa's conduct under Blatter in settling with ISL's liquidator, then the settlement of Fifa's own threatened prosecution with the 2.5m CHF payment by court order. Despite his formidable CV as a prosecutor and judge, the way it went gave no great cause for confidence in a new culture for Fifa. On 12 March 2012, while Eckert was still considering the case, Teixeira suddenly resigned from the presidency of the CBF, and therefore came off the Fifa executive committee. He also stepped down from chairing the organising committee of the World Cup due to kick off in Brazil two years later. Teixeira, sixty-four by then, did not say his resignation had anything to do with the revelations of the bribes he banked, or the pending verdict of the ethics committee; he said it was due to ill health.

That was the same reason Teixeira had given a decade earlier, when he avoided questioning by a Brazilian senate investigation into the CBF, following years of concerns and allegations of corruption. There were longstanding complaints that the brilliance of Brazil's playing talent, its golden football heritage, were being betrayed by corrupt officials lining their own pockets. The former national team striker Romário, a stand-out star of the 1994 World Cup in the USA won by Brazil, was becoming a prominently forthright critic, a senator, speaking with the voice of exasperated experience. Teixeira, citing ill health, stepped down when his time came for an appearance before the senate, and his deputy sustained the inquisition instead.

When the senate committee delivered its 1,600-page-long conclusions in December 2001, its chairman, Álvaro Dias, famously described the CBF under Teixeira as: 'Truly a den of crime, revealing disorganisation, anarchy, incompetence and dishonesty.'

Alex Bellos, the journalist reporting on the inquiry for the *Guardian* at the time, who later wrote a book, *Futebol*, about the wonders and ugliness of the beautiful game in Brazil, said that the game's bosses 'have long been symbols of authoritarianism and impunity, one of the last areas of public life to modernise since the [military] dictatorship ended in 1985'.

Teixeira had won an election for the presidency of the CBF in 1989, four years after the end of the dictatorship in which Havelange himself had flourished and been supported by the military generals. In the senate report, Teixeira was heavily criticised, accused of taking unauthorised salaries and of corruption, and of having bought power and political influence, for protection in the country. The inquiry called for him and other senior CBF figures to be prosecuted for alleged crimes including tax evasion and money laundering, but no charges were brought and no formal action was taken following this extensive investigation. Teixeira, who always denied wrongdoing, recovered from his bout of ill health, and remained the CBF president and on the Fifa executive committee right up to his resignation in March 2013.

The news that Havelange had also resigned came on the day Eckert delivered his verdict, 30 April 2013. The ethics committee report stated that Havelange, ninety-six by then, had actually stepped down from his position as honorary president twelve days before, on 18 April – the very day that the Concacaf integrity committee was delivering its devastating findings of fraud by Jack Warner over the Dr João Havelange Centre of Excellence. Havelange's reputation, record and legacy were sunk, here at the end of a long and epic life, but his resignation put him beyond the reach of any sanction.

Leoz, another Fifa boss in South America, president of the confederation, Conmebol, for a staggering twenty-seven years, member of the Fifa executive committee since 1998, also resigned, citing 'health and personal grounds'. That came on 24 April 2013, six days before Eckert's report. In it, Eckert noted the resignations of both Havelange and Leoz – not Teixeira, an omission which was not explained – and confirmed that he believed that put them beyond sanction:

'Any further steps are superfluous.'

It was just one element of a judgement which was poorly explained and deeply unconvincing.

In the new ethics committee split, Eckert had received a report from Garcia into the ISL bribes, Fifa cover-up and the extent of Blatter's knowledge. He recommended no action be taken against anyone. Eckert's report was, though, plain-speaking about the payments made by ISL to the Fifa president of twenty-four years, the CBF boss and the president of Conmebol:

'From money that passed through the [ISL] group, it is certain that not inconsiderable amounts were channelled to former Fifa president Havelange and to his son-in-law Ricardo Teixeira as well as to Dr Nicolás Leoz, whereby there is no indication that any form of service was given in return by them,' Eckert concluded.

'These payments were apparently made via front companies in order to cover up the true recipient and are to be qualified as "commissions", known today as "bribes".'

It is difficult now, with so many towering Fifa names demolished by exposed corruption, to remember how significant that simple admission was, as recently as 2013. Finally, after all the years of cover-up and denial in Zurich, this new ethics committee within Fifa itself had come out with it, in a public statement: these were bribes. For years, millions had indeed been paid, as a matter of course and endemic culture, from the Swiss rights company founded by Dassler, to the president himself and his clan.

Eckert then rehearsed the argument that being paid bribes was not a crime in Swiss law at the time; it was regarded as commission. This seemed to be at odds with the view of the prosecutor who had been convinced there were grounds for a criminal case, but Eckert was apparently persuaded by it.

'However,' he judged, 'it is clear that Havelange and Teixeira, as football officials, should not have accepted any bribe money, and should have had to pay it back since the money was in connection with the exploitation of media rights.

'[The fact that it was not a crime in Switzerland at the time] does not change anything with regard to the morally and ethically reproachable conduct of both persons,' Eckert stated.

On Blatter, Eckert went out of his way to clear Havelange's successor of taking bribes himself, even though that had not been suggested. Blatter has always said, throughout the unmasking of corruption at the heart of Fifa, that he never took any money improperly himself. Eckert supported this, on the basis of the documents he had seen: 'There are also no indications whatsoever that President Blatter was responsible for a cash flow to Havelange, Teixeira or Leoz, or that he himself received any payments from the ISL group, even in the form of hidden kickback payments.'

Then Eckert went on to clear Blatter of knowing about the bribes to Havelange. He referred to the UBS bank transfer, which showed that, on 3 March 1997, a payment of 1.5m CHF was sent by ISL to a Fifa account, with a note that it related to 'a guarantee for Mr Havelange'. Eckert recited that: 'It is undisputed that the former chief accountant of Fifa brought this to the attention of then secretary general Blatter, and the former arranged for the return transfer to ISL.'

When Blatter was shown this payment to Havelange from ISL, a company bidding for and buying Fifa's marketing and TV rights, he was extremely experienced in the ways of Fifa and the sports rights world. After an initial career in other sports governing bodies and at Longines, he had been at Fifa for twenty-two years, secretary general under Havelange for nineteen, and was ready, just one year away, from standing to take the top job himself. Yet about this payment, when interviewed by Garcia, he was nonplussed. He 'couldn't understand that somebody is sending money to Fifa for another person', Eckert's report states.

'But at that time,' Eckert records solemnly, '[Blatter] did not suspect the payment was a commission.'

The accusation made against Blatter by many observers of this episode is that he must have known this payment was improper. Even he had acknowledged, when he said he couldn't understand it, that there was no explicable reason for it. The same suspicion prevails against him now, that even though there is still, to be fair, no evidence of him taking bribes while those around him were helping themselves insatiably, he must have known. That Warner, his arch-supporter, was a fraud and embezzler, including of massive money from Fifa, that bin Hammam was a payer of bribes, that Havelange, Teixeira, Leoz were all at it. He denies it; says, in effect, he knew nothing.

The further accusation is that, faced with this payment which had no explanation, he should have confronted Havelange about it, found out the truth of what was passing under his nose at Fifa. That he should have blown the whistle on it, because it was clearly bribery and corruption, as a culture. Blatter, though, does not do whistleblowing, as he would tell me in my interview with him for this book.

Eckert's summary of all this was that perhaps Blatter should have sought some 'clarification' of what the payment was for, but, 'President Blatter's conduct could not be classified in any way as misconduct with regard to any ethics rules.'

Without explaining that conclusion further, Eckert decided: 'The conduct of President Blatter may have been clumsy because there could be an internal need for clarification, but this does not lead to any criminal or ethical misconduct.'

And there it was. Blatter, Havelange's trusty secretary general through the 1980s and 1990s, as Fifa sold sponsorships for millions of dollars to multinationals, TV rights for ever-burgeoning fortunes and did exclusive deals with its entwined agency ISL, had been 'clumsy' when he did nothing about the 1.5m CHF payment from ISL for Havelange. Nobody had ever thought Sepp Blatter had got where he was in the world by being clumsy. Rather, he was always considered exceptionally smart in a formidably complex web of global sport, huge money flows, intricate power politics and personal alliances, but 'clumsy' was the verdict of the German judge.

Of Fifa's cover-up under president Blatter in 2004, Eckert did actually conclude that Havelange and Teixeira would have had to pay back the money they pocketed, at least 41m CHF, if Fifa had demanded it. However, the judge said that Fifa 'was under no obligation to demand the repayment of this money', and that it was 'within

Fifa's discretion in applying its business judgement to decide whether to seek repayment'.

Blatter had actually told Garcia that he had not authorised the lawyer who had made the settlement of 2.5m CHF on Fifa's behalf, for the whole issue to go away and to avoid publicity. Eckert did indulge that possibility, saying that 'it could not be determined with certainty' that this lawyer had involved Blatter in the 'deliberations and decisions'. So it was possible that the president of Fifa, contemplating the catastrophic insolvency of ISL and the revelation that his predecessor and senior supporters on the executive committee had taken bribes, was not involved in the discussions of what to do about it, or the decision finally to settle it and hush it all up.

Eckert said that he did agree with Garcia that this settlement 'may very well be seen to have been affected by a conflict of interest'. But Eckert then explained why he was not recommending any action be taken about this: 'At the time of ... the settlement [in February 2004], there were no ethics rules.'

So neither Blatter nor anybody else could be held accountable within Fifa for the settlement, which meant Fifa allowed Havelange, Teixeira and Leoz to keep the money they took in bribes, because there had been no explicit, written 'ethics rules' at the time. And the fact that these former barons had resigned from their positions appeared to satisfy Eckert that, like other 'major corruption proceedings' involving German or US companies, the employees guilty of bribe-taking had been removed.

'No further proceedings related to the ISL matter are warranted against any other football official,' he concluded – and none ever were.

Havelange had reached the age of ninety-six but was finally exposed; Teixeira had dodged accusations in Brazil but was damned by this. Leoz claimed he had passed on the ISL money to a school project in Paraguay in January 2008, eight years after he received it, but he had not been 'fully candid', Eckert said. Warner and Blazer had been all but finished two weeks earlier by the Concacaf integrity committee. Mohamed bin Hammam was already banned for life following the PWC report into his beneficence with Asian Football Confederation money.

Yet Blatter emerged with only a scratch; 'clumsy' but cleared, from an inquiry and court proceedings which established that corruption had been soaked into Fifa's culture in Zurich, in Europe, for at least two decades in which he worked throughout as the secretary general. He welcomed Eckert's verdict 'with satisfaction', that he had been exonerated. Blatter was home free, to scan the horizon and consider the future, and he began to assess that only he could navigate Fifa through its uncertainties, that he should stand to be at the helm yet again.

CHAPTER 11

The Dirty Linen

In May 2015 the remaining chief officers of Fifa, and the substitutes for those thrown overboard, assembled in Zurich for the annual congress and inevitable re-election of the president, a gathering suffused with gloom, grey and ennui. Sepp Blatter, masterful survivor, was not only still afloat, but in command, at seventy-nine the unquestionable favourite to be elected for his fifth term, extending his tenure to beyond twenty years. To the trail left in the wake of his political acumen and relentless self-advancement could be added another sulking victim: Michel Platini, nursing a grumble that Blatter had reneged on a promise to step down this time. Since his very first entwining with Blatter in 1998, Platini always believed the older man was grooming him for the Fifa presidency, but now he felt betrayed: he was never going to stand against Blatter, worried that he would always lose a nasty fight. So the one realistic candidate prepared to oppose the long-term crowd-pleaser was really no more than a stalking horse, a symbol of opposition, backed by Platini for having a go in his place: the game prince of Jordan, Ali bin Al Hussein.

The planes flew in, the pampered delegates were met at the airport by smart young Swiss greeters holding Fifa names aloft, then leading their visitors to their Mercedes saloons and familiar grand hotels. After the scandals and so many impregnable reputations sunk, including that of Havelange, it was nevertheless business as always. Reforms were being introduced, initially developed by Mark Pieth and his independent governance committee, which featured some prominent names in anti-corruption, including the British former attorney general Lord Goldsmith. But they had pulled out and dismantled their process when, in the autumn of 2014, Blatter had pondered all the options and decided it would be for the best if he stood again.

'That was partly why we stepped down,' Pieth told me in an interview for this book. 'We found it indefensible for him to run again, because he was so discredited. It was a slap in the face for us, it would have meant our work was useless.'

Domenico Scala, the Swiss corporate executive recruited by Blatter, on Pieth's recommendation, to steer the reforms in as the chairman of a new audit and compliance committee, was continuing his work. His immediate perception on arriving at the House of Fifa had been that there was a howling vacuum where some basics of governance should be expected of a modern organisation. Scala recommended oversights of the finance; a committee to set the pay of the president and executive committee, which had never existed before; reformation of the executive committee and president, and their powers.

'As far as good governance is concerned, I am convinced that we remain on the right track,' Scala said in the annual report published at the congress.

Long-term allies Warner, Blazer, Teixeira, Leoz and bin Hammam were gone, replaced in their confederations and on the executive committee by new men who had been in the system for years. There had not been a major scandal since all the unpleasantness in the Trinidad hotel and its aftermath, and Blatter had sailed through the scrutiny of the ISL bribe revelations. The New York *Daily News* had run its splash on 2 November 2014 about Blazer, revealing 'the secret life of soccer's Mr Big', but not much had been heard about that supposed US investigation since.

Also in November 2014, Judge Eckert of the ethics committee's 'adjudicatory' chamber gave his verdict on the long-awaited investigation by Michael Garcia into the bidding process which sent the 2018 and 2022 World Cups to Russia and Qatar. Eckert said Garcia's findings did identify some possible malpractice by bids, including England's and Australia's, and by executive committee members, including Warner and bin Hammam, but none were sufficient to undermine the 'integrity' of the outcome. The Spain and Portugal bid for 2018, accused of colluding with Qatar in a pact of votes, appeared not to have cooperated at all with Garcia; their bid was not included in Eckert's summary and the Spain FA president, Fifa executive committee member and vice president, Ángel María Villar Llona, was later given a warning by the ethics committee and fined 25,000 CHF.

Franz Beckenbauer, the world football icon for forty years and member of the Fifa executive committee from 2007 to 2011, who was one of the twenty-two voters in 2010, was also fined, in February 2016, for failing to cooperate with Garcia. This was despite, the ethics committee said, 'Repeated requests for his assistance. This included requests to provide information during an in-person interview and in response to written questions presented in both English and German.'

The Russian bid, led by the minister for sport in Vladimir Putin's government, Vitaly Mutko, had told Garcia that it no longer had any of its emails or computer records, because they had only 'leased' the computers, then given them back to their owner.

'The owner has confirmed that the computers were destroyed in the meantime,' Eckert's report said.

Nor could the Russian bid's emails from Gmail accounts be recovered because, the bid said, Google USA had not responded to its request. Eckert accepted this, made no criticism of it, and on 'the evidence available' found nothing 'sufficient to support any findings of misconduct by the Russia 2018 bid team'.

Bin Hammam was found to have paid Reynald Temarii €305,640 to help the Oceania president with legal costs to fight his one-year suspension imposed after the undercover sting by the *Sunday Times*. Garcia found that bin Hammam's funding of Temarii's appeal was directly intended to help the Qatar bid. It meant that Temarii did not have to step down and be replaced on the executive committee, which would have been by David Chung, his then deputy, who is from Papua New Guinea and would have voted, as mandated, for Australia. However, Eckert concluded that because it was only one vote, it did not make a 'significant' difference to the outcome. Despite all the allegations and suspicion loaded on to the Qatar result, Eckert said no other evidence of serious corruption had been found.

Garcia, extraordinarily, joined those protesting that Eckert's report was a whitewash, issuing a statement complaining publicly that the summary of his investigatory report contained 'numerous materially incomplete and erroneous representations' of the facts he had established and his conclusions. But an appeal to Fifa's own appeals committee failed, and Eckert's decisions stood. Garcia then explicitly questioned Eckert's independence, and the culture of Fifa, saying there was 'a lack of leadership on these issues'. He resigned, but has never since broken his confidentiality agreement to explain his objections to Eckert's summary. He was replaced by his deputy, a Swiss lawyer and prosecutor, Cornel Borbély.

The ethics committee announced it would proceed against some of those identified for misconduct, including Warner, bin Hammam and Temarii, who had, anyway, already been discarded. On 18 November 2014, Fifa even stated that it had lodged a criminal complaint with the Swiss authorities based on some of the misconduct identified. But these were evidently fringe issues, not sufficient to annul the vote and rerun it. The contracts with Qatar were signed, and the multi-billion-dollar stadium and infrastructure programme was going ahead in the boomingly wealthy statelet in the Gulf.

The 2014 World Cup in Brazil had begun with anti-Fifa and anti-inequality demonstrations by thousands of citizens in Rio de Janeiro appalled at the tournament's cost to the country. But as so often – and as is likely in Qatar in 2022 – once the tournament started the action was globally engrossing, and the experience was mostly acclaimed as a carnival of football. Germany's rebooted generation were a mature and intricately unified team by then, and they produced one of the most extraordinary results in World Cup history when they sliced open a dishevelled Brazil side 7–1 in the semi-final. Joachim Löw's team beat Argentina 1–0 in extra-time of the final with an exquisite cushioning of the ball on his chest by midfield substitute Mario Götze and a seamless left-foot volley. German football's revival, begun in 2000 and accelerated by the World Cup hosting *Sommermärchen* of 2006, was complete, a model achievement to other European countries, including England, who failed again at the group stage.

So in May 2015, Blatter was in Zurich welcoming the voting delegates from around the world with well-timed helpings of good news and lavish promises of money. The financial report showed that while Fifa's month of football cost Brazil a reported $13bn to host, Fifa went home with $2.4bn from the worldwide TV rights, $1.6bn from the marketing rights and sponsorships by Adidas, Coca-Cola, Hyundai, Emirates, Sony and Visa. Fifa's total income from the 2011–14 cycle was $5.1bn. Payments to the FAs, gathering to vote for a president, had exceeded $1bn in a four-year period for the first time, which included a special payment of $261m, part of a total $538m paid directly to them in the financial assistance programme.

Making his presidential address in the report, Blatter, pictured smiling, paid tribute to Julio Grondona, who had passed away in July 2014, having been a key ally as the chair of the finance committee. He had served 'with dedication and commitment' for fifteen years from 1999 to 2014, Blatter said, 'overseeing a period of growth and success for global football and for Fifa'. The new chairman of the finance committee was Issa Hayatou, the Cameroonian long-serving president of CAF.

'The Fifa World Cup™ [sic] in Brazil … was a truly unforgettable tournament,' Blatter said in his statement. 'From the first kick of the ball to the last, fans around the world were hit by football fever.'

Explaining that 'Fifa redistributes the majority of [its] revenue back into football,' and outlining a $100m legacy fund in Brazil, Blatter said: 'As we embark on a new commercial cycle, we have many reasons to be optimistic.'

So, people were kicking their heels in Zurich, seeing normal service resumed after the upheavals and corruption revelations, watching the delegates and executive committee high-ups arrive for their gilded few days, to culminate in another syrupy Sepp Blatter victory speech on the stage at the Hallenstadion.

The serenity of this lakeside coronation was shattered on the morning of Wednesday 27 May, just two days before the vote would take place. As the heads of the Fifa family were still sleeping beneath plumped-up duvets in the suites of their elegant Zurich haunt, the Baur au Lac hotel, Swiss police launched a dawn raid and arrested seven of them. Wanted – in fact, as it turned out, already charged in thunderous detail – by the US Department of Justice, the men were dragged from their dreams, awoken, told to get dressed and taken out to meet their nightmares. Some of them were led out of back doors into waiting cars, and shielded from photographers by thoughtful hotel staff holding Baur au Lac bed sheets in front of them. That produced the timeless photographs, perhaps the ultimate flipside of Fifa's great images, like Pelé and Bobby Moore embracing in sportsmanship, of its dirty linen finally being washed in public.

Timed to coincide with and explain these arrests, the US Department of Justice published its stunning allegations: fraud, $200m bribes taken over twenty-four years, racketeering, money laundering and other serious criminal charges against fourteen defendants, including the seven who had been whisked away from the Baur au Lac. Nine occupied senior offices at Concacaf and Conmebol, and commensurate positions at Fifa. Already, that privileged world had gone, given way to the bare reality of police stations, cells, questioning and extradition proceedings. The few stories of an FBI investigation which had leaked over the four years since the Trinidad debacle turned out to have been mere fragments; the US authorities really had been constructing a barrage.

Several big beasts of Fifa were on the indictment; Warner, Leoz, Teixeira would be added within months. Grondona, not yet dead a year and Blatter's praise for him barely published, was there as 'Co-conspirator #10', accused of taking millions in bribes. But some of their successors, too, those who had replaced the former presidents of Concacaf, Conmebol and the CBF, were also accused, including, extraordinarily, Jeff Webb, who had endlessly preached reform and appointed the Concacaf integrity committee to forensically expose Warner and Blazer.

On the same day, Michael Lauber, the attorney general in Switzerland, whose governments had for so long been accused of indulging Fifa and ignoring alleged corruption, announced an investigation into suspected criminal mismanagement and money laundering in connection with the awarding of the 2018 and 2022 World Cups. Lauber announced that Fifa, on a 'cooperative basis', had handed over data and documents from its granite bunker on the hill, and that 'relevant bank documents had already been ordered beforehand at various financial institutes in Switzerland'. Lauber said ten people gathered in Zurich – understood to be the members of the Fifa executive committee who voted on the World Cups – would be interviewed, although 'persons unknown' were suspected of the wrongdoing.

'It is suspected that irregularities occurred in the allocation of the Fifa World Cups of 2018 and 2022. The corresponding unjust enrichment is suspected to have taken place at least partly in Switzerland.'

In New York, at a press conference live-streamed around the world hours after the arrests, the attorney general, Loretta Lynch, who was in charge of the prosecutions, James B. Comey, director of the FBI, and Richard Weber, chief officer of the Internal Revenue Service, competed with each other to produce the phrase most damning of Fifa. Lynch trademarked some which have been repeated ever since, saying:

'The indictment alleges corruption that is rampant, systemic and deep-rooted, both abroad and here in the United States. It spans at least two generations of soccer officials who, as alleged, have abused their positions of trust to acquire millions of dollars in bribes and kickbacks. And it has profoundly harmed a multitude of victims, from the youth leagues and developing countries that should benefit from the revenue generated by the commercial rights these organisations hold, to the fans at home and throughout the world, whose support for the game makes those rights valuable.'

Comey said: 'As charged in the indictment, the defendants fostered a culture of corruption and greed that created an uneven playing field for the biggest sport in the world. Undisclosed and illegal payments, kickbacks and bribes became a way of doing business at Fifa.'

Alleging 'corruption, tax evasion and money laundering', Weber came up with the money quote, asserting that what had been uncovered was: 'The World Cup of fraud.' Comey would admit, a little ruefully, that he wished he had thought of the phrase first.

The indictment itself – the charge sheet against the named defendants – and other key documents including guilty pleas are public in the US, so we had access to the details that day. Expanded six months later when more arrests were made and twenty-seven defendants were accused, along with several others, including Blazer, who had already pleaded guilty, it was an astonishing and gripping read. The indictment charged that there was a culture of bribes paid routinely, almost compulsorily, to Concacaf and Conmebol presidents and officials for the TV and marketing rights of all international tournaments in South, North and Central America and the Caribbean. It was like a densely detailed version of the ISL bribery conduct, replicated in the Americas. The media rights for the Concacaf Gold Cup and its club Champions League were alleged to have been awarded always with the payment of bribes, as was Conmebol's Copa America – the world's oldest continuously running international tournament – and its Copa Libertadores for clubs.

Blatter and others in Switzerland would later complain at the US authorities launching these corruption allegations against Fifa itself, and staging arrests of South and Central American citizens in Zurich, so explosively sabotaging his election cakewalk. Although nobody listened, given the unprecedented drama, that did have some justification: almost all the corruption charged was in systematic kickbacks paid by marketing companies for Conmebol and Concacaf tournaments, in the Americas, in which Fifa itself had no financial involvement at all.

The only charges relating directly to Fifa were the Trinidad cash in brown envelopes, thrown in on page 120, and major further claims against Warner. The indictment accused Warner of being paid bribes by South Africa's bid to host the 2006 World Cup, when the country was beaten by Germany, claiming that: 'At one point, Warner directed [his son] Daryan Warner to fly to Paris, France, and accept a briefcase containing bundles of US currency in $10,000 stacks in a hotel room from co-conspirator #13, a high ranking South African bid committee official.'

In accusations which appeared clearly to have come from Blazer, it was also alleged that when he and Warner once flew to Morocco, which was bidding to host the 2010 World Cup, an unnamed representative of the Moroccan bid committee offered to pay $1m to Warner for his vote.

That was peanuts compared to the most powerful accusation in the indictment. It was based on the South African government having offered to pay $10m to Warner's Caribbean Football Union for a World Cup-linked legacy programme. Blazer, the indictment said, understood that offer to have been a bribe, the $10m was in exchange for Warner, Blazer and an unnamed Conmebol representative to vote for South Africa to host the 2010 tournament. Blazer's account – which Warner was understood to deny; he has been fighting extradition since – was that Warner told him he had accepted the offer and agreed to give Blazer $1m of the $10m.

The indictment framed these charges in an historical narrative. It claimed that the partnership of Warner and Blazer, once they were in control at Concacaf from 1990, generated 'the initial corruption' of Fifa. Alleging that Warner diverted Fifa, Concacaf and Caribbean Football Union money into 'numerous' bank accounts he controlled, the indictment stated: 'Beginning in the early 1990s Warner, often with the assistance of Charles Blazer, began to leverage his influence and exploit his official positions for personal gain.'

Although it was now evident that, as reported, Blazer had indeed been helping the authorities with their inquiries for a long time, it is clear from the indictment that a principal witness for the majority of the charges was another who pleaded guilty: José Hawilla. He was the founder and owner of the South American marketing company which had been prominent and renowned for years, with a slick and glamorous image: the Traffic Group. This company was perhaps best known for the deal it brokered for the CBF to do its famous ten-year sponsorship of the Brazil national football team with Nike, in 1996, which was always billed as a $160m deal. The indictment stated that when buying up rights he had paid bribes to football officials, who demanded them, ever since 1991. On that CBF deal, Hawilla's evidence was that the CBF itself had directed Nike to also pay Traffic a $40m agency fee – and that Hawilla had then split this $40m fifty-fifty with Ricardo Teixeira. Brazil's congressional inquiry had examined the Nike deal without quite finding major corruption; now the US Department of Justice was alleging that Teixeira received a $20m kickback on the deal. Teixeira, who had moved to Miami for a while, was reported to have moved back after the indictment to Brazil, whose law does not allow citizens to be extradited to another country. That meant he has not yet been required to plead guilty or not guilty to the charges, but he has always angrily rejected allegations of wrongdoing.

Hawilla, it emerged, had pleaded guilty on 12 December 2014, at a court in Brooklyn, to charges of conspiracy to conduct racketeering, with 'multiple acts involving bribery, in violation of New York State Penal Law'; wire fraud; money laundering of the proceeds and obstruction of justice. District judge Raymond Dearie, who would hear further guilty pleas, told Hawilla that on just one of the conspiracy charges the maximum possible sentence the judge could impose was twenty years in prison; in fact all four counts carried a possible twenty-year imprisonment. Bribery is very definitely considered a crime in the US.

On the same day, Hawilla had signed an agreement to cooperate with the US authorities which would reduce his sentence. The agreement, also made public, revealed that Hawilla, like Blazer, had clearly been cooperating for many months before December 2014. Hawilla agreed that he must 'at all times give complete, truthful and accurate information and testimony, and must not commit or attempt to commit any further crimes'. He also agreed to forfeit to the US authorities the incredible sum of $151m, which he agreed 'represents profits that the defendant made from certain contracts obtained through the payment of bribes and kickbacks'. These included the Copa America, 2016 Copa America Centenario, Gold Cup and Concacaf Champions League contracts, and a 2012 contract Traffic agreed with the CBF for the rights to its club tournament, the Copa do Brasil. Hawilla had already paid $25m of his ill-gotten profits to the law enforcement authorities, and agreed to pay the further $126m in instalments.

Hawilla also confessed that when he first heard from an associate that the FBI was asking questions and looking into bribes paid by Traffic, 'I asked him not to mention my name or the name of Traffic to the FBI,' and that when he was finally questioned he withheld information 'about ongoing criminal activity'. That was a guilty plea to the other criminal count, of obstructing justice, by intentionally impeding a grand jury investigation.

'I knew that this conduct was wrong,' said the former multimillionaire. 'I repent very much and apologise for what I did.'

In his guilty plea, Hawilla furnished the court with a little of his background. He was Brazilian, was seventy-one at the time, with various age-related health problems: he had recovered recently from cancer underneath his tongue, and suffered from pulmonary hypertension in one lung which meant he had to sleep with oxygen apparatus. He had, like João Havelange, originally studied law, and said he was a lawyer. The way he told his sorry story, he had begun Traffic as a decent business, in around 1980, buying rights to football events and 'promoting them in a legitimate way throughout the world'. Then he ran into Nicolás Leoz, when negotiating for Traffic to buy the rights to the Copa America. Hawilla claimed it was Leoz who corrupted him, and the TV rights process throughout the following years.

It happened in January 1991, Hawilla said. He had already bought the Copa America rights, and went to a signing ceremony at Conmebol's headquarters in Asunción, Paraguay, Leoz's base. There, the indictment alleges, Leoz, already by then the president of Conmebol for five years, declined to sign the contract.

'In a private meeting, Leoz told Hawilla … that Hawilla would make a lot of money from the rights he was acquiring and Leoz did not think it was fair that he [Leoz] did not also make money. Leoz told Hawilla that he would only sign the contract if Hawilla agreed to pay him a bribe.'

So there it was, the allegation that the president of the South American football confederation who lasted twenty-seven years, for fifteen of them one of the elite few in the Fifa executive committee, for whom the English FA had considered an honour when they wanted his vote for the 2018 World Cup, did not think it 'fair' for him not to take a bribe on a TV contract. This alleged sense of routine entitlement runs throughout the staggering picture painted by the US indictment, as it had been implicit in the drier Swiss legalese of the ISL documentation, in which Leoz had been one of the men paid bribes.

Hawilla said in his guilty plea that when Leoz demanded that bribe to sign the deal in Paraguay, he had to pay it because – as was explained in relation to the ISL bribes having continued unstoppably for years – 'I needed that contract because I had already assumed future engagements … commitments and even though I didn't want to, I agreed to pay the bribe to that official.'

Hawilla had a six-figure US dollars payment made to an account designated by Leoz, he said. From then, Hawilla admitted, Traffic's operation was corrupt. Bribes, he alleged, had to be paid as a matter of course to the officials selling the rights, who expected and demanded them – then to their successors who worked their way up within this culture. The indictment gave an overview of the 'racketeering conspiracy' which it claimed had been the underbelly of the lucrative increase in football TV and sponsorship deals' value during the same period:

'Over a period of approximately 25 years, the defendants and their co-conspirators rose to positions of power and influence in the world of organised soccer,' it said. 'During that same period ... a network of marketing companies developed to capitalise on the expanding media market for the sport, particularly in the United States. Over time, the organisations formed to promote and govern soccer in regions and localities throughout the world, including the United States, became increasingly intertwined with one another and with the sports marketing companies that enabled them to generate unprecedented profits through the sale of media rights to soccer matches. The corruption ... arose and flourished in this context.'

Leoz's personal role in this process, from its early days, was alleged in some eyewatering detail:

'In approximately 1993 or 1995, the defendant Nicolás Leoz began demanding additional bribe payments around the time each edition of the [Copa America] tournament was played,' the indictment stated. 'José Hawilla agreed to make these payments and caused them to be made. The defendant Nicolás Leoz solicited and received bribe payments from Hawilla in connection with every Copa America edition until 2011. The payments increased over time, and ultimately reached the seven figures.'

Leoz, eighty-six by the time all this caught up with him, was in the Migone private hospital in Asunción – which he reportedly owns – being treated for high blood pressure. A judge, Humberto Otazú, went to the hospital and told the media crowded outside that he had ordered Leoz to be under house arrest when he was released, as people over seventy are not held in prison before trials in Paraguay. Leoz's lawyer, Fernando Barriocanal, told the reporters that Leoz was in good spirits and would defend himself 'when the right time comes'.

Hawilla's guilty plea and cooperation agreement continued, admitting to corruption having become endemic over twenty-four years, during the time of the TV and sponsorship rights boom.

'After this and until 2013, other soccer officials came to me and those with whom I associated in business, to demand bribes to sign or renew contracts. I agreed that undisclosed bribe payments would be made to those soccer officials for contracts for the marketing rights to various tournaments and other rights associated with soccer.'

He said that Grondona, the chairman of the Fifa finance committee from 1999 until his death in 2014, pocketed millions of dollars which were due to the Argentinian FA from Traffic for the Copa America. Starting in the 1990s, Hawilla agreed to pay the AFA millions for each tournament so that Argentina would field its best players, and therefore increase the quality of the football and value of the TV rights. Hawilla was at times told not to send the payments to AFA, he said, but to a travel agency which, the indictment alleged, was 'used to facilitate payments to [Grondona] personally'.

From 2001, Hawilla similarly agreed to pay the CBF money to field its best players, for a tournament the two South American giants might otherwise consider not their highest priority. Teixeira, the indictment alleged, would tell Hawilla to make payments to strange bank accounts, which were not CBF accounts. Hawilla said Traffic also paid bribes to Teixeira for almost twenty years, from the 1990s until 2009, when buying the rights from the CBF to the Copa do Brasil. When in 2011 another company, unnamed, supplanted Traffic and bought the rights, it too agreed to pay a bribe to Teixeira, the indictment alleges. Hawilla took issue with that company, and they agreed a settlement to jointly pool the rights to the tournaments from 2013 to 2022, and, as part of that, 'Hawilla agreed to pay half the cost of the bribe payments,' which totalled almost $1m. The bribes had become so soaked into the ways of football, they were a business expense

With Blazer and Hawilla, the selling and buying parties on the Concacaf deals, both pleading guilty, the indictment alleges that bribes were kicked back to Blazer and Warner when Traffic paid $9.75m in 1994 for the rights to the 1996, 1998 and 2000 Gold Cups, and when Traffic subsequently bought the 2002 and 2003 rights as well.

'Traffic caused hundreds of thousands of dollars in bribe payments to be made to the defendants Jack Warner and Charles Blazer,' it alleges, noting as an example $200,000 wired by Traffic to Barclays bank in New York in March 1999 for the credit of a company Blazer owned in the Cayman Islands. Three weeks later, half that money was transferred from Blazer's Cayman Islands account to one of Warner's accounts in Trinidad.

Throughout the indictment, the $200m money flows of alleged bribes and kickbacks are traced, through banks in the US and sundry tax havens, and these major figures in football are also charged with wire frauds and money laundering, for seeking to conceal that the payments were bribes.

The Copa America Centenario competition was a special historic moment, celebrating 100 years since Argentina, Chile, Uruguay and Brazil had played the first Copa America tournament as long ago as 1916, itself held then to mark 100 years of independence for Argentina. After discussions, the tournament became a pan-American affair, opened up to Concacaf countries as well as Conmebol, so featuring countries throughout the Americas and the Caribbean. It was held in the US, where the gradual growth of soccer's popularity, and increase in value for TV rights and sponsorships, underpins the wave of corruption alleged against the football bosses. The Copa America Centenario, a romantic landmark, is alleged to have turned into a frenzy of fraud. Another dispute between Traffic and a marketing company, Full Play, owned by brothers Hugo and Mariano Jinkis, who were also charged, led to the two companies and a third, Torneos, joining together to form a new umbrella company, Datisa. It would take on and share the rights to the 2015, 2019 and 2023 Copa America tournaments, which were the subject of the dispute, and the Centenario competition in 2016. The total paid by Datisa to Conmebol was $317.5m, and the company would agree to pay a further $35m to Concacaf for its countries' participation in the Copa America Centenario.

Hawilla's evidence was that Full Play and Torneos had already bought the Copa America rights, although he had argued he had an option to buy them, and their executives had told him they had already agreed to pay bribes to Conmebol officials. As his part in resolving the new Datisa joint venture formed to give Traffic a share of the TV rights, Hawilla actually agreed to pay a third share of the bribes already committed. He ended up paying $13.33m, suggesting that a total of $40m in bribes was paid. The list of those alleged to have been paid these bribes included the senior citizens of Fifa entitlement, Leoz, Teixeira and Grondona, but a clutch of their successors were also indicted.

'The corruption ... became endemic,' the indictment alleged. 'Certain defendants and their co-conspirators rose to power, unlawfully amassed significant personal fortunes by defrauding the organisations they were chosen to serve, and were exposed and then either expelled from those organisations or forced to resign.

'Other defendants and their co-conspirators came to power in the wake of scandal, promising reform. Rather than repair the harm done to the sport and its institutions, however, these defendants and their co-conspirators quickly engaged in the same unlawful practices that had enriched their predecessors.'

Eugenio Figueredo, the Uruguayan former player who replaced Leoz as the Conmebol president when Leoz stepped down just before the ISL corruption revelations in 2013, was one of the seven arrested in Zurich. He was alleged to have taken bribes from Datisa on this deal, and 'annual bribe payments', together with Leoz, for the sale of the rights to the club competition, the Copa Libertadores. Figueredo would be extradited from Switzerland to Uruguay, where, at eighty-three, he was reported to have been remanded in prison while awaiting trial.

Figueredo's successor, Juan Ángel Napout, fifty-eight, was a Paraguayan who had risen to become president of Conmebol in the classic, apparently model pattern: a businessman who became president of his local club for years, then president of the Paraguay FA, then involvement in the committees of the confederation. He was added to the indictment in November, arrested in Zurich – while lounging in the comforts of the Baur au Lac hotel – and charged with taking bribes from the massive Datisa contract with Conmebol, as well as 'annual six figure bribe payments' from the sale of rights to the Copa Libertadores. He was reported to have travelled voluntarily to the US, where on 16 December 2015 he pleaded not guilty to the charges and was released to home detention with twenty-four-hour video surveillance, in a $20m bond package agreed by the judge.

So, the past three presidents of the South American football confederation, formed in 1916, home of Argentina and Brazil, two of the greatest playing nations on earth, have each been charged with criminal involvement in massive corruption when selling the rights to televised tournaments. At the CBF itself, José Maria Marin, a former politician, took over as the president when Teixeira finally stepped down in 2012. Marin became the head of the committee organising the 2014 World Cup in Brazil, but a year after that triumph he was one of the Fifa high-ups arrested at the Baur au Lac in May 2015. Marin was charged with taking bribes from the Datisa contract, and to have 'solicited and received bribe and kickback payments' on the sale of the rights to the Copa Libertadores.

Marin was photographed in November 2015 outside a federal court in Brooklyn following his extradition from Switzerland, where he pleaded not guilty. The judge allowed him, too, to avoid being remanded to prison, sanctioning him to stay in a New York apartment, reported to be in Trump Tower, with tight restrictions and a $15m bond. Court reporters described Marin, eighty-three by then, looking: 'Haggard ... slumped down in a chair while lawyers remained standing in front of the bench discussing his bail conditions. He later rose for a long embrace with his wife, who was required to sign the bond.'

His lawyer, Charles Stillman, said Marin would be 'preparing to deal with the charges'.

Marin had been replaced as the CBF president in April 2014, adhering to a prior agreement, by Marco Polo del Nero, another lawyer, then seventy-three, a long-term football politician who made it to the Fifa executive committee in 2012. In his official profile on Fifa's website, asked what football meant to him, del Nero proclaimed: 'The magic of the ball. I feel responsible by representing a sport which is so popular amongst millions of people. As a member of the management, I want to do something in order that the game stays clean and healthy.'

He left Zurich to fly back to Brazil early the week of the May 2015 congress, before the vote for president, and before he could be arrested for the charges of racketeering, involving alleged bribery, wire fraud and money laundering. Del Nero was charged with taking his share of the Datisa bribes along with Teixeira and Marin, and with soliciting 'systematic' bribes and kickback payments on the sale of rights to the Copa Libertadores. Hawilla had also told the authorities, in a startling story in the November indictment, that he and another, unnamed, sports marketing company had to pay Marin and del Nero, as well as Teixeira, bribes when the companies bought the rights to the club tournament, the Copa do Brasil. This was after the pair succeeded Teixeira as CBF president. Hawilla said he had a meeting with Marin in Miami in April 2014, to discuss these bribe payments, and had asked whether it was 'really necessary' to continue to pay bribes to Teixeira, who had stepped down from his football positions by then.

Marin, according to the indictment, stated: 'It's about time to have it coming our way. True or not?'

'Hawilla agreed, stating: "Of course, of course, of course. That money had to be given to you." Marin agreed: "That's it, that's right."'

Del Nero is reported to have remained since the indictment in Brazil, free from the threat of extradition, and said he was preparing a response to the charges. In April 2016, charged with racketeering, wire fraud and money laundering relating to these alleged massive bribes demanded and paid for the sale of rights to tournaments, he brazenly reclaimed the presidency of the CBF. At the time of writing, he is still the president of the football association in Brazil, attacked by Romário as 'the great plague of our football'.

While the world gazed upon these revelations and gasped incredulously at the sight of Fifa executive committee chiefs arrested, led away and charged in their vault of Zurich, Fifa itself still claimed it was in control. There was no question of postponing the election or of Sepp Blatter withdrawing for the mere matter of nine senior Fifa figures being charged with bribery and racketeering. On the day of the arrests and indictments, Fifa argued for a distance to be acknowledged from the US investigation, pointing out that 'the individuals [were arrested] for activities carried out in relation with Concacaf and Conmebol business'.

That was not the full truth, as Warner, Blatter's supporter for years, was charged with accepting bribes for previous World Cup votes, and he and Jeff Webb, a current executive committee member and Warner's reforming successor, were accused of embezzling Fifa money. The indictment alleged that endemically, habitually corrupt men had been with Blatter on the executive committee, in the inner sanctum of Fifa House for decades, including the long-term chair of the finance committee being thanked for his service in the annual report. Yet Fifa sought to portray the alleged corruption as wholly separate, and nothing for it to worry about.

It was true enough that, in the fevered perception that the organisation was finally being exposed, some of the small print in the Swiss attorney general's statement had been missed. He had indeed said, right at the end, that Fifa itself had filed the 'criminal charges against persons unknown' on 14 December 2014, after the completion of its own ethics committee's report into the 2018 and 2022 World Cup bidding process. So, Lauber explained, Fifa itself was being treated as 'the injured party', and cooperating with the investigation. This, being the victim rather than the accused, would be the legal position and strategy which Fifa would seek to adopt throughout the trauma of the indictments and investigations, during which football's world governing body was effectively in the hands of its lawyers, a US firm, Quinn Emanuel. In its own statement, Fifa emphasised that victim status, reiterated that the organisation had itself presented the file to Lauber, and at the end of a day of unimaginable scandal, on which it was plunged into the most shocking crisis in 114 years of history, it stated blithely: 'We are pleased to see that the [Swiss] investigation is being energetically pursued for the good of football and believe that it will help to reinforce measures that Fifa has already taken.'

Efforts were then made to carry on as if the calm of the coronation had not been so rudely interrupted. Blatter was still standing again, on his record, and went on with the congress in the Hallenstadion, unveiling the financial figures which showed that $1bn sent between 2011 and 2014 to the gathered FAs. The staged presentations went on regardless, blissfully distanced from all that unpleasantness which had befallen colleagues from South America and the Caribbean who would otherwise have been in the hall. The good works of football – underwritten by Fifa's motto: 'For the Game, For the World' – were proclaimed in videos and presentations, football as a vehicle for hope, anti-racism, peace. All of which was still true; the game was beloved worldwide, and a great frustration of Fifa staff was that some tremendous development work, by many committed people, done in difficult areas and countries was going largely unrecognised beneath the heap of corruption scandals involving the bosses. Here, the projects were presented as Blatter's vision, legacy and achievement – which to a degree is true, too – to national FAs which were receiving more money than they could ever have conceived before he became president.

People new to all this in 2015, who were baffled that the incumbent president for seventeen years could be re-elected two days after members of his executive committee were indicted for 'the World Cup of fraud', did not know the culture or the politics. Prince Ali bin Al Hussein doughtily spoke to the assembly to warn them that 'Fifa does not exist in a bubble' and that change was needed. Michel Platini, the Uefa president, had now told Blatter to resign and rallied the Uefa associations to back Prince Ali.

Blatter, though, was supported by an increasingly prominent power broker in Asia, the Kuwaiti Sheikh Ahmad al-Fahad al-Sabah, who had said: 'If you speak about Sepp, you have to speak about the change of football. He has maintained and developed football. He funded a lot of football projects and made it more international.'

To a majority of the football associations around the world it remained a record not worth breaking with. After the standard interminable vote of 209 associations in alphabetical order from Afghanistan to Zimbabwe, Sepp Blatter, aged seventy-nine, was accepting the congratulations of 133 countries which had voted to keep him for another four years. Prince Ali's seventy-three votes in the first round were a creditable statement of protest, and Platini gave him a pat on the back:

'I congratulate my friend Prince Ali for his admirable campaign,' he said.

Blatter, acceding to a fifth term, called for unity then, for football to pull together, and insisted that he was best equipped to lead Fifa through its choppy waters.

'You have seen the results of the congress, and they think that I am still the man to solve these problems,' he said.

He argued that the spectacle of so many senior people with whom he worked as allies for years having left or been banned by the ethics committee showed that Fifa had taken a tough stance on corruption. Asked if he was worried himself about the US investigation, he replied:

'I have no concerns. I especially have no concerns about my person.'

Even an operator with the ambition and obsession of Sepp Blatter, though, could not convince himself that he had retaken the Fifa presidency in a manner untainted by the arrests and allegations of twenty-four years of endemic bribery involving $200m. Just four days after the Friday of his fourth election triumph, on Tuesday 2 June 2015, Blatter announced a press conference at the House of Fifa. The world's media had written and broadcast their fulminating coverage on the Friday, aghast that Blatter seemed to be carrying on regardless, then gone home. The conference room so often packed with indignant questioners, in which we had been told that elegance was an attitude, was eerily empty.

On the fifa.com live stream, he was a little shakier than normal as he walked in, then quite croaky as he read from a prepared statement:

'I have been reflecting deeply about my presidency and about the 40 years in which my life has been inextricably bound to Fifa and the great sport of football,' he read. 'I cherish Fifa more than anything and I want to do only what is best for Fifa and for football.

'I felt compelled to stand for re-election, as I believed that this was the best thing for the organisation. That election is over but Fifa's challenges are not. Fifa needs a profound overhaul.

'While I have a mandate from the membership of Fifa,' he had noticed, 'I do not feel that I have a mandate from the entire world of football – the fans, the players, the clubs, the people who live, breathe and love football as much as we all do at Fifa.

'Therefore, I have decided to lay down my mandate at an extraordinary elective Congress. I will continue to exercise my functions as Fifa President until that election.'

The decision and promise, a completely uncharacteristic turnaround, was that he had accepted four more years was untenable, and would stand down within months. His statement included the assertion, again, that the scandals involved members of the executive committee who were representatives of confederations 'over whom we have no control, but for whose actions Fifa is held responsible'. He railed against the blocking of two key reforms, the setting of limits to how long people could serve and integrity checks on their fitness to do so, by Platini's Uefa. But he had recognised he could not continue for years and promised to 'focus on driving far-reaching, fundamental reforms', which Domenico Scala would oversee.

He declined to answer questions, so afterwards there was a scramble to understand what had inclined the great survivor to accept that this time it was all over. It was clear that he had not had the celebratory weekend in Zurich he had envisaged for himself when the development money, and his strategies and wiles, secured him his fifth term. It was said that his one daughter, Corinne, had urged him to step down, for his health and for his chance of a respectable legacy. It was speculated that the US authorities were investigating in particular his role in the $10m paid to Warner relating to the South Africa World Cup bid of 2010, which was undoubtedly true, and that he could face charges any moment, which turned out not to be. Other informed people told me that it was vital legally to show the US authorities that Fifa was committed to change, because that way it could maintain its victim status and fend off the allegation that it was indeed a racketeering organisation and become itself subject to criminal charges.

Scala, who was involved with Blatter in the discussions over that traumatic weekend, confirms that people close to him were counselling him, not demanding of him, to stand down.

'It was not black and white,' Scala recalls. 'It was multiple factors. I think he did have a choice, it was not inevitable for him. It was not legal factors; his position had become untenable because public opinion and the media had decided he had become the personification of the ills of Fifa. That may be not completely fair – the alleged crimes were committed in the confederations which Fifa does not control – but there comes a point where you have to protect the organisation you are leading.

'The pressure was tremendous; in public life, how many people have suffered such pressure?'

Scala said that people around Blatter were persuading him he could still shape the future and end his tenure with some dignity this way, but he could not sustain four years of criminal investigations, global criticism and ordure. Presenting the prospect for Blatter of seeing the reforms implemented, then handing over some months later, Scala said, 'I was trying to give him a direction to move out in a controlled manner; to have a good exit, salvage some creditable legacy and image.'

In the face of multiple arrests, indictments and Fifa being accused of the 'World Cup of fraud', even Sepp Blatter, the lifer at the captain's table, had had to recognise his position was unsustainable.

'He should have resigned earlier; in 2011, or after the World Cup in 2014; that would have protected Fifa better,' Scala reflected, before summing it up: 'He was out of time.'

Blatter ended his oration with an emotional plea and self-justification, complete with a reference to the politics: 'It is my deep care for Fifa and its interests, which I hold very dear, that has led me to take this decision,' he read. 'I would like to thank those who have always supported me in a constructive and loyal manner as President of Fifa and who have done so much for the game that we all love. What matters to me more than anything is that when all of this is over, football is the winner.'

Then he turned around and began to walk out. A door opened for him, showing light in the corridor outside, in the House of Fifa he had built, inhabited, protected and never wanted to leave, even into his eighties.

CHAPTER 12

'Tell Me What You Did'

The way Chuck Blazer's story is told, his outsized appetites and lust for money, status, women and excitement sprang from a hunger to escape a lower-middle-class upbringing in Queens, New York, where he would help out in his parents' small stores and snack joints. Soccer was never a route to wealth and a fantasy life of luxury hotels and the deference of statesmen when he began volunteering to help out with his own children's teams in the 1970s. But as he climbed the local soccer political structures, then regional and national associations, and when in 1983, as he said himself, he saw the opportunity to help Jack Warner become the president of the continental confederation, he came to see riches within reach. From 1990 when he became the Concacaf secretary general, earning fabulously and, by his own admission, sharing huge kickbacks and bribes with Warner and avoiding tax, spreading across a whole floor of Trump Tower in Manhattan, including the apartment for his cats, he had really made it. Presidents, princes, emirs wanted his patronage, and the floors of the world's palaces were his to bluster along. With Blazer, then, there is the sense of a bleak full circle travelled, that the crumbling of that life of lies and frauds finally happened back in Brooklyn.

It was ten o'clock in a deserted courtroom on the winter morning of 25 November 2013. There, Charles Gordon Blazer formally pleaded guilty to ten criminal charges. He had not filed a tax return at all for the years 2005 to 2010, when he had been piling the money up from Concacaf at his base in Trump Tower. This swindle was easily checked by the US agencies after Warner's heedlessly public accusations about Blazer's earnings following the Trinidad fallout. It was the big break which led the tax authorities to tap Blazer confidently on the shoulder as he trundled along East 56th Street in November 2011, and tell him it was all over.

It would be confirmed, after the arrests at the Baur au Lac, when in June 2015 Judge Raymond Dearie agreed to make Blazer's plea public, that Blazer had indeed begun cooperating with the authorities very quickly, in December 2011. Similarly to Hawilla, Blazer had agreed to 'provide truthful, complete and accurate information' to the investigators, and also to 'participate in undercover activities pursuant to the specific instructions of law enforcement agents'.

There does not appear to have been much glamour for Blazer on the November 2013 morning of his guilty plea. The investigation was continuing, so Dearie agreed to a bar on publicity and closed the courtroom. The only people in attendance were court staff, lawyers for the government agencies and for Blazer, and three agents from the Internal Revenue Service and the FBI. From the transcript, Dearie seems to have had a polite, even kindly manner as he led Blazer through all the formalities necessary to make a guilty plea permanent, to ten criminal counts carrying a maximum penalty of 100 years in prison. After asking Blazer to confirm his name, age – sixty-eight then – and education (Blazer said he had been 'partially through graduate school'), Dearie asked Blazer about his health, observing: 'I know you are wheelchair-bound.'

The purpose of this was to confirm that Blazer, as with any defendant, was mentally fit and therefore able to consciously plead guilty, and waive his right forever to a trial. Blazer filled Dearie in on his many physical ailments.

'Personally I have rectal cancer,' he said. 'I am being treated. I have gone through twenty weeks of chemotherapy, and I am looking pretty good for that. I am now in the process of radiation, and the prognoses is [sic] good.

'At the same time I have a variety of other less significant ailments dealing with diabetes 2 and coronary artery disease, but holding up reasonably well.'

'Good luck,' Dearie replied.

The judge took Blazer through the implications of pleading guilty, the rights he was giving up by doing so, and the charges. The transcript of the hearing makes it clear that, although Blazer committed most of his offences just over the Brooklyn Bridge in Manhattan, the US authorities were targeting Fifa, in Zurich, and portraying Concacaf, whose head office was down the road in Trump Tower, as just a constituent part. In a passage which would doubtless further enrage Sepp Blatter, who always fumed that the investigation targeted Fifa because the USA lost the bid to host the 2022 World Cup, Dearie told the court he did not even know how to pronounce Fifa. Then, once he had been put right by Evan Norris, a lawyer for the attorney general, Dearie proceeded to tell Blazer that the charges identified Fifa as a RICO enterprise, an acronym, as he explained, for a 'Racketeering Influenced Corrupt Organisation'.

So football's world governing body, formed in that backroom of a Paris office block by a handful of European gentlemen enthusiasts in 1904, ended up in a court in Brooklyn 111 years later, being labelled with a criminal accusation conceived for the mafia.

Blazer had been cooperating for two years and had accepted with his lawyers that doing so, and pleading guilty, gave him the best chance of staying out of jail, or at least limiting the time of any sentence. After all the preambling and gentle explanation, Dearie then turned to the required procedure whereby the accused has to himself state the crimes to which he is pleading guilty.

'Mr Blazer,' Judge Dearie said to him, 'tell me what you did.'

Blazer then explained, that from 1990 to his sudden resignation in 2011 he was employed by Concacaf and, he said, by Fifa; he earned annual fees as a member of the executive committee from 1997 to 2013, which were never published by Fifa until 2015 when they were $300,000 a year. He then proceeded to admit to his own crimes and associate Warner, described as co-conspirator #1 in Blazer's own indictment, with them.

'I and others agreed that I or a co-conspirator would commit at least two acts of racketeering activity,' Blazer said. These were: agreeing in 1992 to accept a bribe from the Morocco bid in return for Warner's vote for the country to host the 1998 World Cup. Blazer's indictment stated that after their trip to Morocco at the invitation of the bid committee, when the bribe offer was made, Warner 'directed' Blazer to chase the payment. The money was actually paid, the indictment alleged, at Fifa's executive committee meeting of 2 July 1992, although Morocco lost the vote to France.

'Beginning in or about 1993 and continuing through the early 2000s,' Blazer, in his wheelchair, read out in the empty Brooklyn courtroom, 'I and others agreed to accept bribes and kickbacks in conjunction with the broadcast and other rights to the 1996, 1998, 2000, 2002 and 2003 Gold Cups.'

He also admitted to having accepted bribes 'in conjunction with the selection of South Africa as the host country of the 2010 World Cup'. That was all count one. Then he ran through the wire transfers and cheques, transmitted between the US and the Caribbean, which amounted to money laundering. It was important for the US authorities to prove the crimes took place under their jurisdiction, hence the emphasis of the US geographically as a place where the money was received or passed through.

'I agreed to and took these actions to, among other things, promote and conceal my receipt of bribes and kickbacks,' Blazer stated. 'I knew that the funds involved were the proceeds of an unlawful bribe, and I and others used wires, emails and telephone to effectuate payment of and conceal the nature of the bribe. Funds procured through these improper payments passed through JFK Airport in the form of a check.'

The indictment of Blazer stated that as identified by the Concacaf integrity committee, he had often been paid via his company, Sportvertising, registered in the Cayman Islands tax haven. That, it was alleged, was 'to further disguise the source and nature of the funds'. On receipt of one payment, $600,000, to that Cayman company, his bank, FirstCaribbean International Bank (Cayman), asked him to inform it as to the source of the money, with supporting documents, to comply with anti-money-laundering regulations. Blazer, the indictment said, forwarded the email to the secretary of the person who paid him the money, referred to as co-conspirator #2, apparently Hawilla, and said: 'We will need to construct a contract regarding this and other transfers.'

Blazer subsequently received a false, backdated 'consulting services agreement' purporting to be between Sportvertising in the Cayman Islands and a Panamanian company, and Blazer sent this to his bank, to justify the $600,000 he had been sent.

For criminal counts four to nine of tax evasion, each carrying a maximum five years in prison, which could be added to twenty years for each of the previous racketeering and bribery crimes, Blazer recited: 'Between 2005 and 2010, while a resident of New York, New York, I knowingly and wilfully failed to file an income tax return and failed to pay income taxes. In this way I intentionally concealed my true income from the IRS, thereby defrauding the IRS of income tax owed. I knew that my actions were wrong at the time.'

Finally, he admitted to a financial crime carrying a maximum ten years in prison: having bank accounts in a foreign country with more than $10,000 in, and not disclosing them for tax. Blazer agreed to pay back more than $11m in taxes he had criminally evaded, and to testify at future trials of his former Fifa colleagues. A bond was set at $10m for Blazer to be allowed not to sit on remand in prison. Judge Dearie reminded him that the cooperation, admissions of his wrongdoing and reports of other people's and now his formal guilty pleas, did not mean there were any assurances 'as to what I will do when it comes to sentence'.

Dearie told Blazer: 'Good luck with your health,' then each of them signed a form.

The hearing was over at 11 a.m.; one hour in which Chuck Blazer had sat in his wheelchair in a court in Brooklyn and admitted that he was part of corrupting Fifa, Concacaf and the game of football. The indictment against him read:

'Though they helped pursue the principal purpose of [Fifa and Concacaf, to promote football], Blazer and his co-conspirators corrupted the enterprise by engaging in various criminal activities, including fraud, bribery and money laundering, in pursuit of personal gain. Blazer and his co-conspirators corrupted the enterprise by abusing positions of trust, engaging in undisclosed self-dealing, misappropriating funds and violating their fiduciary duties. To further their corrupt ends, Blazer and his co-conspirators provided each other with mutual aid and protection.'

And with his admission of guilty to all that, to a judge in an empty courtroom on a cold morning in Brooklyn, the brilliant career of globe-conquering Charles Gordon 'Chuck' Blazer was over.

CHAPTER 13

Mr President Integrity

Jill Fracisco worked hard for Jack Warner and Chuck Blazer, all hours of the day and night, organising the Gold Cup and Concacaf's other competitions down to all the overwhelming logistical details, for seventeen years: from 1994 until the pair resigned in 2011 in the fallout from the Trinidad scandal. So when I talked to her, I had thought she would be seething with resentment, at the overtime she put in, the sacrifices she made, for moderate pay, while they were now revealed to have been racketeering all along. Yet, surprisingly, she wasn't. She told me she had been grateful for the opportunities, a woman involved with soccer at that level in the Americas; she had loved working with players, coaches and referees, and felt greatly satisfied when the tournaments worked well. She gives Warner and Blazer credit for successfully having run and grown the confederation, and says that, overall, they treated her pretty well.

'In different ways I had respect for Chuck and Jack,' she told me. 'Chuck was the wheeler-dealer; he set policy and oversaw the money. Jack was the warrior who fought for Concacaf – I did see him as a Robin Hood figure, that he wasn't just taking money for himself, he was making sure the Caribbean countries had it.'

Fracisco said they had a good time, too, in the years before Blazer and Warner began to clash, when Warner became preoccupied with politics in Trinidad and, as Blazer would later say, acted as if he was above it all at Concacaf. She remembers when they would be on a football trip to somewhere in Central America or the Caribbean, in a place where security was not guaranteed, holed up together in some hotel:

'Then Jack and Chuck, when they used to get along, they were fun. I'm not talking strip clubs and steak houses [as Blazer would be known for in his Trump Tower, New York pomp], it was just sitting in a room, having drinks and talking and laughing, making our own snacks.'

Blazer, she said, was good to work for overall; he had an open-door policy, although it worked like that anyway because the door was literally open and he had a very loud voice. She said she was surprised at the revelations about Warner, because he always seemed to live quite humbly, his wife Maureen 'not over the top', staying in the same hotels as the staff, his only obvious extravagance the flowery ties he was known for. Clive Toye, too, worked for Blazer and Warner happily enough for thirteen years. He began doing the PR for Concacaf from 1998, the year Brazil agreed to send a full team to the Gold Cup, and Toye told Blazer he hadn't done anywhere near enough to publicise that. When Toye finally retired in 2011 after a remarkable career, aged seventy-nine, he says Blazer agreed to pay him a handy pension, of $3,000 per month.

'Even though I know now a lot of the wickedness Jack and Chuck got up to, I find it hard to dislike them because they were so pleasant,' Toye says. 'You could have a laugh with them.'

Fracisco said it was a shock and 'a nightmare' when the Trinidad cash scandal happened; she was in New York and remembers Blazer getting the call from Anton Sealey, and realising he had to inform on Warner. They had the Gold Cup to run imminently; referees, she said, were calling wondering if they would be paid for officiating and threatening not to turn up. She was worried the offices would be raided and the computers taken away, she remembers staff working till 3 a.m. scrambling to save the tournament, and they got through it. She was acting deputy secretary general after Blazer and Warner bowed out, and she hoped that with her knowledge of procedures, all her expertise, and relationships with people at all levels of football, she might be offered a senior role permanently.

Then, in May 2012, Jeff Webb came in as the president, and within two months brought in as the secretary general Enrique Sanz, who had been a senior executive, a vice president, at José Hawilla's marketing company, Traffic. It is for these two new brooms, not Warner and Blazer, that Jill Fracisco reserves her seething resentment.

Within days of his election as the president, Webb set up the integrity committee chaired by David Simmons, to investigate Concacaf's affairs under Warner and Blazer. At Fifa, Webb was now on the executive committee and one of the six vice presidents; he was the chairman of the internal audit committee and had been a member of the transparency and compliance committee. Among the many similar statements Webb made after arriving as the Concacaf clean-up man and bringing in Sanz, he said of his own credentials:

'As Concacaf president, the core focus is to restructure the confederation by building solid foundations to manage, develop and promote the game with a resilient commitment to inclusiveness, accountability and transparency.'

He was seriously being talked about as a future president of Fifa, an upstanding man with the kind of integrity necessary to restore the organisation's credibility. Sepp Blatter had even mentioned that possibility in a throwaway line – making Webb another rising figure on a vague promise of the top job. Fracisco had known Jeff Webb around the circuit for twenty years; he had been the president of the Cayman Islands FA from 1991. He was not a guy overblessed with charisma or personality; he worked in a bank on the tax haven island and, she says, he always liked the luxuries of life. Although she had been working as the interim deputy secretary general in the vacuum, working with other staff to keep the confederation from collapsing, and they made a lot of sacrifices with the hours and weekends they put in, when Webb and Sanz arrived she found herself closed out.

She says that Webb, whom everybody had always known as Jeff, now made it known he was to be called Jeffrey. Then Sanz let it be known that Webb was to be addressed as 'Mr President'.

'Probably it didn't help me,' Fracisco reflects, 'because I'd just laugh.'

The open-door policy was over, then they took away Fracisco's responsibilities, hiring an outside travel company to do the logistics for the tournaments. She was kept on to talk to lawyers and accountants sifting through the horrors Warner and Blazer left, but then, within months in 2013, she was told – not even by Webb or Sanz personally, but by a woman from the human resources department – that she was fired.

'After nineteen years, there was no goodbye; nobody was allowed to talk to me,' she says. 'I didn't do anything wrong; I worked really hard, I am not accused of anything, so you question it. I should have been OK because they knew I knew how to do the work, so the reason had to be something else: maybe to keep me away from what they were doing.'

Everybody – Fracisco, most of the Concacaf establishment, its integrity committee, the Caribbean football officials who had stuck their necks out for honesty, integrity and transparency, Fifa and the good people who had believed in Jeff Webb as the man he claimed to be – were stunned when he turned out to be one of the seven Fifa big shots hauled out of the Baur au Lac hotel by Swiss police on that morning of 27 May 2015. The indictment alleged a backstage predilection for corruption which exposed Webb's public displays, actions and pronouncements of integrity to have been a curtain of spectacular, still almost unbelievable hypocrisy.

The Department of Justice alleged that Webb had asked for a $3m bribe from 'co-conspirator #3' before Webb even became the Concacaf president, and while Sanz was still working for Traffic. 'Co-conspirator #3' was unnamed in the indictment, but described as a high-ranking executive of Traffic USA who joined Concacaf as secretary general in July 2012; he was therefore widely identified in the media as Sanz, who has not been charged or indicted. Webb was charged with perpetuating, not ending as he publicly claimed, schemes for personal enrichment first conceived by his notorious predecessor. The indictment accused Warner of having had for years a cunning way of diverting money in bribes to himself when selling TV rights to World Cup qualifiers on behalf of the CFU. It said that although the sale by the CFU included all its thirty-one member countries' matches, including those of Trinidad and Tobago, Warner would ask Traffic to create another contract purporting to be for the sale of Trinidad and Tobago's rights separately. So although Traffic had already bought those rights under the contract with all the countries in the CFU, the false side contract paid extra money to accounts controlled by Warner.

As an example, Traffic agreed on 17 July 2000 to pay $900,000 for all the Caribbean countries' qualifying matches for the 2006 World

Cup, including those played by Trinidad and Tobago. But at the same time, Traffic signed a separate contract with the Trinidad and Tobago FA, of which Warner was the president, to pay $800,000 'for the same ... rights it had [already] purchased as part of its contract with the CFU'.

Webb, still only the Cayman Islands FA president, replaced Warner as the CFU representative negotiating the sale of World Cup qualifiers, after Warner resigned from all his football positions. Preaching the need for reform and integrity after the scandal, Webb had also become chairman of a 'normalisation committee' for the CFU, responsible for steering the FAs back to decency and normality by working up new statutes. These new regulations embodying enhanced accountability and protections were unanimously approved by the CFU member countries on 7 March 2012.

At the same time, Webb was negotiating with Sanz for the sale to Traffic USA of the rights to the CFU countries' qualifiers for the next World Cups, scheduled for Russia and Qatar in 2018 and 2022. The value of the matches was greatly increasing with the growing popularity of football in the US particularly; ultimately, Traffic would agree to pay $23m for the rights. Webb's secretary general at the Cayman Islands FA then, who is also accused of involvement in the bribes, was Costas Takkas. He was a UK citizen with, according to the indictment, a number of businesses registered in Caribbean tax havens, including the Cayman Islands and the British Virgin Islands.

'During the negotiations, co-conspirator #3 met with the defendant Costas Takkas, a close associate of Jeffrey Webb,' the indictment states, 'who informed co-conspirator #3 that Webb wanted a $3m bribe in exchange for his agreement to cause the CFU contract to be awarded to Traffic USA. Co-conspirator #3 agreed.

'When he returned to the United States, co-conspirator #3 advised the defendant Aaron Davidson, at the time the Traffic USA president, of the bribe.'

In the spring of 2012, Traffic then agreed a joint venture for these CFU rights with another marketing company. Both treated the bribe as a business expense, according to the indictment, and agreed to share the payment to Jeff Webb, $1.5m each.

After Webb was elected to become the president of Concacaf in May 2012, he quickly brought Sanz in as his secretary general, to advance the causes of integrity, transparency and accountability. Takkas became Webb's 'attaché'. While Sanz had agreed the $23m CFU rights deal with Webb when still a Traffic executive, it was actually signed on 28 August 2012 by Davidson, a few weeks after Sanz had gone to join Webb at Concacaf. Nevertheless, the indictment alleges, at the same time as Sanz and Webb were setting up the Concacaf integrity committee and securing David Simmons and his well-respected colleagues to staff it, 'co-conspirator #3' was helping Takkas sort out the payment of Webb's bribe. He put Takkas in contact with Traffic executives in Brazil, put calls in from the new Concacaf office in Miami and went to meetings himself in Brazil.

The bulk of the $1.5m bribe from Traffic USA, initially $1m, was allegedly routed to Takkas in November 2012 via banks in Miami, New York, Hong Kong, back to New York, then to Takkas' company's account at Fidelity Bank in the Cayman Islands. An unnamed 'co-conspirator #23' was paid a fee of $200,000 for allowing his company to be used as a front for the payment to and from Hong Kong. The remaining $500,000 promised to Webb by Traffic USA was, the indictment states, paid through an associate of José Hawilla's, to another of Takkas' accounts in the Cayman Islands.

Next, in the way Takkas transferred the money to Webb, came a glistening detail, which seems to encapsulate the whole shameless, excessive, different planet these football chiefs inhabited and helped themselves to, from exploiting the people's game.

'Takkas subsequently transferred the funds to an account in the name of a swimming pool builder at United Community Bank in Blairsville, Georgia, for the benefit of Jeffrey Webb, who was having a pool built at his residence in Loganville, Georgia.'

So, these huge bribes paid to Webb for selling TV rights of Caribbean football matches were wired to a man who was building a swimming pool at his home in the US.

In late 2014, Webb received $250,000 from the other $1.5m he had demanded. The indictment states that the second media company did not make any more payments because, in the winter of 2014 they got wind of the authorities' investigation into Traffic and José Hawilla.

Once installed at Concacaf, while they were intoning publicly about their new era of transparency, Webb and Sanz began negotiating with Aaron Davidson for Traffic USA to buy the rights to the upcoming Gold Cup and club Champions League tournaments. Immediately, according to the indictment:

'Jeffrey Webb directed co-conspirator #3 to seek a bribe payment in connection with the negotiations.'

In November 2012, Davidson agreed that Traffic USA would pay $15.5m for the exclusive worldwide commercial rights to Concacaf's 2013 Gold Cup and the Champions League for the 2013–14 and 2014–15 seasons. The indictment alleges that 'co-conspirator #3 solicited from Traffic USA its agreement to pay Webb a $1.1m bribe in exchange for Webb's agreement to award the Gold Cup/ Champions League contract to Traffic USA. The defendant Aaron Davidson and José Hawilla agreed to the bribe payment.' The money was eventually agreed to be paid to the Panama bank account of an unnamed kit company, for which Webb is alleged to have instructed his co-conspirator to submit a false invoice.

A year later Sanz, on behalf of Concacaf, and Davidson, for Traffic, agreed a renewal contract for exclusive sponsorship rights to the four Gold Cups and seven seasons of the Champions League between 2015 and 2022, for the payment by Traffic of $60m.

'Again,' the indictment states, 'Jeffrey Webb directed co-conspiator #3 to solicit a bribe for Webb in exchange for Webb's agreement to award the … contract to Traffic USA. Though Webb wanted more, the parties eventually settled on $2m as the size of the bribe payment.'

The indictment then cites a meeting held between Hawilla and Davidson in March 2014 in Queens, New York, to discuss how the bribe schemes were going. Talking about the endemic, common practice of paying bribes to obtain commercial rights, Davidson is said to have exclaimed to Hawilla:

'Is it illegal? It is illegal. Within the big picture of things, a company that has worked in this industry for thirty years, is it bad? It is bad.'

The anecdote was apparently based on the testimony of Hawilla himself, who had by then begun cooperating with the authorities and committed in a legal agreement to tell them his experiences truthfully.

Webb, seemingly insatiable, also sought a bribe from the next tournament which came Concacaf's way: the joint Copa America Centenario with Conmebol. His interim predecessor as Concacaf president, the Honduran lawyer Alfredo Hawit, who began the negotiations, had announced that he hoped the tournament would be held in the US because, he said: 'The market is in the United States, the stadiums are in the United States, [and] the people are in the United States. The study that we have made [shows] that everything's in the United States.'

Already infamous by the time it took place for the bribes allegedly paid to the football men who organised it, the Copa America Centenario did indeed take place in the burgeoning soccer 'market' of the United States. It ran from 3 June 2016, when the hosts lost 2–0 to Colombia at Levi's Stadium in Santa Clara, California, to the final on Sunday 26 June at the Metlife Stadium in New Jersey, where Chile beat Argentina 4–2 on penalties after a 0–0 draw. The tournament featured all of Conmebol's ten national teams, including Brazil, and the national teams of six Concacaf countries: the USA, Costa Rica, Haiti, Jamaica, Mexico and Panama.

Datisa, the joint venture of the marketing companies Traffic, Full Play and Torneos, had already bought the rights to this and other Copa America tournaments from Conmebol for $317.5m – and, according to the indictment, agreed to pay $40m in bribes to Conmebol officials. After Concacaf agreed that its member countries would also play in this landmark tournament, Datisa separately contracted on 4 March 2014 to pay $35m to Concacaf for the rights to the matches involving those countries. The indictment alleged that Webb negotiated with senior executives of the three Datisa companies and that:

'Datisa also agreed to pay Webb a bribe in exchange for Webb's agreement to cause Concacaf to enter into the 2014 Centenario contract.'

On 1 May 2014, Eugenio Figueredo and Webb held a press conference in Miami to announce that this pan-American Centenario tournament would take place at major stadiums in the United States in the summer of 2016. Hawilla, of Traffic, Alejandro Burzaco, of Torneos, who has also since pleaded guilty to agreeing bribes and kickbacks on that and other Copa America tournaments, and the Jinkis brothers of Full Play, who are charged, were all there. After the press conference, the indictment states that the marketing company bosses had a meeting at which they discussed the bribery plans.

'At one point,' the indictment alleges, 'Burzaco said: "All can get hurt because of this subject ... All of us can go to prison"'.

At his appearance to plead guilty in the Brooklyn courthouse on 16 November 2015, Burzaco, then fifty-one, said that he acquired a minority stake in Torneos, an Argentinian sports TV production company, in 2005, and became the chief executive the following year. He said that he was told early in his Torneos career by a founding owner of the company that they paid bribes and kickbacks to Conmebol chiefs, to secure the rights to South American tournaments.

'I was informed that the agreement had been in place for some time,' Burzaco told the court in his statement of guilt. 'I know that I should have walked away at that point, but instead I agreed to work for Torneos and agreed to take an active role in the bribery schemes. I regret the decision. I was wrong.'

He confessed to paying bribes and kickbacks to 'multiple Conmebol, Fifa and other officials affiliated with ... soccer to obtain and maintain the marketing rights to various tournaments'.

Burzaco then admitted the alleged Datisa conspiracy, that they paid 'multiple bribes or kickbacks totalling tens of millions of dollars to Conmebol and Fifa officials in exchange for their endorsement of the new contract' to buy the rights to the Copa America for 2015, 2019 and 2023. For the Centenario tournament in 2016, he said that 'officials who held positions of authority and trust within Conmebol and Concacaf approached our joint venture and demanded that we ... pay a bribe or kickback in connection with the rights of this special edition of the tournament'.

Ultimately, he said, he decided not to pay a bribe to Conmebol or Concacaf officials for the Centenario, following the deal signed in 2014, 'because of fear of law enforcement scrutiny', but accepted that it was wrong to have agreed to pay it, and that a charge of conspiracy still applied to the agreement.

When it all came out on 27 May 2015, Webb arrested at dawn in Zurich and driven into custody, his name first on the indictment as the authorities' biggest catch, I still clung to a thought that there could be some mistake. Loretta Lynch and her fellow US law enforcers had a triumphant relish and hyperbole about their announcements; already Blatter and others around Fifa were complaining that the sabotaging of his election week sprang from the US losing the 2022 bid. Webb lived in the US now, not even in the Cayman Islands, so it did seem unnecessarily melodramatic and publicity seeking to have him arrested in the statement-making Fifa hotel in Zurich, for financial swindles allegedly all hatched in the Americas.

Contemplating the scale of the allegations, I could just about digest that this corruption happened, the persistent taking of bribes by men grown cynical or greedy. Perhaps the culture of football administration bred in them a belief that they were entitled to the millions, telling each other that everybody else was getting rich from the football rights boom except them, the committee men who kept the game running. I still found it difficult to picture the pact of dishonesty between briber and bribe-taker, the corrupt conversations and channelling of the money itself, that behind their grand rhetoric about the good football does these men would conspire to fill their boots with booty.

But that is still easier to comprehend than the image which was presented of Jeff Webb. It was the scale of hypocrisy, of double-talk, the ability to be two people at once, the hard-faced enormity of it. It was beyond anything I had ever seen before, to believe of this man who arrived after the Trinidad scandal, talked endlessly in globally reported public forums about integrity and transparency, and solemnly established a committee of top people to investigate Blazer and Warner. Now we were told that all the while, from as soon as he had the opportunity, behind the scenes he was demanding bribes. We who have loved football all our lives do not want to believe that those who run the game, on their manifestos of doing good, are this corrupt and rotten, and so marinated in greed. So I maintained the view that this could be a mistake, that these were only allegations, which seemed to have been quite extravagantly made and staged. Webb pleaded not guilty, so we would see.

Then, on 23 November 2015, Jeff Webb changed his stance. He went to Judge Dearie's court in Brooklyn to plead guilty. To count 1:

racketeering conspiracy, which involved agreeing he had committed 'multiple acts of bribery', money laundering and wire fraud; to count 25: wire fraud conspiracy for his bribes and kickbacks on the Caribbean Football Union countries' 2018 and 2022 World Cup qualifiers; count 29: money laundering of those bribes; count 33: wire fraud conspiracy to take bribes and kickbacks from the Concacaf Gold Cup and Champions League rights; count 37: money laundering of those bribes; count 39: wire fraud conspiracy for the bribes and kickbacks on the Copa America Centenario; and count 40: money laundering of those bribes. All of it; everything he helped himself to in the very short time he was in a position to do so while publicly preaching integrity: guilty.

There was no charge of hypocrisy but the conspiracy charges included accusing him of: 'Knowingly and intentionally conspiring to devise a scheme and artifice to defraud Fifa, Concacaf and the CFU of their respective rights to honest and faithful services through bribes and kickbacks, and to obtain money and property by means of materially false and fraudulent pretences, representations and promises.'

When invited, like Blazer and Hawilla, in the same format of court hearing, to tell Dearie what he had done, Webb recited his career. President of the Cayman Islands FA from 1991, working his way up football politics and committees, first the CFU, then Concacaf, then Fifa. President of Concacaf from May 2012, when he became a vice president of Fifa. He spared Dearie the CV of his work on the normalisation committee, internal audit committee, transparency and compliance committee, and his appointment as Fifa's global pioneer for anti-racism and discrimination. Then he made his admission:

'While I held the position of Cayman Islands FA president, and then Concacaf president, I abused my position to personally enrich myself, through various means … I abused my position to obtain bribes and kickbacks for my personal benefit. Among other things, I agreed to commit at least two counts of racketeering activity …

'For example,' he then said, 'in or about 2012, a co-conspirator told me that sports marketing companies would offer us side payments in exchange for awarding them commercial rights to World Cup qualify [sic] matches for the CFU nations. At the time I understood this to be a bribe offer, and I believed that such offers were common in this business.'

When I first read that, this man telling a court that he believed bribes were 'common in this business', I felt as if the football dreams of small boys, all around the world, were being trampled on.

He also admitted to: 'embezzling funds intended for the benefit of football organisations that I represented'. Without including much detail, the indictment had referred to Fifa's provision of hundreds of millions of dollars to its member associations from the GOAL and Financial Assistance Programme and other development programmes, and alleged that Webb and Warner:

'Took advantage of these opportunities and embezzled or otherwise personally appropriated funds provided by Fifa, including funds intended for natural disaster relief.'

Warner had been accused of keeping money designated for relief to people who suffered in the Haiti earthquake disaster, which he always angrily denied.

So Jeff Webb stood in that courthouse and mumbled through his humble pie: he had defrauded Fifa, Concacaf and the CFU of their right to honest service from him, he had solicited and been paid bribes, sought to conceal the money and laundered it with wire frauds. He said he knew at the time 'it was unlawful to accept bribes and embezzle funds in connection with my duties as a high level official of Fifa, Concacaf or CFU'. He claimed: 'I deeply regret my participation in this illegal conduct.'

Then there was a discussion about the terms of his remand: he was under house arrest and GPS electronic monitoring, but Dearie agreed to allow him to leave his home between 8 a.m. and 5 p.m., limited to a twenty-mile radius, for the sole purpose of running errands relating to the care of his eighteen-month old son. His wife, Kendra Gamble-Webb, a doctor, had 'thankfully' been able to get a job, as a practising physician in the Atlanta area, the court was told – she must have felt her world had crumbled.

The court made public the means by which Webb had met the $10m bond required to keep him out of jail and in his house while awaiting sentencing. Ten properties, their addresses redacted, five owned by him and his wife, others owned apparently by family members, were pledged to secure the bond. Also in the list was a menu of flash, high-living, very expensive possessions of the Webbs: a 2014 Range Rover and 2015 Ferrari – initially these were noted as owned by Webb, but this was crossed out and his wife's name handwritten across it; a 2003 Mercedes; $401,000 in his wife's bank account; her equity interest in a company whose name was redacted, and her diamond wedding ring. Then there were eleven watches owned by Webb: four Rolexes, one Cartier Roadster, a Hublot gold watch, a Breitling. His wife had to put up diamond and pearl jewellery, a Hublot and a Rolex watch.

Jill Fracisco told me that if people were shocked to see that list of Rolexes and luxury motors, she wasn't: 'That was the way he was; he always had a taste for luxury items and a taste for the good life,' she said. 'It wasn't because he became the president; that just gave him more opportunities.'

Four people had also agreed to indemnify the government for any costs if Webb were to break his agreement, forfeit bail or become a fugitive: they were noted as John Bodden, Webb's uncle; Olive Bodden, Webb's aunt, who was described as retired; Thelma Phipps, Webb's sister-in-law, and Rynlee Thompson, his niece.

But this spectacle of Warner's successors at Concacaf, pledging their devotion to integrity while helping themselves to oceans of bribes, goes further than the epic swindles and deceptions of Jeff Webb. The indictment alleged that Alfredo Hawit, as soon as he replaced Warner as the interim Concacaf president in 2011, took $250,000 in bribes from Hugo and Mariano Jinkis, as an agreement to use his influence, with others, to get Concacaf to switch the sale of rights to the Jinkis' company, Full Play.

Hawit was alleged to have put the question of selling Full Play the rights on to the agenda for a Concacaf executive committee meeting in Miami, in January 2012, but ultimately, despite further efforts, it never came to fruition. Three years later, in July 2015, the indictment claimed, Hawit instructed an intermediary to create a sham contract for 'consulting services' to account for the payment from Full Play, and to create a sham land purchase with Hawit's wife. Hawit was then alleged to have told another suspect that he was not worried about law enforcement because the intermediary 'did not pay me … he bought land in Honduras … from my wife'.

Hawit, like Webb, pleaded not guilty at first, then on 11 April 2016 he changed his plea, to guilty, on four of the ninety-two criminal counts in the indictment. In three, he was charged, alongside others, with a racketeering conspiracy and two counts of wire fraud involving bribes and kickbacks. Count 92, to which he also pleaded guilty, was accusing him alone of a conspiracy to obstruct justice, based on the sham contract and property sale.

Jill Fracisco says that somehow she does not really feel betrayed by Warner and Blazer, despite now knowing what they did. Jeff Webb and Enrique Sanz she says, were cold from the day they arrived and they sacked her without having the 'decency' to tell her themselves or give her a reason. Clive Toye said that when he retired, Blazer saw to it that the agreed pension of $3,000 a month was paid, but when Webb and Sanz arrived the cheques stopped. When he finally asked them what was happening, he says: 'They were rude, there was silence, they said: "Why are we paying you anything?" They were appalling, it was terrible behaviour, and there was no need for it. And I am sure that happened to some other employees to whom it mattered a lot more than me.'

Concacaf say they have reformed now and really are putting this past behind them. Webb is helping the authorities, presumably, following his guilty plea. I did ask if he would talk to me about his admitted crimes and incredible hypocrisy, but his lawyer, Ed O'Callaghan, said he would be making no comment while the cases are still ongoing. Sanz is not actually charged. In June 2015, immediately after the arrests, Fifa's ethics committee provisionally banned him from football. Then in August 2015, following a review into the allegations against this man who, with Webb, had led its previous integrity investigation, Concacaf sacked him.

Jill Fracisco is not suspected of having been involved in any of the wrongdoing, only recognised to have done her diligent best. But since, she has been able to find few other opportunities. That is despite having run major international football tournaments for many years, often in the most trying of circumstances.

'I was fortunate, a lone female in that position, on the road, working with the players and referees. A lot of us gave up part of our lives to do it but we travelled the world together; it was like working with family,' she said.

'Then when Jeff Webb and Enrique Sanz arrived, I was shut down and shut out. But now we see Jeff was planning to make a lot money from overcharging for the tournaments, from kickbacks. I haven't done anything, but it is extremely difficult to find work; I'm sending résumés out, frequently getting no replies.'

She paused, and reflected, after speaking of her years given to football. 'The story is told as the bad people getting their comeuppance,' Fracisco said, 'but there are good people too, who have been collateral damage.'

CHAPTER 14

The World Cup of Fraud

Fifa's scrambled response to the tsunami which swamped the Baur au Lac was to sniff at the accusations in the indictment, say it was cooperating as 'the injured party' and argue the charges all related to deals done in the Americas, not the clean Alpine air of Zurich. Sepp Blatter would complain forever after that 'the Americans' were sore at losing the 2022 World Cup vote and had sought to sabotage Fifa and his presidential election by portraying American corruption as Fifa's. The men arrested, and Blazer who had pleaded guilty already, were foisted on Fifa by the confederations' right to seats on the executive committee: Fifa could not control them, they argued.

But there was that one particular allegation lurking in the centre of the indictment which did strike at the heart of Fifa, and it was the most monstrous and unpalatable of all. It was the jaw-dropping story, which had come from Blazer's own admissions, that the South African government, and its FA's 2010 World Cup bid committee, had paid the $10m bribe to Jack Warner to buy his, Blazer's and another Fifa executive committee member's vote. The indictment said that this payment was to be paid to the Caribbean Football Union for apparent legacy inititatives, to 'support the African diaspora'.

It was indeed the case that as part of the rhetoric in which the South Africa World Cup was wrapped, the tournament's historic significance for the country liberated from apartheid and for Africa itself, one of the promised legacies was some work, never really defined, for the diaspora. The appalling nature of this crime, if it is true the money was a bribe, is that the African diaspora is understood to be, essentially, the descendants of people wrenched out of their African homes over generations and taken into slavery. To provide some tangible social programme in the name of addressing that historic crime, or, anyway, just to share with deprived African-descendant communities some of the fortunes from the first World Cup in Africa, which made Fifa $3.5bn, was consistently expressed as a noble purpose. The South African president himself at the time of the World Cup, Thabo Mbeki, made this legacy part of his bid to the Fifa executive committee, saying: 'The millions of Africans on the continent and the African diaspora have embarked on an exciting human journey. This is a journey away from a history of conflict, repression and endemic poverty.'

If, though, the 'African diaspora' had been conjured as a disguise for money which was just a bribe, to be pocketed by three men personally for their votes, this was cynicism beyond conscience.

The denials would pour in immediately after Loretta Lynch unleashed her indictment. While the South African government initially said it was looking into the claims, its FA and Danny Jordaan, the football official turned politician who had been garlanded for leading the successful bid and the tournament organising committee, were indignant. Fifa distanced itself completely at first, and claimed anyway that the money was for a legacy programme.

Blazer was clear in his guilty plea that he had understood, from what Warner told him, that the $10m was, plainly, a bribe for their votes. He had given the US authorities a narrative of the money trail, which was set out in the indictment. Now, years after the Trinidad fallout in 2011, it finally provided an explanation for the $750,000 paid to Blazer which Warner had complained so publicly about: Blazer was saying that was his share of the South Africa bribe.

Blazer's account was that when Warner told him the South African government and bid committee 'were prepared to arrange for the government of South Africa to pay $10m to the CFU to "support the African diaspora"', he was clear that it was 'in exchange for the agreement of Warner, Blazer and co-conspirator #16 [an unidentified Conmebol member of the Fifa executive committee] to all vote for South Africa, rather than Morocco, to host the 2010 World Cup'.

The indictment accuses two unnamed 'co-conspirators' of having been involved: a 'high-ranking official of Fifa' and a high-ranking official of the South African FA and World Cup organising committee.

When Blazer pleaded guilty to the ten charges against him on that November morning in 2013, he included this bribe from South Africa as one of the crimes to which he was admitting.

'Beginning in or around 2004 and continuing through 2011, I and others on the Fifa executive committee agreed to accept bribes in conjunction with the selection of South Africa as the host nation for the 2010 World Cup,' he recited to Judge Dearie in the Brooklyn courthouse. That was included with Blazer's admissions of being paid bribes and kickbacks when selling the rights to the Concacaf Gold Cups to Traffic in his guilty plea to count 1: the racketeering conspiracy.

Blazer was clear and had made an admission of criminal guilt that the money was a bribe for his vote, Warner's, and a third member of the Fifa executive committee. There is a baffling contradiction in the evidence about the third person: in the indictment of Blazer personally, the US authorities allege it was the third Concacaf executive committee member. They were thereby accusing Isaac David Sasso Sasso, a businessman, president of the Costa Rica FA and Fifa executive committee member from 1990 to 2007, who died in 2011 aged eighty-five with no allegations of wrongdoing having been made against him. However, in the main indictment of Warner and the other twenty-six defendants, the authorities allege the third voter to have been involved in taking the bribes was an unnamed 'co-conspirator #16', described as a high-ranking official of Conmebol, not Concacaf. It seems rather a shame for Sasso Sasso's family, to say the least, that the authorities have not moved to clarify this.

It was not made clear if the third voter is alleged to have taken a share in the money, but Blazer confessed that he did. He said that Warner had told him that he had accepted the offer of $10m from the South African bid team and government, and that he would give $1m of it to Blazer. This is the clearest admission ever of a Fifa executive committee member accepting a bribe for his vote on a World Cup host, although Warner has not admitted that it was.

Warner had during the bidding process already extracted a burdensome price from the South Africans to win his favour. Fixated on the prestige and status it would give him, Warner lobbied relentlessly for Nelson Mandela himself, the global embodiment of humanity, truth and reconciliation, to come to Trinidad to meet him personally. It might have been thought that Jack Warner could make up his mind about the objective merits of the rival countries bidding to host the World Cup without needing a personal visit from Mandela. But Jordaan and the South African bidders were so keen this time to secure the hosting of the World Cup, after being pipped by the German bid for 2006, that Madiba was persuaded to make the long, arduous journey to Warner's Caribbean island. He was eighty-five, frail, his health faltering, and he never made a journey this exhausting again. In its denial that the $10m it subsequently agreed should be paid to Warner was a bribe, the South African FA said:

'Our world icon, the late former state president, Mr Nelson Rolihlahla Mandela, made one of his last foreign trips on 29 April 2004 and visited Trinidad and Tobago to encourage the head of its football association to vote for South Africa to host the 2010 World Cup. He undertook this 17 hour trip because of his deep desire to fulfil his dream of hosting the world's biggest sporting event in our country.'

The involvement in the bid of Mandela, a universally admired and adored figure, and his personal entreaty to Jack Warner in Trinidad, have always been presented as sainted blessings of the bid, and the tournament as an indivisible part of his humanitarian gifts to his nation. On the small Gulfstream jet, that photograph of him was taken, a blanket over his lower body, face fixed in a grin, with Blazer and Mary Lynn Blanks posing for the camera.

To see the image of a man as distinguished as Mandela forced to abase himself this much, towards the end of his hard and exemplary life, before corrupt thieves like Blazer and Warner, to have Fifa locate its World Cup in South Africa, is repugnant now. The picture was top of the blog Blazer maintained – which was still up, years after his guilty plea – boasting about his life among kings and presidents, living the high life on Fifa. Written across the picture, above Madiba's head, in big yellow letters, is the blog title: 'Travel with Chuck Blazer and friends'.

Warner, a Trinidad and Tobago MP and government minister by then, was in the official party to meet Mandela straight off the plane. During the two-day trip, Mandela was carted to a dinner hosted by

Warner – at the Dr João Havelange Centre of Excellence. This long journey at Warner's insistence was always portrayed as the clincher for the three votes Warner controlled. The vote, on 15 May 2004, just two weeks after Mandela's visit, was 14–10 in favour of South Africa over Morocco, so the three votes were, as Warner always knew to his advantage, crucial. It was hailed as the historic landmark to bring the great and dazzling World Cup to Africa, sealing South Africa's journey from the constitutional racism of apartheid to liberation and modernity.

'Madiba's personal diplomacy paid off,' the SAFA said, 'when Fifa decided to grant this privilege to South Africa.'

Until the US Department of Justice alleged it was a $10m bribe based on Blazer's criminal confession, it seems that few people even knew that an actual payment had been made relating to the rhetoric about an African diaspora legacy. In the five years since the 2010 World Cup, no legacy programme had been announced in the Caribbean, and there were no activities relating to it, according to the journalist vigorously covering and investigating Warner, and football on the small island, Lasana Liburd.

The grim payment trail, and some supporting documentation, were disclosed or leaked, in the frenzy after the allegation was made. Fifa had issued a denial that either Blatter nor Valcke had anything to do with it; they were not 'involved in the initiation, approval and implementation of the ... project'.

Within hours, a letter was leaked to the Press Association, whose correspondent, the sports news reporter Martyn Ziegler, immediately Tweeted it to the world. It showed that Valcke had been directly asked to implement the $10m payment to Warner by the South Africa FA. The letters released subsequently showed that in December 2007, three years after the vote, three before the World Cup itself, Jordaan had written to Valcke to initiate $10m for a '2010 Fifa World Cup Diaspora Legacy Programme'. Jordaan, in his capacity as chief executive of the World Cup organising committee, told Valcke that the South Africa government had committed to paying that money. He said that two government ministers had been involved, saying the money should be paid to the organising committee.

So Jordaan suggested to Valcke that, as the government was to make good the $10m, Fifa should deduct the money from the overall budget for the organising committee, and 'deal directly with the Diaspora legacy support programme'.

The next leak was of correspondence before that, dated 19 September 2007, in which Valcke had referred to the South Africans' $10m diaspora legacy programme being 'specifically for the Caribbean countries'. On 7 December 2007, strangely, the very same day as the letter Jordaan had sent to him, Valcke wrote what appeared to be a chasing email to a South African government minister asking when he could make the transfer of $10m. In that email, Valcke said this had been discussed by Sepp Blatter and the president of South Africa:

'This is based on a discussion between Fifa and the South African government and also between our president and HE President M'Beki [sic].'

Fifa, responding to that leak, insisted that Blatter was not involved in implementing the scheme, but was 'simply referring to an update' Mbeki had given Blatter.

By 4 March 2008, three months later, crucial detail had been added to the discussions. It came in a letter from Molefi Oliphant, then the president of SAFA and a vice president of the Confederation of African Football, to Valcke at Fifa in Zurich, confirming the arrangement. Now, however, the recipient of the money had become more specific: 'SAFA requests that the Diaspora Legacy Programme be administered and implemented directly by the president of Concacaf [Jack Warner himself] who shall act as a fiduciary of the fund.'

How the idea of a development fund for the African diaspora had come to be directed into the control of Jack Warner, personally, as the ideal person to administer it, nobody has explained at the time of writing. After the letters emerged, Fifa released another statement, clarifying its first one, saying that although Valcke was indeed clearly involved in the correspondence about the $10m, he was not 'initiating' it, and the payment had been authorised by the chairman of the finance committee, the late Julio Grondona.

For so much money presumably intended to do good, transformative work in impoverished areas of the Caribbean, to which African people had been transported as slaves, and for so high a purpose as an African diaspora development programme, there appears to have been very little follow-up about what was actually done with the $10m. The indictment, giving Blazer's account, alleges that no programme was ever going to be put in place and it was always simply a bribe from the South Africa government and bid, for Warner's and the two other votes. It says that for some years after they voted, Blazer 'periodically' asked Warner about the $10m and chased up his promised $1m share. Blazer said that he was told that 'the South Africans' were for some time unable to arrange for the government to make the payment:

'Arrangements were thereafter made with Fifa officials to instead have the $10m sent from Fifa [to the CFU],' the indictment states, 'using funds that would otherwise have gone from Fifa to South Africa to support the World Cup.'

Then, in early 2008, three payments totalling $10m – two of them in January, before that 4 March request from Oliphant to Valcke – were paid by Fifa to Bank of America accounts in New York which the indictment states were in the name of Concacaf and the CFU, 'but controlled by the defendant Jack Warner, at Republic Bank in Trinidad and Tobago'.

The FBI had investigated what happened to this money which had landed in US bank accounts, and the indictment alleges that Warner 'caused a substantial portion of the funds to be diverted for his personal use'. It sets out as examples $200,000 of an initial $616,000 from Fifa which Warner allegedly transferred to his own personal loan account, then more than $4m which he is accused of laundering via a middleman. This was a Trinidadian businessman, unnamed in the indictment but whom the US authorities state they have identified, and to a large supermarket chain and property company which this person owned.

'During approximately the same period, funds equating to at least $1m were transferred from these same accounts into a bank account held in the name of Warner and a family member, at First Citizens Bank in Trinidad and Tobago,' the indictment states.

Warner took his time to pay Blazer, who said he finally heard 'from a high ranking Fifa official' that Fifa had indeed paid Warner the $10m. Blazer then asked for it again, according to the indictment, but ultimately Warner only ever gave him $750,000 of the

$1m promised. It is alleged that Warner told Blazer he would have to pay it in instalments because he had already spent the money. He eventually paid it in three instalments, which appeared to be eerily similar to the three payments to Blazer which Warner complained about in 2011.

The indictment alleges that the first was for $298,500, wired from a Trinidad bank account in the name of the CFU, on 19 December 2008, to one of Blazer's accounts at a bank in the Cayman Islands. The next instalment of his bribe money was stated to be for $205,000, a cheque, which Blazer paid into his own account at Merrill Lynch in New York. The third payment involved another cheque, this time for $250,000, drawn on the account in the name of CFU at the Republic Bank in Trinidad and Tobago, being transported in and out of the US. It was physically delivered to Blazer by an intermediary, who flew over to JFK airport from Trinidad and then took it to Trump Tower to put it in Blazer's hand, the indictment states. Then, a representative of a bank in the Bahamas, where Blazer had an account, flew over to New York to take it off Blazer, then flew back to the Bahamas and, on 3 May 2011, paid the cheque into Blazer's account. The indictment claims that Warner sent Blazer an email in March 2011 to tell him the payment was coming. Blazer never received the final instalment, of just under $250,000, which he claimed was due for his share of the bribe. In his public complaint about Blazer in 2011, Warner had indeed said that Blazer was chasing him for another $250,000.

When this hideous allegation, confessed by Blazer, broke and shattered Sepp Blatter's coronation week, SAFA issued a long denial. It included the sugary credit to Madiba, a reminder of the legacy for Africa and its diaspora which the bid had promised, describing this as a 'noble effort to support football development' and arguing that the $10m was paid in good faith to Warner who appeared ideal at the time to administer it.

'We categorically deny that this was a bribe in return for a vote,' the SAFA statement said, again praying Mandela in aid of its argument. 'It belittles the hard work done by Madiba, Archbishop [Desmond] Tutu, the South African government and numerous others who sacrificed their time and money and family lives to make our country proud! It tarnishes their images in the most unscrupulous manner.'

SAFA referred to some other football development programmes, to justify including a diaspora legacy programme in its bid and having Fifa pay $10m to Warner, which SAFA accepted it did. However, nowhere did it say that any actual work had been done on this legacy programme, and did not explain whether it had made any efforts with Warner to check on whether a programme had been set up. In fact, SAFA appears to acknowledge that the money had gone and that Warner and Blazer appeared to be the culprits:

'That the money may have been siphoned off by individuals after it was donated does not make the donor complicit or a co-conspirator,' it said.

Jordaan himself, who became the mayor of Nelson Mandela Bay in Port Elizabeth, has repeatedly denied that the $10m he asked Valcke to pay was a bribe to Warner, and also argued it was a betrayal of Madiba's work to suggest it.

In March 2016, Fifa threw a rock through the window of its previous denials. The embattled governing body, which had been in the hands of its US lawyers for months, seeking to maintain 'victim' status and avoid being condemned as a RICO, sued all the charged defendants itself. In the list were its former long-serving executive committee barons and allies of Blatter: Warner, Teixeira, Leoz, Blazer and the others in Concacaf and Conmebol alleged to have taken bribes. In effect, Fifa was now saying it believed everything in the indictments to be true, and that this criminal activity had indeed damaged Fifa, which made a 'victim statement'.

In that, it set out its own history as the basis for its hurt: that Fifa was founded in 1904, had 209 member associations, 'giving it greater global reach and diversity than even the United Nations'. Fifa stated its constitutional purpose and that it had been a 'global force for good', proclaiming its achievements – the World Cup, 'tireless efforts' to promote football; $550,000 a day going to development projects, the social initiatives and children playing the game in troubled regions.

'Fifa is the driving force behind football throughout the world, ensuring that it is on solid ground everywhere,' was the claim.

The lawsuit argued that the 'brazen corruption of the defendants' had tarnished the Fifa 'brand', obscured its role as a 'positive global organisation' and also caused it financial damage which it was claiming from the defendants.

Within that startling legal position taken by Fifa against men it had paid, pampered and indulged for decades, it included Warner and Blazer's $10m bribe from South Africa, adopting the allegations in the indictment.

'It is now apparent that multiple members of Fifa's executive committee abused their positions and sold their votes on multiple occasions,' Fifa itself stated, remarkably, having overseen these votes and never itself found any bribes to have been paid.

Fifa claimed that Warner had developed 'strong, illicit ties to the South African bid committee', having received the briefcase with $10,000 in cash, as alleged in the indictment, which his son Daryan, acting as 'his father's bagman', picked up in a Paris hotel and took back to his dad in Trinidad. Then, to secure Warner's vote for the 2010 tournament, Fifa now claimed:

'The South Africans offered a more attractive bribe of $10m in exchange for Warner's, Blazer's and a third executive committee member's votes. Warner and his co-conspirators lied to Fifa about the nature of the payment, disguising it as support for the benefit of the "African diaspora" in the Caribbean region, when in reality it was a bribe. They breached the fundamental duties they owed to Fifa, CFU and Concacaf, and stole $10m.'

Fifa specifically sued Warner, Blazer and their – unnamed – co-conspirators for the $10m it now said was 'theft', money they 'funnelled as bribes for their personal use'.

Claiming that they also took their salaries and allowances on false pretences because they did not give 'honest service' in return, Fifa claimed repayment from all the defendants, $28m in total. In Blazer's case, from all his years at Fifa, the claims was $5.3m; from Warner, Fifa wanted $4.4m on top of the $10m. Oddly, there was no mention of suing to reclaim the money from the Dr João Havelange Centre of Excellence, and the new regime at Concacaf did not respond to my question about whether they are seeking to repossess it from Warner. In its claim, Fifa was also suing the defendants for the damage to its reputation and its legal costs, which will not be cheap.

The day after this claim was issued, the South African sports minister, Fikile Mbalula, criticised as 'despicable' Fifa's adoption of the bribe allegation and implication of the South African bid. He maintained that SAFA had asked for a $10m fund for a diaspora legacy programme in the Caribbean, and that if Warner took the money, that was 'frowned upon'. He argued that the Fifa lawsuit was not aimed at the South African government, but only at the defendants in the US indictment. And Mbalula mounted a platform of indignation again, at the accusation being made:

'The South African government maintains its position that the African Diaspora Legacy Programme was a legitimate programme of the South African government,' he said. 'We will not apologise for our progressive stance to the African diaspora for including the diaspora in the pride and honour of hosting the Fifa World Cup. To infer or insinuate anything else, including to diminish such an important part of the continent's history as an elaborate ruse to issue a bribe, is despicable.'

I have a number for Jack Warner, and an email address he responds to – Trinidad is a small place, and he is surprisingly accessible. When I called him, I introduced myself, said I was writing a book about the events at Fifa, and wanted to hear his perspective. He replied:

'I have nothing to say about Fifa, now or ever. You can write the book, without my support.'

I decided to email him, invite him to give his perspective on all the issues in which he has been accused or implicated of wrongdoing. It was a long list: the issues raised by the Concacaf integrity committee report which found he had perpetrated a $26m fraud to own the Dr João Havelange Centre of Excellence; the allegations in the indictment, particularly the alleged $10m bribe to vote South Africa for the 2010 World Cup; whether there ever was a diaspora programme; the brown envelopes of cash with bin Hammam in the Hyatt Regency; bin Hammam paying him $1.2m after that, which some people have alleged was so that Warner would not contest the charges and give evidence; his alleged ticket scams over the years, the current status of the Dr João Havelange Centre of Excellence; several other allegations of improper conduct against him; and to clarify his current stance: whether he is denying the claims in the indictment and contesting extradition, and, if so, on what grounds. In September 2015 the Fifa ethics committee, using new powers investing it with the authority to proceed against people even after they have resigned, banned him from football for life. It cited, without giving details, that he had been involved in 'schemes involving the offer, acceptance and receipt of undisclosed and illegal payments'. The ethics committee said this related to its investigation into the bidding process for the 2018 and 2022 World Cups investigated by Garcia, not for the alleged South Africa bribe.

Warner replied quite promptly to my email, saying:

Dear Mr Conn

It is clear that our interests at present veer along divergent paths and what seeks to attract your attention is quite irrelevant to me.

Please be advised accordingly,
Regards,

I replied, trying once more, telling him I was still very interested in hearing his thoughts and perspective, including about his experiences at Fifa in general. He responded promptly again:

'While I am impressed with your insistence [sic] please be advised that I do not share your interests and have no desire to assist you or the Fifa or anyone else in this matter.'

The US law enforcement authorities also want to talk to him about these issues, for which they have issued major criminal charges, including this most terrible allegation of all. The accusation is that he abused the history and legacy of African slavery, pretending he would implement a programme of good works for the descendants of those whose lives were stolen, and instead he stole the money himself. At the time of writing, he has very skilled and expensive lawyers arguing against his extradition. So he may never be forced to 'assist', and face the question about what he did with $10m for a South Africa World Cup 2010 Africa Diaspora Programme, paid to him after Nelson Mandela, at eighty-five, was made to fly seventeen hours over the ocean, to beg for his support.

CHAPTER 15

Le roi se Meurt

The FBI and Fifa ethics committee had come for all these former allies whom Sepp Blatter had supported for years, but largely he had been unmoved and said it did not reflect on him, because he was unaware of their wrongdoing and had no part in it. He had worked eagerly at Havelange's side for twenty-three years, made it as an unlikely, unpresidential-looking character to outflank the attacks of Johansson for the presidency in 1998, then flourished through seventeen years and five elections. He had survived the dossier amassed against him by his own secretary general, Zen-Ruffinen, in 2002, and the exposure of the ISL bribes in 2013. Now a ferociously well-resourced, lengthy US criminal investigation had not produced the name Blatter on any indictment, charged with any offence. He had agreed to step down due to the intolerable pressure, and because even he recognised his time was up. But it would be at his choosing, designated for February 2016, with a legacy of reform in place, when he, unblemished, could retire to acclaim. So when the Swiss criminal authorities and Fifa ethics committee finally came for him, Sepp Blatter was disbelieving, indignant to his core. The evidence they had, to finally overthrow a president of forty years' tenacity, would also sweep away his likely and once-chosen successor: the former playing genius turned Uefa president, Michel Platini. For Platini, just when his time had finally arrived to step up to the Fifa presidency and attain the summit of a starry career he believed was his destiny, this would be a catastrophic fall, and humiliation.

It was the attorney general in Switzerland, the country so long accused of leniency towards the sports bodies it shelters, who emerged brandishing the piece of paper which felled the presidents of Fifa and Uefa. On 25 September 2015, attorney general, Michael Lauber, made a brief, lethal announcement: that he was investigating a 2m CHF payment from Fifa, made on Blatter's instruction, to Platini, in February 2011. That was just three months before the vote in which Blatter had been standing again to be the Fifa president against Mohamed bin Hammam, an election in which Platini supported Blatter and encouraged Uefa's fifty-three European FAs to do the same. This was neat, and devastating, and it turned out to be rooted in the very beginnings of Blatter and Platini's entanglement in football politics, seventeen years earlier.

Blatter, Lauber announced, had been 'interrogated' as a suspect of criminal mismanagement, and Platini interviewed as 'a person asked to provide information', a particular status in Swiss law. Both men said, extraordinarily, that the 2m CHF was Platini's back pay, for that dimly remembered stint Platini had served as Fifa's football adviser after Blatter won the 1998 election. Still a glittering figure then, from his feats as a player, then France coach, then lead organiser of his country's triumphant 1998 World Cup, Platini had lent stardust to the secretary general's hustings and been given that job afterwards. Blatter had then supported his man, who believed he was on a promise to succeed him one day, to be elected on to the Uefa executive committee in 2002. Then in 2007 Platini, with Blatter's political support, moved in to oppose and replace Blatter's rival, Johansson, as Uefa president. Since that first election, Platini had eased comfortably into the role, status and politics as Uefa president, was elected for another term in 2011, then again in March 2015 after it became clear Blatter was digging in at Fifa. Platini was biding his time to move across from Lake Geneva to Lake Zurich, and after the traumatised Blatter had finally announced he would step down, Platini, on 29 July 2015, had actually declared himself a candidate to succeed him.

Yet here it was, this sudden bombshell, that while he was the Uefa president Platini had been paid 2m CHF on Fifa president Blatter's order, shortly before the 2011 Fifa election. And Platini was claiming it was money he was owed for the job he did at Blatter's side which finished fully nine years earlier. It looked awful for both of them, and it turned out to be awful for both of them.

It was established very quickly that Platini had no written employment contract with Fifa for the 2m CHF he had been paid. He had worked as Blatter's football adviser, and as the deputy chairman of the newly established GOAL programme alongside bin Hammam, for a contract paying him 300,000 CHF a year. As the ethics committee and the Court of Arbitration for Sport would both state, there was no documentation or written note, evidence of any sort, for a further 2m CHF to be payable. Both Blatter and Platini claimed they had made an 'oral agreement' back in 1998 that he would in fact be paid 1m CHF a year, but that Blatter had only felt able to pay 300,000 CHF of it at that time, so had owed a further 700,000 CHF a year.

The reason, both Blatter and Platini claimed, was that Zen-Ruffinen, the then secretary general who turned whistleblower and Blatter's accuser, was only being paid 300,000 CHF. Blatter said he agreed to pay Platini 1m CHF, but could not be seen to pay him three times more than Zen-Ruffinen, so had said they should defer the remaining 700,000 CHF a year. In the actual contract, which I have seen, the salary figure was left blank, and Blatter had handwritten it, in blue pen: 300,000 CHF.

Platini claimed he had not been paid the extra money he was owed because Fifa was having financial difficulties in 2002 following ISL's collapse, and he did not need it. He let it be known that he is not a man interested in money, having always had plenty of it all his life since he started earning as a midfield prodigy at Nancy aged seventeen. He went off to his new life and upward ascent of the Uefa elevator without giving it a great deal of thought, he said; he had been owed money often in his life and did not greatly pursue it.

Then, years after the work at Fifa finished, when he had moved a great deal further on in football's political system and was Uefa president, in 2011 Platini had suddenly decided to go back to Blatter and ask for this money he was owed. He said he actually underclaimed, because he forgot he had only been paid 300,000 CHF a year; he had thought it had been 500,000 CHF, so he was only still owed 500,000 CHF for each of his four years at Fifa rather than 700,000 CHF. Hence his demand for 2m CHF, rather than 2.8m CHF.

Platini tried to set out this version of events, and his innocence, in an interview for *Le Monde* in France, where it was most important to him to safeguard his cherished reputation and national hero status. In it, he said:

'*Je ne suis pas un homme d'argent.*' (I am not a man obsessed by money.)

Seeking to explain why he didn't ask for the money he claimed he was owed until nine years after the work he did was finished he said:

'I didn't ask for the money because I didn't miss it. I started earning money at 17 years old. I didn't even know it was possible in football [then]. I remember my father [Aldo Platini, who also had a bar and ran the local football team in Joeuf, the mining town where Michel grew up] who was a maths teacher, he couldn't believe it either and he asked at Nancy: "And you are going to give him money to play?"

'I have kept those values,' Platini claimed. '*L'argent, j'en ai assez.*' (Money, I have enough.)

He invited *Le Monde*'s journalist, Raphaelle Bacque, to ask his wife whether it was true that he does not care about money or look at his bank account, and Bacque noted that Christèle Platini, who was sitting in on the interview at their duplex apartment in the village of Genolier near Geneva, agreed by rolling her eyes in mock exasperation.

Platini's matey, banterous, working man way of expressing himself had won him friends and influenced people all along his journey, where he had seemed a greatly refreshing, authentic football man among the suits and blazers of commercialised European football. He had waved away concerns about his vote for Qatar to host the 2022 World Cup while admitting he changed his mind after his lunch at the Élysée Palace with the French president, Nicolas Sarkozy, and the Emir of Qatar. Platini maintained that Sarkozy had not asked him directly to vote for Qatar, and he had made his own mind up. He voted for Qatar, he reiterated to *Le Monde* in this interview, because he thought a World Cup across the Gulf in the winter would be '*magnifique*' – even though the vote was for a summer World Cup and no other Gulf country except Qatar will be a host. He dismissed with the same bar-room insouciance the questions about his son, Laurent, having been recruited by the kit company Burrda, which was owned by Qatar Sports Investments, after Platini did cast his vote for Qatar. That had nothing to do with it, Platini insisted; it was a year and a half after the vote, and he did not intervene in his son's life:

'*Il n'y a aucun conflit d'intérêts,*' (There was no conflict of interest at all) Platini stated.

This 2m CHF payment, however, was discovered and had come to be considered by serious authorities in a newly forensic climate of arrests, indictments and a massive clampdown on financial wrong-doing at Fifa. It was a proper, formidable test of that payment's legitimacy, money passed between the holders of football's two highest offices, and of Platini's man-in-the-dressing-room approach to football, money and politics.

Platini gave a consistent account of his alliance with Blatter. He said Blatter first approached him in 1998 at a hotel in Singapore, when Platini was joint president of the 1998 France World Cup organising committee, for which he said he did not get paid. He said Blatter asked him then if he planned to stand for Fifa president, because João Havelange had suggested it, saying: 'Platini as president and Blatter as secretary general, would be a very elegant solution.'

Platini just took it as flattery; he was only starting in the game's polit-ical snakes and ladders, still quite fresh from playing and coaching. In his telling of his story, he declined Blatter's approach, then Blatter said: 'I will stand, but I need you.' And Platini then entered an imme-diate embrace with the master of manoeuvres, Blatter, twenty-four years in this game at Fifa by then, with experience before that, too.

Lars-Christer Olsson, the Swedish secretary general at Uefa who worked for Johansson, describes Blatter as a brilliant political strat-egist. He would be stunned and appalled at Blatter's virtuosity at politics when he saw him flourish it in 2007. Blatter had initially supported Johansson as the candidate to serve another term, as the best character to protect and develop European football. Olsson, a long-term ally and admirer of Johansson's, believing him to have good values of governance for football, saw Blatter's support warn off other potential challengers, and believed it also lulled Johansson into a sense of security. Then, in November 2006, a late stage before the elections in the spring, Blatter declared his backing for Platini, his ally. Olsson was so dismayed that he pledged he would resign if Platini won the election. When that did happen, Olsson did resign.

'Blatter was very shrewd,' Olsson says, 'he was a very clever politi-cian in that way, technically good, a strategist, and he always landed on his feet. I thought it was so wrong and against good governance, I believed that the Fifa president should not intervene in other elections, so I resigned as my way to support Lennart Johansson. Blatter was always nice to the losers afterwards; he was clever in that way, too. And he groomed Michel Platini in the politics.'

Platini lent his name and fame to support Blatter, and after the win in Paris, Blatter offered Platini the job of football adviser. At the same time Jérôme Champagne, a former French diplomat with a high-achieving CV, who had been head of protocols for the France 1998 World Cup, hosting the heads of state and other dignitaries, was recruited as Blatter's international adviser. Platini, the star who grafted his way to the very top of football with Juventus and as captain of his country, with his professed man-of-the-people roots, seems never to have taken to Champagne, the highly educated career diplomat working in the elaborate international relations of Fifa.

Platini claims that when they discussed money for the role, Blatter asked him how much he wanted to be paid, and he replied: 'One million.' Then that Blatter replied: 'Of what?' and Platini, in his telling, says he replied that he did not care which currency it was: 'Whatever you like,' he says he told Blatter: 'Roubles, pounds, dollars.' He said Blatter had replied: 'OK: 1m Swiss francs a year.'

Blatter tells the same story, that Platini asked for 'a million', but didn't specify the currency, and Blatter decided it should be Swiss francs, although Platini worked from an office in Paris, not at Fifa in Zurich.

Jean-Philippe Leclaire, the editorial director of *L'Équipe* and author of the Platini biography, *Platoche: Gloire et déboires d'un héros français* (The glory and woes of a French hero), believes the one million figure does have some significance, and that it reveals Platini's attitude to money was a little more insistent than laissez-faire. When he was still a young player, aged twenty-two, at Nancy, Platini played for France in midfield at the 1978 World Cup in Argentina, including in the 2–1 defeat to Italy in the first group match. After the World Cup, Inter Milan were interested in signing him and they had talks. Platini was still on only a modest salary, the story goes, but when the chairman of Nancy heard Platini had been talking to the giant Italian club, he halved the player's salary.

'After that, Platini promised it would never happen again,' Leclaire says. When Platini moved up the football ladder, from Nancy to St Étienne, he asked for 1m francs a year.

'He is a family guy and he is not flash with his money,' Leclaire says, 'but he sees it as his value, a way his talent is recognised.'

The title of the book, *Platoche*, a jokey, not particularly reverential nickname for Platini, Leclaire explains as the French attitude to arguably the country's greatest ever football man, his generation's Zinedine Zidane. 'He is a French hero and we see through him the development of football in France, but we don't worship our heroes,' Leclaire says. 'The nickname is a way people are brought down to earth. The Italians, when he was at Juventus, called Platini "*le roi*" ['the king']; the French didn't.'

Platini did work for Blatter from the office in Paris, advising on the football calendar, distributing development projects to the poorer associations in those first transformative years of the GOAL project, and accompanying Blatter on his travels, which Platini is said not to have particularly relished. In 2002, he left, with Blatter's support, to sit on the executive committee at Uefa, where the president and senior representatives around the table had fought so bloodily to unseat Blatter at Fifa, without success.

After he beat Johansson in the 2007 election, I interviewed Platini for the *Guardian* that autumn, at Uefa's headquarters in Nyon, Switzerland. The building is attractively modern, with clean lines and open spaces of wood, glass and chrome, like a designer cabin on the banks of Lake Geneva. Platini was new in the job and he seemed to brim with energy and genuine enthusiasm for nurturing football in Europe, which had so gilded his life. He told me that although he had been a great and well-paid player, he learned his 'conviction and philosophy' from the coaching he saw his father do for the love of it in their small town of Joeuf, and from their base in the bar. His mission at Uefa, he told me, was to maintain the soul of football in the era of mega-money: 'To protect the game from business.'

He talked about the investors arriving to buy English Premier League clubs, like the Glazer family, from the US, who bought Manchester United in 2005 and leveraged the club with their £525m bank debts, and said he was 'afraid' of the effect it would have on the game.

'My philosophy is that football is popular because of the identity of the clubs, because the people of Manchester played the people of Liverpool, and the fans take care because the clubs belong to the people. Now, because football is popular, people are coming to take control of this popularity, to make money. That is not correct. I don't like that.'

It was a message I and many people wanted to hear, at a time in English football when money was dominant, and the FA had allowed historic, beloved football clubs to be bought and sold as financial investments. Platini and his advisers had not yet developed into coherent policies his protests about business, and the '*ultra-liberalisme*' of the English and Premier League approach, but they would soon produce the 'financial fair play' rules, at least to stem the losses clubs were making across Europe. The rules were then criticised for themselves cementing the power of the big clubs which made most money, but they prevented a further round of hyper-wage and transfer fee inflation fuelled by oil-rich owners buying clubs, as Russian oligarch Roman Abramovich had at Chelsea in 2003, Sheikh Mansour at Manchester City in 2008 and Qatar Sports Investments at Paris Saint-Germain, after Platini's lunch with Sarkozy, in 2010. It is true that Platini did not really reshape European football and curb its exploitation as a business; gradually the big clubs garnered more influence with him, but he seemed in those early months genuinely committed to trying.

He had won his election in the classic, Havelange and Blatter-patented manner at international federations, by appealing to the votes of the smaller countries, as he illustrated to me:

'My job is to develop the football in Europe, for the youth – to help the children of Georgia, Armenia, Lithuania to enjoy the game. The smallest associations do not receive money from the governments; that's finished. Only from Fifa or Uefa or the richer countries. If we don't give money, mini-pitches, footballs, they can't play, it's finished. My job is not the games between Arsenal and Manchester but between the smaller clubs; that's more important, and that's football. The day when I don't take care of that, I leave.'

I asked him about his rapid rise in football administration, his alliance with Blatter, which was still fresh and strong then, and he portrayed it as a continuum with his fabulous career as a player, leaving no doubt that he believed he would one day be president of Fifa, too:

'It was destiny. When I stopped being coach of the [French] national team in 1992 I had the opportunity through President Mitterrand to be co-chairman of the World Cup in France. And because I was co-chairman, I began to have a rapport with Havelange and Blatter. Then in '98 Mr Blatter asked me to help him to be president of Fifa and I went inside this way, and at the end of being the adviser of Mr Blatter, I decided you are more influential if you are elected and I was elected in Fifa and Uefa and at the end, I decided to stand to be the president. And now I am here, by the Lac de Genève ... It was the destiny, the fatality that I went through this.'

About his quite uniquely successful journey and segue from playing and coaching into top administrative roles, which so few former footballers have ever managed to secure, Platini again said it was his fate to reach the top, that he was a natural leader:

'I was not captain of Juve, but [I was] of France, and every team. Some people are born leaders at certain ages, five, or fifty-two. I used to organise games in my street, four against four, or sometimes it was one against four because I was too strong. Then I organised games for my clubs, then for France, then Uefa; it comes straight from my youth, my *jeunesse*. A professional habit – don't send me a psychologist to understand why I am a leader. It was my destiny, I wanted to do something, I am afraid of what happened to football and I think we need to come back to the game.'

Presenting his credentials as an ideal character to be in charge, he opined: 'If I was a football fan, then I would be very happy that a football person is finally in charge of a football house. Because we are not a bank, or a tribunal, or a political, or a stock exchange, we are a house of football.'

Asked about Blatter, and their relationship, he described him as a man who also cared about football and who grappled manfully with the political complexities of a global organisation. He included an intriguing assessment of the 'morality' and culture of people in the

Fifa executive committee, which he claimed was different from the ethics of Europeans:

'Blatter is a good football man ... I know him very well, I stayed with him a long time; he's a guy who loves football and who loves players. The people have to know that, but I am sure they know. Those who are with Sepp in the executive committee, many times they don't share our philosophy, our morality, our policies because they are coming from another world, another morality. Sepp is in the middle of everybody and he has to take care politically of many people.

'It's easier for me because in Europe we have broadly the same philosophies, but in many other countries the culture is totally different – the president for political reasons has to take care of it. That is why he is not so popular.'

As the Uefa president, Platini said he would not be moving against Blatter, as his predecessor had:

'Now it is a benefit that Uefa has a president who is close to Fifa and we can come together,' he said. 'I know him, perhaps he will defend the interests of Fifa and I will defend interests of Uefa, we will never share all ideas, but it will be in a positive way and we will work to find a solution. It will not be a war. We will share the values of football – I don't want to take his place, as Uefa wanted to do in 1998.'

As the years wore on and the politics of football became Platini's life rather than a bonus of destiny, he seemed to lose some of that vim and lustre. You would see him in his Uefa blazer at the European Champions League draw or other event in the sunshine, and he could seem gloomier, sometimes sulky, the throwaway one-liners still there, but his character sunk in the tedium of administration. He seemed more sucked in, at times, to the politics of his organisation and Blatter's, rather than being able to maintain his focus throughout as the pure football man, and there were fewer leaps of progressive reform.

The happy partnership with Blatter and Fifa did not survive many years either; once Platini was no longer at his side but heading the most powerful confederation, the political rivalry of Uefa inevitably reasserted itself. For Blatter, who had dedicated his adult life to achieving and maintaining his position of Fifa president, the status was a precious prize, and perceived slights revealed how fragile he could feel it was. As early into Platini's Uefa presidency as the summer of 2008, Blatter fell out with him because at the opening ceremony of the European Championships his designated seat was eight along from the Swiss president.

In an outburst to the Russian news agency TASS, given in October 2015 after both men were suspended for ninety days while the Fifa ethics committee considered the 2m CHF payment, Blatter attacked Platini for 'envy and jealousy', and recalled that seating plan which he considered a snub:

'After he was elected Uefa president in 2007 … one year we were the best friends,' Blatter said. 'And one year later in the 2008 European Championship in Switzerland and Austria I was sidelined by Uefa. And since then I never went to Uefa competitions because it's non-respect, not to me as a person but to the office and the people I represent. He could not [explain it]. Uefa is affected by anti-Fifa virus for years. They have an anti-Fifa virus.'

Blatter also attacked Platini for wanting to be Fifa president but not having the backbone to stand against him. In his interview with *Le Monde*, Platini was emollient, and revealing, when asked about his relationship with Blatter:

'I had respect, friendship,' he said. His wife, Christèle, spoke up to remind him that he admired Blatter. 'Yes, I admired the politician. He had a lot of charm … Although he wanted to kill me politically, I still have a little affection for what we achieved together.'

Yet in that long interview, in which Platini concertedly put on the record for France his good intentions, homespun philosophy and lack of care for money, there was no actual explanation for why he suddenly decided to ask for 2m CHF from Blatter so many years after he left his employ.

He first asked for the money on 26 February 2010, telling Markus Kattner, Fifa's deputy secretary general and chief financial officer, that he was still owed it from his time at the organisation eight years earlier. At that time, he argued in his evidence when challenged about the timing, the Fifa presidential election was a long way off, so his request for the money could not be said to be related to it. In March 2010, at the Uefa congress in Tel Aviv, Platini was on record, before he was paid his money by Fifa, saying that he was happy at Uefa and wanted to stay on for a second term. That was true; he was enjoying the role, and the prestige and attention which came with it; he was comfortable and feted in Europe and was notching up achievements. It felt too soon to leave after only four years, and anyway Blatter was now unlikely to step down.

People close to Platini have said the most likely motivation for him requesting the money then was that Jérôme Champagne left, and received a large settlement, thought to have been more than €3m. Urs Linsi, the secretary general who replaced Zen-Ruffinen, had also left with a big payoff, although that had been in 2007. So, the suggestion is that Michel Platini recalled he was only paid 300,000 CHF a year (although he thought it had been 500,000 CHF) when he worked for Fifa, that he had an oral agreement to be paid 1m CHF, and that now, if people like Champagne were getting huge settlements, he should have the money he was owed.

That is not, it has to be said, a description of somebody who does not care about money. In fact, you could argue it is the opposite: the reaction of a man who cares robustly about it, who felt slighted when he saw what others got, and wanted more for himself. Perhaps it illustrates the attitude to money Leclaire believes Platini has: that it offended his sense of his own value to see Champagne paid so much. Champagne himself makes no apology at all for receiving a payoff; he said that he had his family to provide for, he worked hard at Fifa on difficult international governance problems, and believed his own sacking was political.

'I have nothing to hide,' he told me. 'I had a contract with a determination that I would remain as long as Sepp Blatter was president. I was outraged to be fired for political reasons when I had done nothing wrong. The reality is that this is a post-rationalisation of Michel Platini's own greed: he pretends not to care about money, and to only care about football.'

Platini asked again in June 2010, shortly before the World Cup in South Africa. When, on 2 December 2010, Platini voted for Qatar to host the 2022 tournament, Blatter, who believed he had secured the necessary support for the USA to host it, was, as he later acknowledged publicly, furious. Blatter began to make it clear that he would stand again for the Fifa presidency in 2011, and Mohamed bin

Hammam, who felt this was a betrayal, asked Platini if he would mount a challenge. Platini had decided to stay at Uefa and was not going to stand against Blatter, and bin Hammam began to consider challenging himself.

In January 2011, Platini asked for the money once again. Blatter's account of it is that Kattner referred the request to him, and he said Platini should send an invoice for what he was owed. So, to his ultimate great cost, Platini did; he put his request in writing. I have seen a copy of the invoice. It is headed at Platini's address in Genolier, dated 17 January 2011, addressed to Kattner at the House of Fifa in Zurich. Platini titled it: 'Re: salary payments 1998–9, 1999–0 [sic], 2000–1, 2001–2.'

It said, in English, this having been the agreed language of Fifa's multi-lingual organisation for many years: 'I would appreciate it if you would pay me the following salary payments for the four years in question, which were deferred by mutual agreement.'

Then Platini, Uefa president at the time, listed 500,000 CHF for each of the four years, a total of 2m CHF. Out of that, he said, Fifa should take care of his pension and other social security benefits. He put his bank details on the invoice.

Fifa paid him in February 2011. At that time, bin Hammam was becoming more serious about standing to challenge Blatter, and, just weeks later, on 18 March 2011, he did declare his candidacy as Fifa president, saying Blatter should not have stayed on beyond two terms, and famously promising 'transparency'. Four days later at the Grand Palais in Paris, Platini was re-elected as Uefa's president 'by acclamation' of its fifty-three national football associations, because nobody stood against him. He had promised to increase the money paid to national associations, from €408m in Uefa's 2008–12 cycle, to almost €500m for 2012–16. Blatter made a guest speech at the congress, saying he was emotionally moved to be in Paris – because it reminded him that he had first won the Fifa presidency in the city in 1998. He thanked and praised Uefa and the strength of European football, and appealed for solidarity: 'to fight all the little devils that exist in the world'.

Platini took a little time to announce which man he would support for the Fifa election, but ultimately the leader of fifty-three European football associations came down on Blatter's side. When it was explosively revealed in 2015 that Blatter had authorised the 2m CHF to be paid him just weeks before that endorsement, the timing did not look pretty for either of them. The Swiss attorney general stated that his criminal investigation into Blatter was examining whether the 2m CHF was a 'disloyal payment', in serious breach of Blatter's duties of trust to Fifa as its president. Platini's status as 'a person asked to provide information' meant that he was not a criminal suspect, but that he had not been cleared either, and could become a suspect depending on the course of the investigation.

Neither man could at first believe the trouble they were in over this bit of business between them, which had been done with a proper invoice and gone through Fifa's financial systems. On 8 October 2015, the 'adjudicatory' arm of the ethics committee, chaired by Judge Eckert, suspended both the presidents of Fifa and Uefa for ninety days, pending an investigation into the payment by the 'investigatory' arm chaired by Cornel Borbély, Garcia's replacement.

Platini pleaded complete innocence over a payment he said he was owed for work done according to their oral agreement, and denied it was related in any way to his support for Blatter in the 2011 election. He still thought he could come through it, be cleared, and actually stand for the Fifa election in February 2016, in which he was the favourite to achieve his destiny and become president. Blatter, too, believed he had done nothing wrong, and would be restored to see an orderly handover in February, at which his legacy of eighteen years' development, commercial success and reforms could be celebrated. He made a plea of innocence which he repeated several times in public, saying that he had always kept to advice his father had given him: 'Don't take any money that you haven't earned, and pay your debts.'

But in this very self-contained issue, a 2m CHF payment, as with other scandals and criticisms of his period in charge, Blatter had not been accused of taking money. He was alleged to have improperly paid money to somebody else, to aid and serve his own advancement.

It was a major test for the ethics committee, and the impression of its independence, which Garcia had furiously questioned. Borbély's investigators went to work on this issue which, by definition, had very little documentation to look into.

That was fatal to them. The ethics committee was not persuaded by either man's account of an oral agreement. Borbély sent his report to Eckert, who delivered his decision on 21 December 2015, just in time for Blatter and Platini to have a crestfallen Christmas. They were both banned from all football activities for eight years, an unimaginable fall. The ethics committee looked at the money owed from the other way round, from what concrete evidence there was: a contract, which stated the salary as 300,000 CHF. There was therefore 'no legal basis' for the 2m CHF Platini was paid by Fifa in 2011, Eckert ruled. Platini is understood to have been asked by Vanessa Allard, a lawyer who conducted the ethics committee investigation, what he believed the validity was of the actual written contract, which noted a 300,000 CHF salary, if there was a side oral agreement for more. Nobody found the answer persuasive.

'Neither in his written statement nor in his personal hearing was Mr Blatter able to demonstrate another legal basis for this payment,' Eckert's judgement stated. '[Both Blatter and Platini's] assertion of an oral agreement was determined as not convincing and was rejected.'

The judgement cleared them of bribery and corruption, which was seriously considered by the ethics committee. In effect that was a finding that the 2m CHF was not a straightforward payment by Blatter to Platini to support him in the 2011 Fifa presidential election. But they threw four other breaches of the Fifa ethics code at them: finding them guilty of 'offering and accepting gifts and other benefits'; having a conflict of interest; breaching their duty of loyalty, and breaches of the general rules of conduct.

'Mr Blatter's actions did not show commitment to an ethical attitude, failing to respect all applicable laws and regulations as well as Fifa's regulatory framework to the extent applicable to him and demonstrating an abusive execution of his position as president of Fifa,' Eckert determined.

Of Platini, Eckert said: 'Mr Platini failed to act with complete credibility and integrity, showing unawareness of the importance of his duties and concomitant obligations and responsibilities. His actions did not show commitment to an ethical attitude', and so he too was found to have demonstrated 'an abusive execution of his position' as a Fifa executive committee member and vice president.

Toppled with this much shocking finality from such summits of power and prestige, both presidents disputed the verdict, adamantly protesting, as they still do, that they had done nothing wrong. They appealed against the decision of the Fifa ethics committee to the Court of Arbitration for Sport, which really tests the fairness of the procedures. Platini's case was heard first, and he did not have much luck at CAS in Lausanne either. The judgement by a panel of three European professors, delivered on 9 May 2016, explicitly linked the payment of 2m CHF to the Fifa presidential election. Referring to Platini's explanation that it was paid on an oral agreement made in 1998 that he could have 1m CHF a year, and that he had forgotten that he was only paid 300,000 CHF not 500,000 CHF, the CAS determination was not indulgent:

'It was not until 1 February 2011 – four months prior to the Fifa presidential elections and at a moment when Sepp Blatter and Mohamed bin Hammam were both still candidates to the election – that Fifa paid the amount of CHF 2m in favour of Mr Platini,' the panel concluded.

'Mr Platini justified such payment as back pay, explaining that he had orally agreed with Mr Blatter in 1998, when the future Fifa president was negotiating with him, to an annual salary of CHF 1m. The panel, however, was not convinced by the legitimacy of the 2m CHF payment, which was only recognised by Mr Platini and Mr Blatter, and which occurred more than eight years after the end of his work relations, and was not based on any document established at the time of the contractual relations and did not correlate with the alleged unpaid part of his salary (CHF 700,000 X 4 = CHF 2,800,000). Moreover, the Panel took note that Mr Platini benefited from the extension of a pension plan to which he was not entitled.'

The Fifa appeals committee had already reduced his ban to six years, and CAS did reduce it to four. Its panel stated that Platini was guilty of obtaining an undue advantage and a conflict of interest, but should not have been sanctioned for breaches of loyalty and the general rules of conduct as well. The panel also reduced his fine from 80,000 CHF to 60,000.

That was the end of the line for him. When the Swiss attorney general had announced the criminal investigation in September

2015, Platini, the lifelong leader, was a declared candidate for the Fifa presidency and just five months from the destiny of attaining it. Now he was banned altogether from any football activities, which had been his whole life and identity, except going to watch a match in the stands.

Blatter, too, was two months away from his planned, orderly hand-over of the ship to the next elected skipper when he was thrown overboard into the night. After he was suspended, he had told the Swiss newspaper *Schweiz am Sonntag* the same as he told Mark Pieth when he recruited him to advise on anti-corruption reforms: that he did not want to leave the House of Fifa by the back door:

'I want a dignified departure after forty-one years,' Blatter had said. 'Otherwise, I would fear visiting my father's grave. What do you believe will happen when I tell him that I give up? He'd step out of his grave.'

Within days of talking in such terms about his struggles and fear of disappointing his dead father, Blatter collapsed and was taken to hospital. He spent several days recuperating in Zurich, then went to rest back in the haven of his home in the Valais. His long-term PR adviser, Klaus Stoehlker, told the media that Blatter, under all the stress and pressure, had suffered 'a small emotional breakdown'.

The decision from Eckert confirmed Blatter's worst fear: he was banned, and he would not be leaving at the time of his choosing, by the front door. The day after the announcement, he held a press conference. He chose the old Fifa House, on Hitzigweg, where he had worked and made his way up so busily all those years. He looked a suddenly fallen, shrunken figure from the slick, controlled operator of four decades in Fifa. He was rough-shaven, dishevelled, looked dramatically aged, and he had a plaster on his cheek, having been found to have melanoma cancer and had some of it removed.

To the media, Blatter raged against the unfairness of it all, disbelief that the ethics committee had not believed his and Platini's identical stories about their oral agreement. He said he was being used as a 'punchbag', and that it was still rooted in the USA's failure to be given the hosting of the 2022 World Cup. He was asked if that was still valid, given that most members of the ethics committee which banned him were Europeans, and he suggested there were forces within Fifa who did not want Platini to be president. Facing this shock of the worst moment of his career, right at the end of it, and the pressure of global attention again, he was not always at his most coherent. In his hour of trouble, he referenced Nelson Mandela, 'the great humanist', who had said: 'Humanity needs no other thing but human beings being respected.' Blatter said he had been shown no respect because the media was given the news of his ban before he was himself. He declined to talk about his health, and promised at the end: 'I am doing better; I'll be back.'

But on 5 December 2016, CAS announced its decision to reject his appeal outright. Its panel had decided that the written contract invalidated any oral agreement the men claimed they had, and therefore the payment of 2m CHF was an 'undue gift'. Blatter, seeing no way back, described that summation as 'incomprehensible' and 'difficult to accept', but this time managed a gracious kind of quote for the media:

'I have experienced much in my forty-one years in Fifa,' he said. 'I mostly learned that you can win in sport, but you can also lose. Nevertheless I look back with gratitude to all the years, in which I was able to realise my ideals for football and serve Fifa.'

Platini, after his defeat, barely spoke in public again, although he was given a dispensation to say farewell at the Uefa congress. He watched as his former secretary general at Uefa, Gianni Infantino, seized the chance to leap into his shoes, and went for the presidency of Fifa himself, winning the vote in February 2016. Platini never accepted he had done anything unethical, and took his fall hard.

In the summer of 2016, Uefa's European Championships were held in France, a month which had been gift-wrapped for Michel Platini. The former great player, World Cup and Euros captain of France, would have been there, in the best seat, as the Uefa or Fifa president, at a tournament he had overseen and expanded to twenty-four countries for the first time. Paris was given a makeover in devotion to football; a splendid fanzone was marked out around a wide, stately stretch of central Paris centred on the Eiffel Tower, which was resplendent in fresh gold paint, a giant ball at its base. His whole country was given over to football, but Platini did not go to a single game. He turned invitations down, and stayed private at his holiday home in Cassis, in the south of France, with family and friends, nursing his pride. In the tournament, after a hesitant start, the France team found its rapid, attacking confidence, spearheaded by the sharp Antoine Griezmann, blew away Iceland, who had beaten England, and made it to the final. Having a heart for the French hero who had done so much in his life for football, the national team, and the championships which should have been his stage, the organisers had Platini's picture shown on the big screen of the Stade de France before the final. At the grand stadium in the heart of Paris, the home team waiting to take the field and sing the Marsellaise, the crowd full of Frenchmen looked up and saw that picture of Michel Platini, icon of France – and there was an audible chorus of boos.

CHAPTER 16

'The Money of Fifa is Your Money!'

Gianni Infantino, jumping onto the trajectory from which his former boss, Michel Platini, had been ejected, became the reform candidate for the presidency of Fifa after these events of incomparable scandal. Born in Brig, another Swiss Alpine town not far, in fact, from Blatter's birthplace and spiritual home of Visp, Infantino studied law at Fribourg University in Switzerland, then worked as the secretary general of the International Centre for Sports Studies at the University of Neuchâtel, before joining Uefa in 2000. He worked his way up and had been known since 2009 as a cautious, deeply ambitious secretary general, from the graduate class of Swiss administrators educated to service the forest of sports governing bodies nestling in the country. Infantino had worked closely with Platini, secured the financial fair play regulations and increased Uefa's own income while the organisation strengthened its anti-racism stance and supported some progressive social programmes. He had tied his rise to Platini's star, too, and was also associated with the increasingly presidential style at Uefa and the lack of further stand-out reforms. His polished manifesto for the Fifa presidential election made the promises the world's football supporters, media and campaigners needed to hear: 'transparency', 'good governance', and to implement the organisational reforms proposed by Domenico Scala. But at its heart was the language Infantino had seen the national football associations always understood: more money. There were – literally – large dollar signs printed in the middle of his document, as if to underline for them that Infantino knew what big bucks looked like.

In the frantic weeks preceding the 26 February 2016 election after Blatter and Platini were banned on 21 December 2015, the money promise at the centre of Infantino's offer was perhaps overlooked, in favour of the perception of him as the European candidate for reform. That was partly because of the unattractiveness, to many, of his opponent, the president of the Asian Football Confederation who finally replaced Mohamed bin Hammam in 2013: Sheikh Salman bin Ebrahim al-Khalifa, a member of the extended ruling family in Bahrain. He was thought to be the favourite, able to garner enough support in Asia and Africa to win, yet his candidacy was beset by allegations that he had been involved in the crackdown against popular dissent in his country during the Arab Spring of 2011.

The Bahrain Institute for Rights and Democracy (BIRD) wrote to Fifa in November 2015, objecting to Salman's fitness to stand, alleging he had 'aided and abetted gross human rights abuses', including against Bahraini footballers. These complaints were rooted in Salman having chaired a commission whose role, the Bahrain Ministry of Information had announced, was to identify athletes, including footballers, who had taken part in a pro-democracy protest rally in Bahrain, and 'breaches by individuals associated with the sports movement during the recent unfortunate events in the Kingdom of Bahrain'. Prior to the commission meeting, two prominent Bahraini footballers, with other athletes, had been arrested and severely tortured, BIRD wrote in their letter to Fifa, and the Bahrain FA, of which Salman was the president, had also promised a crackdown on dissidence.

Salman had vehemently denied the allegations and insisted that this commission never sat, but his ruling family had without question conducted a brutal response to the pro-democracy outpouring. Prince Ali bin Al-Hussein of Jordan, who was boldly standing again, criticised Sheikh Salman and accused him at least of not having defended footballers who had been persecuted. Nicholas McGeehan, the Gulf researcher for the campaign group Human Rights Watch, was scathing of Salman's candidacy:

'Since the peaceful anti-government protests of 2011, which the authorities responded to with brutal and lethal force, the al-Khalifa family have overseen a campaign of torture and mass incarceration that has decimated Bahrain's pro-democracy movement. If a member of Bahrain's royal family is the cleanest pair of hands that Fifa can find, then the organisation would appear to have the shallowest and least ethical pool of talent in world sport.'

In that context, Infantino seemed like a gleaming candidate to stand for integrity and reforms desperately needed to Fifa's processes and structures. So, it was not greatly emphasised that his experience in football administration at Uefa, and his antennae for the route to the Fifa votes, had clear similarities with the Blatter and Havelange candidacies in their time. Infantino, like those two presidents before him, flew all around the world – the equivalent of five times, he said – to talk directly to as many voting FAs as he could, particularly seeking crucial numerical support among Africa's fifty-four FAs. He noted that he had begun his whistle-stop campaign in Cairo, and finally ended it in Cape Town.

On his record at Uefa, he stressed the increase in income which he had secured, partly from a change by which Uefa, rather than each individual national association separately, sold the TV rights for European Championship qualifying matches. In the 2014–15 financial year, Uefa's income grew from €1.7bn the previous year, to €2.1bn, and Infantino could stress that 'solidarity' payments to each country's FA, including the smaller ones, had also greatly increased. He made a promise which echoed down Fifa's history from Havelange's pledge in 1974, that he would expand the World Cup to forty countries' teams, which appealed to smaller countries who struggle to qualify, and, presumably, enlarging the TV experience Fifa can sell. In the section of his manifesto headed with the big dollar sign, Infantino promised each of Fifa's 209 countries' FAs a hugely boosted $5m over four years in financial assistance, and $40m for the confederations. Particularly attractive to the delegates from other continents gathered at the Hallenstadion in Zurich, many of which still struggle for the basics, Infantino also promised $1m a year for travel costs.

He was, though, still considered an outside bet; the replacement for the fallen Platini, callow at forty-five, lacking a little in stature, having only ever been the secretary general, never a president. Salman was the president of his large confederation, and a ruling figure in the Gulf, whose money was becoming so dominant in the top strata of football and in the granting of the 2022 World Cup to Qatar. His manifesto promised reform, too, and transparency, but when he took to the stage at the Hallenstadion, he carried an aura of power, and, I thought, of inherited entitlement. There seemed also to be a reassurance to the FAs and football barons, alarmed at the corruption fallout and seeing the prosecutions by the US law enforcement authorities as an invasion.

'At the end,' he said, asking for their votes, 'I am one of you.'

Infantino, by comparison to the Sheikh, had the look of a schoolboy dressed in his best for his big day, his tie ever so slightly askew. He worked his way through a speech which was impressively multi-lingual but lacking grand inspiration for delegates who had heard interminably many of these before, until he reminded them of his $5m commitment, and made a clinching promise:

'The money of Fifa is your money!' he shouted to them from the stage. 'It is not the money of the Fifa president, it is your money!'

There was, in response, a ripple of spontaneous applause. Many of those in the Hallenstadion said the mood in the hall changed. Kohzo Tshima of Japan, a new member of the executive committee, was quoted by Graham Dunbar of the Associated Press, saying: 'Gianni's speech was a president's speech,' and that his words changed the atmosphere.

Infantino overturned the expectation of Salman in the first round of voting, for which a two-thirds majority was required, edging him by three votes, 88–85. Candidate Tokyo Sexwale, a South African former ANC activist in the apartheid era turned multi-millionaire businessman, who had been encouraged in growing Fifa activities by Blatter, withdrew before the voting, seeing that the African FAs were not behind him and he had too little support. Jérôme Champagne, who had declared himself and run an energetic campaign with a platform of detailed proposed reforms, received only seven votes. Prince Ali held the balance for the second round, which would be won just with a majority of the votes. Having been a critic of Salman's, and supported by Uefa when he stood against Blatter at the last election in May 2015, almost all his votes went to Infantino in the second round.

Declared the winner, with 115 countries' football associations for him, beating Salman whose vote nudged up by only three, Infantino was overcome. He did not look like his old boss, Platini, who had long learned to accept that podiums and triumphs were his given destiny; he looked more like a Swiss student, who could not believe he was really there, actually becoming the president of Fifa. Accepting hugs and handshakes, patting his heart, giving gestures of thanks to the arena, Infantino gathered himself to make a victory speech.

'We will restore the image of Fifa and the respect of Fifa. And everyone in the world will applaud us,' he promised. 'I am convinced a new era is starting.'

At the congress, before the vote, the internal changes proposed by Scala and his reform committee had been passed by 87 per cent, 179 of the 207 voting FAs (Kuwait and Indonesia were suspended at the time). The new structures had a long gestation, beginning with Blatter's appointment of Mark Pieth in 2011. Pieth told me that he had suggested Scala's appointment for the job of implementing the proposed reforms:

'I didn't know him intimately, but people told me good things about him,' Pieth said, explaining that he was impressed by Scala's sense of independence. 'He had stepped down three times in his career when he didn't like what he saw; he would not be held hostage.'

Pieth described his general perception of Fifa as like a system of patronage: FA delegates from around the world who had done very well in Blatter's era and benefited from his development money and appointments. He said Blatter had given him the familiar defence to the suspicion of corruption, emphasising that he never took money to which he was not entitled.

Pieth said he had replied: 'Yes, but giving can be a problem, too.'

When he first arrived at Fifa to examine its governance, Pieth said he had asked Blatter why he was implementing reforms, what his motivation was for cleaning up, as he could have got away with just carrying on as before.

'That was a good question, we can see now,' Pieth told me. 'Because he killed himself [with the implementation of an independent ethics committee and other measures]; it was an own goal.'

That was when Blatter, he said, told him: 'I want to leave the house by the front door.'

'We said: 'OK, even if you have not excelled in the past, you can leave this place [with changes] that your successors will find it difficult to dismantle.'

Yet in a book, *Reforming Fifa*, written after his committee stepped down in 2013, Pieth recorded that, surprisingly, the greatest opposition to the recommended reforms had come from Uefa. In particular, Uefa refused to vote for limits to the terms a Fifa president could serve, and for Fifa to carry out integrity tests on proposed executive committee members, arguing the regional confederations should do it themselves.

Pieth saw it as a reluctance to sanction these reforms by Platini – who did go on to a third election as Uefa president – and others who expected to be taking over from Blatter when he finally stepped down: 'They were less than happy to see the ground rules change fundamentally just before they came into office,' he wrote. ' ... They feared for their power basis; the real issue was football politics.'

This was a major factor in the decision of his committee to disband, Pieth said, along with fury in the autumn of 2013 when it became clear Blatter was preparing to stand again in 2015.

'Uefa was blocking the rest of our reforms, and we would have been confronted with yet another congress where they were blocking the introduction of limits to terms of office,' he said. 'We would have looked silly.'

At that 2013 congress when Pieth's committee stepped down, Scala was appointed to chair an audit and compliance committee, which would recommend and oversee the reforms. He was a corporate finance executive, a long-term director of Stock-Exchange-listed companies in Switzerland, with a straight-talking, jovial way about him. He soon showed he was comfortable being outspoken about the governance crisis Fifa was in, and that he saw a stark absence of internal compliance structures comparable to those accepted as normal in large companies. After working at Fifa for some time, Scala, too, perceived it as an operation in which delegates and FAs benefited from the largesse and patronage of the president. But he also sympathised to some extent with Blatter's view that the major corruption, as alleged in the US indictment, was endemic not at Fifa in Zurich, but in the confederations.

'There are certainly questions to answer at Fifa itself,' Scala told me, 'but I did not see evidence of systemic corruption. It was systemic in some confederations, and member associations, over which Fifa has no direct control; in fact via the executive committee, the confederations control Fifa.'

Scala called for the confederations and national FAs also to undertake reforms, including basics such as annual audits, independent ethics committee-style structures and integrity checks for their own officials.

In the reforms Scala ended up presenting to the 2016 Fifa congress before Infantino's election, he had compromised on term limits, offering three terms of four years as a maximum. That still seemed a long time for one person to head an organisation governing world football and handling billions of dollars, but it was significantly shorter than the twenty-four years Havelange had spent cementing the modern culture, and the twenty-one Blatter had planned before he agreed to step down. The other main reforms were designed to reshape Fifa into having a recognisably modern internal form, corporate-style checks and balances. The twenty-four-person executive committee was to be replaced by a thirty-six-member council, which would be responsible for setting overall strategy and direction, to which a separate executive board of professionals would work and manage Fifa and its projects day to day.

This was itself a compromise: Scala is understood to have told the executive committee, when he first presented proposals in July 2015, that they should all ideally resign, and twelve people with no connection to the past should take over. That plan was said to have been met with a stunned silence, and so the new council, with that unwieldy-looking number of members, was proposed as a Plan B.

The president was now to be non-executive; not responsible as Blatter and Havelange had been for running every aspect of Fifa but, as the elected head of the council, setting strategy and ensuring the executive worked to it. Pieth's and Scala's committees also proposed as a basic principle that Fifa should end the secrecy about what Blatter and the other top executives earned, which had long been a focus for complaints, because major corporations publish them as a measure of transparency and accountability. Scala proposed the standard corporate practices of having an independent committee to determine the correct level of pay, and for Fifa to publish them.

That was common sense and was passed by the congress but once Infantino was installed as the president it was to provoke a toxic and unexpected clash, very quickly indeed.

There was little public sign of it in the first weeks after Infantino cleared his desk in the Uefa house of football by Lake Geneva, and moved to one at the House of Fifa on the hill above Lake Zurich. Just three weeks later, Fifa issued its lawsuit for 'restitution' from the defendants charged by the US indictments, positioning the organisation as the victim, rather than involved in the corruption. The accusation, that the defendants 'looked for ways to line their own pockets and siphon off opportunities', could hardly have been stronger had it come from the most vitriolic of critics over the years. As a piece of legal positioning, a break with the past and a reclaiming of Fifa's purpose, it was intended to be very forthright indeed.

Infantino would indeed see the World Cup expanded, gaining approval for a forty-eight-country tournament to be played first in 2026. He also set in train 'Fifa Forward', a more sophisticated and accountable system for paying out the huge new money he had promised to pour into development. Each FA would have its own development plan; they would receive a basic $100,000 for their running costs, then an additional $50,000 was to be available to fund each of the specific initiatives, some of them very basic, like employing a secretary general, a technical director, organising a league, promoting women's football, a good governance programme, a grass-roots or refereeing development strategy.

Infantino's new system was also promising to address the criticism that too much of the GOAL project money had been vulnerable to siphoning off by the recipients, by having stronger detailed involvement by Fifa, and independent audits.

'We are introducing enhanced oversight controls to ensure that this increase in football development spending is transparent, carefully managed and effective,' Fifa promised.

The chairman of the development committee which would run the new programme and allocate its multi-millions of dollars to the national football associations of the world was Sheikh Salman bin

Ebrahim al-Khalifa of Bahrain. Defeated in the election for president after Infantino thumped home his promise to send more of Fifa's millions to the voters, Salman was now in charge of delivering the money. When the programme was launched, he said: 'We are making a qualitative step to improve the impact of Fifa's development projects and better serve the member associations and confederations.'

But some internal rumblings that all was not well inside the new Infantino era at the House of Fifa suddenly blared out at his first congress, in Mexico, on 14 May 2016. Domenico Scala suddenly resigned, and dropped a very strong public statement to announce it. He said that the independence of crucial reform committees had been fundamentally undone: his own, the ethics committee, appeals committee and governance committee. The new thirty-six-person council, he said, had been given by the congress the new power to sack members of these independent committees, including chairmen, which had, in his view, profoundly damaging consequences:

'With this decision, it will henceforth be possible for the council to impede investigations against single members at any time, by dismissing the responsible committee members or by keeping them acquiescent through the threat of a dismissal. Thereby, those bodies are factually deprived of their independence and are in danger of becoming auxiliary agents of those whom they should actually supervise,' his statement read.

'I am consternated about this decision, because it undermines a central pillar of the good governance of Fifa and it destroys a substantial achievement of the reforms.'

And because of it, and because he believed the committees would now be a sham process lacking independence, he was resigning – as Pieth said, Scala had done this three times in his career, on points of principle.

It was true, a rule passed almost unanimously, late at the congress without any discussion, did give the council the right until the next year to appoint and dismiss members of those committees. Scala suspected that it was a ruse to do exactly what he was warning against: sack him as the chairman of the audit and compliance committee.

Just days later, a conversation had by the council in a meeting at this congress, before the measure was recommended and adopted, was leaked to the media. It was a glimpse into the new Fifa in unguarded, unpolished discussion, and it proved Scala's suspicion to be correct. The tape was tremendously damaging to Infantino, and disillusioning. Just three months into the job, he told the council members that he still had no contract with Fifa because he had rejected the one proposed to him by Scala. It was part of Scala's new official responsibility to chair a new compensation sub-committee, which set the president's salary.

'It was a proposal which I found insulting,' Infantino told the council. 'It was less than half of what the previous president was earning the last year. Last year, it was published, 3.6m [CHF]; the offer made to me was less than half of this amount.'

Infantino also told his new colleagues that he had heard from Cornel Borbély, the chair of the 'investigatory' arm of the ethics committee, that Scala had filed a complaint against him. The basis of it was that Infantino and his wife were looking at a house in Zurich costing 25m CHF, which Infantino said was 'complete nonsense' – and that he was claiming expenses, when he had not signed his contract of employment yet.

The 'insulting' salary package Scala had determined for Infantino was quickly clarified: it was 1.95m CHF. That was in fact more than half the 3.6m CHF Blatter was paid the previous year. Scala had made it clear it was not an offer; this was the new system, in which the president's salary was considered by an independent committee, and they had decided that 1.95m CHF was right for the new non-executive-style presidency, and compared well with other, very highly paid roles in similar-sized companies or organisations elsewhere. The two were undoubtedly at odds, and it was understood that Scala did pass on, as he believed he was duty bound to, complaints about Infantino, which grew in the following days, as some employees were made redundant and further stories emerged, including that Infantino and his family had been flown by private jet to meet the Pope in Rome.

The acceptance of the flight on a benefactor's private jet was potentially toxic. Jérôme Valcke, Blatter's faithful secretary general, had been dismissed from his job and then in February 2016 banned from football for twelve years by the ethics committee, for a series of alleged scandals including excessive use of private jets. Valcke was embroiled in a World Cup ticket scheme found to be improper, and was also accused of trying to sell the TV rights for the 2018 and 2022 World Cups to the Caribbean, presumed to be Jack Warner, at an undervalue. The ethics committee stated it had been found that Valcke 'deliberately tried to obstruct the ongoing proceedings against him by attempting to delete or deleting several files and folders relevant to the investigation'.

On the use of private jets, the ethics committee said: 'By travelling at Fifa's expense purely for sightseeing reasons as well as repeatedly choosing private flights for his trips over commercial flights without any business rationale for doing so, Mr Valcke gained an advantage for himself and his relatives.'

On 17 March 2016, the attorney general in Switzerland announced he was conducting criminal proceedings against Valcke 'on suspicion of various acts of criminal mismanagement and other offences', in response to complaints made following the Fifa ethics committee investigation. The 'presumption of innocence applies', the announcement stated.

Valcke's lawyer was reported to have said that his client had done 'absolutely nothing wrong'. I did contact him asking to talk to Valcke and discuss this alleged wrongdoing, but he did not respond.

After all that, and the expectation of reforms and a more befitting culture, the revelation that Infantino had taken a private jet could hardly have sounded a more dispiriting note. But on the leaked tape, as shocking, frankly, as hearing the new Fifa president, who had come from Uefa standing on values of integrity and transparency, describe nearly 2m CHF as an 'insulting' salary, was the quality of what came next. The council, with the exception of David Gill, the FA's representative, who sounded flabbergasted at the turn of the conversation, was as unctuously indulgent of Infantino as the congress sycophants would habitually be of Blatter.

The new president was immediately told that the council shared his astonishment, that 'people are trying to set traps everywhere', and that he had their support. Not one suggested to Infantino that 1.95m CHF was not all that bad and that he had no right to refuse it; in fact the opposite: it turned out that the chairmen of the six confederations had all signed a letter asking Scala to step down. He had refused, and there were no powers for the council to remove him; under the reforms only just adopted, that could be done only by the congress. Then, on the tape, another of the council members is heard saying that Scala should be dismissed, and they should seek the new power from congress to dismiss members of the independent committees. Infantino then actually agreed with that proposal, saying: 'If somebody brings the question to the congress, I advise the congress. It is a democratic decision.'

Gill did protest, saying if congress was going to be told that Scala had to step down and have the new powers to dismiss put to a vote, it would create 'an unbelievable situation'.

Then Infantino himself indicated that Sunil Gulati, the USA FA representative on the council, was going to be an emissary to see if Scala would step down.

'If he doesn't, we will in any case ask for this provision to pass by the congress.'

Infantino talked about the future when they would have a new chair for this committee which set his salary, who would be 'a real world personality'.

The tape confirmed the worst interpretation of the measure which had prompted Scala to resign: Infantino and his council really were seeking the power to remove the chairman of an independent committee if they objected to what he was doing. The fact that it was Scala, who was seen generally as a strong, steadying reformer while Fifa executive committee members were being arrested, indicted and dumped for prodigious corruption, and that it was because Infantino found a 1.95m CHF salary 'insulting', comprehensively ended Infantino's honeymoon period. The publication of the top executives' earnings for the first time in the 2015 financial report also included Scala's, and showed he had given up $200,000 when resigning in principle at the perceived threat to the reforms' independence.

Suddenly the young, reforming Swiss executive who had vanquished the dispiriting prospect of a Sheikh Salman presidency was exposed to look greedy, money-driven and Machiavellian, and the council supine and shifty in support. There was an outcry, particularly in Switzerland itself, then more stories were leaked, of expenses allegedly claimed by Infantino, appointments and sackings without due process, and soon the ethics committee was formally investigating the freshman president.

Just after this ugliness was exposed, with the pressure building on Infantino to justify himself, one week after the congress Fifa suddenly sacked Markus Kattner, the acting secretary general since Jérôme Valcke's departure in February 2016, who had been at Fifa for thirteen years. Fifa sources said that the US lawyers installed at the House of Fifa dealing with the criminal investigations, Quinn Emanuel, had 'uncovered' irregular bonus payments to Kattner.

Days later, Fifa – equally suddenly – announced the results of a Quinn Emanuel investigation into years of earnings for Blatter, Valcke and Kattner. They were very fat, and included huge bonuses for successful organising of the World Cup. Fifa gave a headline figure of around $80m between the three of them over the previous five years. There was plenty to be stunned and outraged by: Blatter was on a most recent basic salary of 3m CHF awarded after he won the post-arrests election in May 2015, with a 1.5m CHF potential annual bonus, and a performance-based bonus of an extra 12m CHF if he worked a successful four years, which clearly he didn't. In December 2010, Fifa now revealed, Blatter had been paid an 11m CHF bonus for the World Cup in South Africa. In 2011, they had each been awarded contractual bonuses if the 2014 World Cup in Brazil was a success: 12m CHF for Blatter; 10m CHF to Valcke; 4m CHF to Kattner.

The Fifa announcement alleged it was a 'coordinated effort' by them to 'enrich themselves', arguing that effectively they were authorising each other's contracts, and there were multiple amendments when contracts were extended or bonuses paid. Julio Grondona, the long-serving Argentinian chair of the finance committee in Blatter's time, had approved many of the contracts, including all of Blatter's, as was the required system at the time. Blatter had had the authority to approve Valcke's contractual terms under Fifa's old regulations, and Valcke and Blatter to approve Kattner's. In a remarkably outspoken announcement, featuring quotes from the Quinn Emanuel lawyer, Fifa said some of the dates of contracts being approved were 'ominous'. For example, on 30 April 2011, shortly before the presidential election at which bin Hammam was then still running against Blatter, and could have won and not retained Valcke and Kattner, both were given eight-year extensions to their contracts. The new contracts handsomely increased their salaries, to 1.4m CHF and 960,000 CHF respectively, with a bonus. If their contracts were terminated, they were guaranteed full pay for the whole of the term to 2019, and also Fifa was committed to pay fees and costs for any legal actions in relation to their employment.

'These two provisions appear to violate mandatory Swiss law,' Fifa alleged.

Kattner's contract was then extended to run until 2023, an extension granted on 31 May 2015, just four days after the US indictments and arrests had plunged Fifa into trauma and disgrace.

It was clear that they had earned on a vast scale, although Blatter's actual salary was not as high as $10m, which had been speculated over the years. Because they had not been published, the world had not known that they were paid huge bonuses for pulling off the World Cup, which did make billions for their employer. Many Fifa staff, in particular, most of them good, smart, multi-lingual professionals who love football and try to do a good job, even minding the pennies while the bosses brought disgrace on the organisation, were appalled at the scale of it. In the eyes of many, it damaged Blatter, who had mostly been a charming and benevolent boss to junior employees in the vaulting corridors of the headquarters.

It was, though, odd that so long after the indictments, with Quinn Emanuel having been embedded in Fifa House for a year, they and Fifa should suddenly, with a scandal looming over Infantino, release all this detail about the earnings of Blatter and his senior executives. The salaries and bonuses of Blatter, 3.6m CHF in total, and Valcke, 2.1m CHF, had just been published by Fifa at its congress anyway, without a murmur that there was anything irregular. There was also an accusation made very pointedly, a persistent theme throughout the lengthy announcement, that Scala was to blame for some of these earnings. The new compensation sub-committee, which he chaired and which came into force in 2013, had approved these astonishing contracts, the new Fifa repeatedly stated. Coming barely three weeks after Scala's public resignation on a point of principle, and the leaked tape which cast Infantino in an awful light, Fifa and Quinn Emanuel were now publicly suggesting Scala had sanctioned excessive pay which could amount to malpractice. Quinn Emanuel said it was referring the contracts and payments to the ethics committee, 'has shared this information' with the Swiss attorney general and 'will brief the US Department of Justice' as well.

Scala never responded to this; he left his resignation statement as his final word. It was pointed out on his behalf that the contracts of Blatter, Valcke and Kattner were agreed in 2010–11 when Scala's committee was not in force, and, when it was, it had no power to end the contracts. The extensions and bonuses, while they are vast, were approved according to the contracts and rules in force at the time, it was said. When Blatter and Valcke's salaries were first published in the 2015 financial report, Fifa said officially that it had carried out independent comparison 'benchmarking', which found their earnings in line with companies of similarly massive turnover. There was a strong feeling that the contract details of Infantino's predecessors had suddenly been revealed in this shocked announcement to help the new president with his difficult battle for credibility, so early in his dream job.

On 5 August 2016, the ethics committee, whose chairmen and members could under the new powers passed by the congress now be sacked by the Fifa council, presided over by Infantino, cleared him of any wrongdoing. It found that the private flights did not involve conflicts of interest, because, it was understood, the rich individual who bestowed on Infantino the use of his jet was not involved in football. Complaints about how Infantino had hired and fired people in his first months, 'as well as Mr Infantino's conduct with regard to his contract with Fifa, if at all, constituted internal compliance issues rather than an ethical matter', the ethics committee said in a statement.

'As such, the final report ... concluded that no ethical breaches had been committed by Mr Infantino.'

And that was that. Infantino, pictured with a beaming smile, issued an official statement saying he was pleased that the truth had prevailed:

'With this matter now resolved, the President and Fifa administration will continue to focus on developing football as well as their efforts to improve the organisation,' he said. 'Tangible progress has been made in key areas such as ensuring that those who have acted against the interests of football are identified and held to account, improving Fifa's governance and repairing its reputation, and restoring trust with its stakeholders. This critical work will continue.'

On 31 August 2016, the new chairman of the compensation sub-committee announced that it had 'agreed' with Infantino a basic gross salary of 1.5m CHF. With pension and benefits, this was understood to be very similar to the 1.95m CHF he had turned down before the congress. Then in September 2016, the Fifa ethics committee announced an investigation into the revelations about the contracts of Blatter, Valcke and Kattner, stating that it related to possible bribery, conflicts of interest and general conduct, while Kattner faced a charge related to allegedly leaking information about Infantino to the media. It stressed there was a presumption of innocence until proven guilty.

And so, in these ways, the old guard at Fifa was supplanted by the new.

CHAPTER 17

Say it Ain't So, Franz

The fame and stature of Franz Beckenbauer through his artistry on the football field attained a scale of global recognition matched perhaps only by his two greatest contemporaries, Pelé and Johan Cruyff. His and their journeys as players were elevated into the expansion of the game itself: from a passionately loved sport to an industry; from star footballers to superstar celebrities, from black and white to colour. Beckenbauer's rise to become the player of such poised control, who entranced me as a nine-year-old boy watching on television his 1974 World Cup triumph, was woven also into the reinvention of his country itself. He was born in 1945, in a ruined and disgraced Munich right after the war; he became a free-flowing star as West Germany found rebuilt confidence in the 1960s, he won the World Cup in 1974 for a modern, capable nation, and won it again as a coach for a reunified Germany in 1990. Then he headed, fronted and chaired the bid and organising committee to bring the World Cup to a happier, more at ease country for that *Sommermärchen* of 2006. Beckenbauer said he had done it for no payment, just for the fulfilment and duty of bringing the World Cup to his mother country, for all that would mean. His status in Germany was beyond *der Kaiser*; he was adored.

In Fifa's own profile of an imperious great who embodied that 1974 period of transformation, another star of his day, his national team colleague Günter Netzer, is quoted saying: 'He's the hero of our nation. It hasn't happened by chance, he's earned it by hard work.'

Michel Platini is quoted, too, with an archetypal quip: 'A truly impressive person. If you don't like him, there's something wrong with you.'

More recently, his advisers and commercial agents, for the Beckenbauer name and 'brand' which still sold so well as an association with class, quality and integrity, even conceived of a conference built around him, to consider how to improve the governance of football. 'Camp Beckenbauer', held in the smart ski resort of Kitzbühel in the Austrian Alps, was a beautifully organised, rarefied gathering, aspiring to be a football and sport equivalent of the World Economic Forum which made another Alpine destination famous, Davos. One among the platform of sponsors lending their name to the event was Adidas, which has a lifetime licensing agreement with Beckenbauer, having from the 1960s striped their brand into his. In 2015, Camp Beckenbauer kindly invited me, to talk about Fifa's crisis, on a panel with Jérôme Champagne, who was at the time campaigning to be Blatter's replacement as president. Champagne talked insightfully about the detailed changes he thought should be made to Fifa's structures; I took a step back and said Fifa, after the indictments and so much corruption exposed, had become toxic, and was still in denial about the scale of its disgrace. I remember the great Franz Beckenbauer, a hero of my boyhood, sitting in the front row of the handsome hall, his hair silver, his glasses on trend, listening indulgently.

There were, it has to be said, stories always around that *der Kaiser* in his grown-up life was not as flawless as the figure we idolised on telly. Very early in my own involvement as a journalist with issues relating to Fifa, I was told that Beckenbauer long-term had quite prolific commercial activities, assisted by one of his advisers, Fedor Radmann.

The world had been quite startled in June 2014 when Beckenbauer was banned from football for ninety days by the Fifa ethics committee for failing to cooperate with Michael Garcia's investigation into the bidding for the 2018 and 2022 World Cups despite, the statement said, he had been contacted in English and German. Beckenbauer had responded to that suspension by saying he had not understood the requests and was in fact willing to cooperate.

Yet when I bumped into Beckenbauer for a couple of minutes during his tour of charming and welcoming delegates to the camp, I came over just a little starstruck, feeling a wave of nostalgia for what he represented to me: a love of football, ever since it blessed my happy childhood. So I just asked him like a fan, about the World Cup in 1966, Bobby Moore and Bobby Charlton, Mexico in 1970; I must have bored him with my sentimental fixation with his 1974 zenith, and told him it was the first World Cup I ever watched. He smiled and indulged me and talked as he must have done a million times to dazzled punters, about how much he had enjoyed it all – in fact, he said how much he had relished life in New York in the mid-1970s, where he was pictured at the Studio 54 disco and could loosen up into something of a playboy.

On 16 October 2015, just nine days after Camp Beckenbauer had happily concluded in the clean, wholesome, Alpine air of Kitzbühel, *Der Spiegel* explosively picked at the lustre of the Beckenbauer legend again. The magazine exposed what it described as a 'slush fund' of 10m CHF, €6.7m, that it alleged had been used to buy Fifa executive committee votes for the 2006 World Cup. Beckenbauer, who had been the president of the World Cup bid, Radmann, who was his vice president, and other senior DFB officials named as having known about it, angrily denied the allegations. Beckenbauer, speaking immediately after *Der Spiegel* published, said:

'I never provided anyone with money in order to secure votes for our World Cup bid, and neither did anyone else on the organising committee, as far as I know.'

The DFB president, Wolfgang Niersbach, also denied it, saying: 'The World Cup was not bought.' He said that 'to clear it up', there was an internal investigation ongoing, and an external investigation to be undertaken by the international law firm Freshfields Bruckhaus Deringer.

While Freshfields was still conducting its investigation, on 17 February 2016, Fifa's ethics committee fined Beckenbauer 7,000 CHF and gave him a warning. This sanction came as a result of its further investigations following the summary by Judge Hans-Joachim Eckert of Garcia's report into the bidding process for the 2018 and 2022 World Cups. The ethics committee stated again that although he had subsequently changed his attitude, Beckenbauer had failed to cooperate with the investigation, 'despite repeated requests for his assistance. This included requests to provide information during an in-person interview and in response to written questions presented in both English and German.'

There was no explanation of what precisely Garcia had been so keen to talk to him about. He was assumed by then to have voted for Australia to host the tournament in 2022 – in fact that he was Australia's single vote. It was known that Radmann, his long-term associate and adviser, had worked for the Australia bid, described as a consultant. Another consultant was Andreas Abold, a graphic designer in Munich, who was taken on by the Australia bid to produce its bid book, the official brochure which was sent to Fifa setting out a bid's credentials, the promotional videos and other work for Fifa's 'technical inspection' visit to the country and its facilities, and the final presentation made to the executive committee on 2 December 2010 in Zurich. That included a film, widely derided, featuring a cartoon kangaroo, which clearly did not do much to bounce anyone into voting for Australia. The Australia bid also hired Peter Hargitay, the former media adviser to Sepp Blatter at Fifa and Mohamed bin Hammam, who had worked for the England 2018 World Cup bid before his contract was not renewed following Lord Triesman's arrival as the chairman.

The employment of Radmann, Abold and Hargitay as consultants to the Australia 2022 World Cup bid had become controversial, particularly after their undoubtedly Fifa directory-like contacts book and long experience in the affairs of the organisation yielded just one vote. The Australian FA (FFA) had convinced the Australian government to spend Aus\$45.6m on the bid to persuade Fifa's executive committee to vote the World Cup to Australia. When the FFA produced its final report to the government in September 2011, it showed that an extraordinary amount of that money had been paid to the consultants, particularly Radmann and Abold.

Radmann's employment as a consultant had not been announced; Bonita Mersiades, who had been head of corporate and public affairs for the bid until she was fired in January 2010 for reasons which were not explained, said she was told not to publicly announce Radmann's appointment, or that of Hargitay. In the final report, the FFA stated that Radmann was not employed directly, but 'sub-contracted' by Abold 'to deliver advocacy services'. The report states that:

'Mr Radmann's role, in collaboration with [Hargitay's company] ECN, was to provide advice on the bid's strategic campaign to the FFA chairman [Frank Lowy] and CEO [Ben Buckley] and to advocate in support of FFA's bid. This included engaging with key decision-makers and facilitating introductions and access to members of the Fifa executive committee for FFA.'

The consultants were, then, substantially to use their close familiarity with the Fifa executive committee members to lobby them to vote for the bid employing them, Australia. The report added:

'Mr Radmann had provided similar services in support of South Africa's bid to host the 2010 Fifa World Cup and Germany's bid to host the 2006 Fifa World Cup.'

Abold, too, had worked on those bids; his consultancy in Munich produced the bid book for South Africa's 2010 World Cup pitch, and Germany's bid for 2006. They were a winning team at Fifa. For those two World Cup hosting votes, Beckenbauer had not been a member of the Fifa executive committee. He was elected on to it in 2007, and so in 2010, when the vote was held for the hosts to the 2018 and 2022 World Cups, Beckenbauer was a voting member of the executive committee for the first time, with his close associate, Fedor Radmann, and Andreas Abold with whom he had worked on the German 2006 bid, working for Australia 2022.

After Germany had won its bid for 2006, and Radmann had become Beckenbauer's vice president on the organising committee for the tournament itself, Abold had been hired, too; he designed the World Cup logo, with its three happy, smiley faces gleeful above the famous trophy. German press criticism of an alleged conflict of interest, because Radmann and Abold were so close they had a business relationship outside of the World Cup work, led to Radmann stepping down on 30 June 2003 and becoming a consultant to the organising committee instead. Theo Zwanziger, later the DFB president, took over Radmann's formal position.

The final report for Australia's 2022 bid submitted by the FFA showed that the work for which Abold was responsible had cost around Aus$10m of the government's public money: $4.89m for the bid book, $3.82m for the final presentation, and $1.36m for work done on the Fifa inspection visit. Fedor Radmann, noted in brackets as a sub-contractor to Abold, was paid Aus$3.63m. Hargitay's bill was less than half that, Aus$1.45m, which he says included not only his work, but four members of staff at ECN. For all that expertise and experience, and contacts in the House of Fifa corridors, and Aus$15m paid for the work of these three people, Australia, with all its attractions as a country, had garnered one vote.

Hans-Joachim Eckert's summary of the Michael Garcia ethics committee report into the 2018 and 2022 bidding process, which is heavily anonymised, presumably to protect Fifa against legal action, said this about the Australia bid:

'[Garcia's] report concludes that the Australia 2022 bid team did undertake specific efforts to gain the support of a particular then Fifa executive committee member and it suggests that there have been efforts to conceal certain key relationships in this context. Certain devices employed by the bid team and its consultants were seemingly aimed at hiding ties with individuals close to the executive committee member concerned while taking advantage of their influence over the member to further the bid strategy.'

It has never been clarified publicly to whom this refers, and whether the executive committee member, whose ties to individuals close to him were attempted to be hidden, was Beckenbauer. Or whether this is what Garcia had wanted to talk to Beckenbauer about. What is now known is that Mersiades, who became a public critic of the Australia bid in central respects, including the employment of the consultants, did express her concerns to Garcia. She was concerned about the closeness of Radmann and Abold, who were paid so much by Australia to drum up support at Fifa, with Beckenbauer himself, a voter on Fifa's executive committee. She is also a critic of the money paid, arguing that, in particular, $10m to Abold for the bid book was hugely more than a normal design-and-consulting company would have charged for work of a similar – or in the case of the final presentation film, better – standard, and it was not clear to her what Radmann did for his $3.63m.

In fact, Mersiades alleges that Abold directly claimed his connection to Beckenbauer as an advantage of hiring him. She says Abold stated that if the Australia bid employed him as a consultant and designer of the bid book, it would bring with it Beckenbauer's vote.

'When Andreas Abold visited us in June 2008,' Mersiades told me, 'he explicitly told us that Franz Beckenbauer was part of the "package" he could offer.'

Mersiades says that afterwards, within the Australia bid, 'it was acknowledged internally as one of the major features of his pitch. Beckenbauer, Radmann and Abold were a package deal. We engaged Abold, and then Radmann through Abold, and that got us – at least in theory – Beckenbauer's support.'

Mersiades' evidence was quite sniffily dismissed by Eckert, under the heading 'Role and relevance of a "Whistleblower"', which was clearly a reference to her. He said that while she provided some useful information, 'the evidence often did not support [her] specific recollections and allegations'.

However, what Mersiades says about the Abold, Radmann, Beckenbauer connections tallies with what I was told from within the England 2018 bid. One senior member of the bid, who wanted to remain anonymous, told me that Peter Hargitay, while working for the England bid as a consultant, had suggested the employment of Abold as a way of winning Beckenbauer's vote.

'He said that if you employ Andreas Abold to write the bid book – and he did say he was the best because he had worked on the South Africa 2010 and Germany 2006 bids – and pay Abold the fees you are asked for, that will be very well received by Franz Beckenbauer.'

He said that the England 2018 bid was not at all interested in working in that way, and they dismissed the suggestion.

Peter Hargitay, whom I have known for years now, as he has liaised with the press on behalf of Blatter, bin Hammam and in other capacities, adamantly denies having said that. He told me that in itself it is not too surprising to say a bid might be seen favourably 'if you have somebody with connections to somebody else'. However he denies making any recommendation to the England bid to employ Abold and says he did not even know Abold at that time, only coming to know him when they worked together on the Australia bid.

When I asked the FFA about its employment of the consultants with close ties to Franz Beckenbauer, a spokesman declined to comment, suggesting I look at statements already made in the press. On 3 June 2015, after the arrests and indictments in Zurich and Sepp Blatter's resignation, Frank Lowy issued an open letter which addressed some of the concerns.

He stated that he 'nursed a bitter grievance' after Australia received just one vote, but said: 'We ran a clean bid.'

About the consultants, he said he recruited them 'on the advice of Fifa's leadership', because Australia were not 'familiar with the powerbrokers in world football'. All he said about them was that they 'ultimately proved less than effective, to say the least'.

Radmann, Abold and Franz Beckenbauer – via his representatives at Camp Beckenbauer – did not respond at all to detailed questions about the Australia 2022 World Cup bid, and their relationships. I put to them that the employment of Abold and Radmann as consultants for a World Cup bid on which Beckenbauer was going to be voting looked at least like he had a conflict of interest, and at worst, given the huge fees paid to Abold and Radmann, could look like an improper commercial relationship. They did not reply to explain.

By the time I asked them, Beckenbauer and Radmann had many other issues to worry about. The Freshfields inquiry, which Niersbach had said would dismiss the story, produced its report on 4 March 2016. It did not dismiss the story at all. In fact, it upheld it in forensic and devastating detail, and it would lead to a great deal of trouble for Franz Beckenbauer. The report said it had not found evidence that votes for the 2006 World Cup were bought, but on the evidence it did find: 'Equally, however, we cannot rule it out.'

It found, in essence, that *Der Spiegel* had been right: the DFB had indeed spent 10m CHF (€6.7m) in 2005, one year before the World Cup was held. It was used, via Fifa itself, to repay the same amount of money, €6.7m, which had been paid out by Robert Louis-Dreyfus, the former chief executive of Adidas, three years earlier, in 2002. At that time, the money was paid directly to Mohamed bin Hammam's company in Qatar, Kemco. Bin Hammam was then the AFC president, and the Freshfields report found that all four AFC representatives on the Fifa executive committee voted for Germany. Beckenbauer and his long-term then personal manager, Robert Schwan, were implicated in the original payment of the money to bin Hammam, in 2002.

The full, 380-page report in German included a cast list and mini-biographies of the main characters involved. It said that Radmann's involvement in sports politics went back to the 1960s, that he had been project leader for the 1972 Munich Olympics, and in 1979 he became a director at Adidas. Working for Horst Dassler's famous operation, he was, the report said, responsible for 'promotion and international relations' for ten years, until 1989. 'At the same time' – that is, until 1989 – the report says, Radmann was active as the German head of International Sport and Leisure, ISL. The Swiss court order, settling the criminal action against Fifa in relation to ISL, had stated that this company had paid bribes to heads of sports governing bodies since its formation by Dassler in 1982, although there was no indication that Radmann personally was involved or implicated. *Der Spiegel* had not held back in its coverage of the rotten, corrupting roots of this company, calling it Dassler's 'bribe company', which paid out, in German, the '*Schmiergeld*' (greasing money). Radmann worked after that for the rights company CWL, where Günter Netzer was now an executive. Radmann worked for other rights companies as well, and in 1996 went back to Adidas for ten years on a consultancy contract. Radmann told the Freshfields inquiry that Beckenbauer had particularly wanted and persuaded him to be involved with the 2006 World Cup bid, because he had all the 'necessary contacts'.

The report also has a cast list of all twenty-four Fifa executive committee members at that time, in 2000, and how completely split it was according to geographical blocks. It listed that all four African representatives had voted for South Africa, as had Blatter, who wanted to make that the continent's first World Cup. The three Concacaf and three Conmebol representatives had all voted for South Africa, too – Warner did, despite benefits bestowed on him by Germany. All eight European representatives were lined up for Germany, so the four Asian votes, for Germany, were crucial. That made it 12–11, and Dempsey's abstention, when his mandate from Oceania was to vote for South Africa, clinched it for Germany. Had he voted, Blatter's would have been a casting vote for South Africa; Germany would have missed its summer fairytale of fanzones, fun and reinvention by football, and the first African World Cup would have taken place four years earlier than it did.

The convoluted but at heart simple tale of the money was described by Freshfields in the report. It began in May 2002, when, in four instalments up to 8 July 2002, 6m CHF was paid into a bank account operated by a law firm in Sarnen, Switzerland. The report states that the 6m CHF came to the law firm from an account 'stated to be held by either Robert Schwan or Franz Beckenbauer'. The law firm itself, however, said that the account was not for the benefit of Beckenbauer. A few days after each instalment was paid to the law firm, the equivalent money, to the total of 6m CHF, was paid to Mohamed bin Hammam's company in Doha, Kemco.

The 6m CHF was repaid to Beckenbauer two months later, on 3 September 2002, and it came from Robert Louis-Dreyfus, who had stepped down the previous year from his position as the Adidas chief executive. After Dassler's death, Adidas' three stripes fell commercially behind the modern swoosh of Nike; the Dasslers had sold it, and Louis-Dreyfus, with partners, bought it in 1993, revitalised the brand and turned the company round. The Freshfields report says that in August 2002, Louis-Dreyfus opened an account at his private bank in Zurich, and immediately paid 10m CHF out of it, going overdrawn, to the law firm in Sarnen. This law firm then repaid the 6m CHF 'to an account belonging to Franz Beckenbauer' which had originally paid it to bin Hammam via the law firm. Schwan, who had made Beckenbauer fortunes in endorsements, principally with the Adidas sponsorships, but also with Knorr soups and other products, had died in July 2002, so he was no longer stated as being possibly involved with the bank account. The report states that when this money flow was put to Beckenbauer he was, according to his lawyer, 'surprised at the insights gained'.

A further payment of 4m CHF was made by the Swiss law firm to bin Hammam's company, two days after Beckenbauer was repaid, on 5 September 2002. The report said it was clear the money was paid to Kemco, but when they contacted bin Hammam, he denied ever receiving it. He was asked what the purpose of the money was, but answered that he could not see any connection between Freshfields' questions about the money and the German bid to host the 2006 World Cup.

A copy of the contract the great Franz Beckenbauer signed with Jack Warner, four days before the 2000 vote on the 2006 World Cup host, was included in the Freshfields report. It is, for a lover of football, horrible. Here was Beckenbauer, signing a brief and pathetic deal to bestow various lucrative benefits on Jack Warner, who was wielding the three Concacaf votes. Beckenbauer signed it on behalf of the DFB itself, with Warner signing as the Concacaf president. There was a commitment to development in it; the DFB promised to provide coaches to Concacaf for four years; soccer equipment – 'Adidas balls, bags, boots etc.', it promised – equivalent to $1m a year for four years; one Concacaf country a year could have a three-week training camp every year for four years, at the DFB's expense. Then the DFB agreed to do some printing for Warner: of 30,000 Trinidad and Tobago flags, and of 30,000 tickets for Trinidad and Tobago World Cup qualifying matches. They even agreed to pay the cost of first-class flights for somebody to pick up the national flags and tickets, and to pay additional costs of air freight if necessary.

Then, at the end, Beckenbauer chucked in the 1,000 tickets to Warner for the 2006 World Cup, should it be held in Germany after all. And there it was on page 4: the signature of the superstar, familiar to any football fan of the 1970s: Franz Beckenbauer, next to a scrawl by Mr Warner. It was stated to have been signed in Rotterdam, on 2 July 2000, four days before Warner would vote alongside the twenty-three other men in the Fifa executive committee, for whether Germany would indeed host the World Cup. It is one of the most disheartening documents you could ever see with the word 'soccer' in it.

Freshfields said it was 'still puzzling' why Beckenbauer should have signed that contract with Warner. There was also no explanation whatsoever as to what it had to do with football development, to promise Jack Warner 1,000 free tickets, which he could sell presumably, at a World Cup for which he was going to vote on the host, four days later.

'This agreement does not appear to have ever formally come into effect,' the report says, 'but a number of the obligations in it have been performed.'

The required approval by the DFB executive committee was never given, but nevertheless the DFB did have the tickets and flags produced for Warner, and paid for him to travel to Germany. There were DFB invoices and other documents related to this, which said 'World Cup 2006 Development Help'.

Beckenbauer finally broke his silence following the Freshfields report with an interview given to the Munich newspaper *Süddeutsche Zeitung*. He came up with nothing more convincing than that he was merely an unworldly ex-footballer. He 'always blindly signed when they needed my signature', he said. 'If I trust someone, I'll sign anything. Blind!'

Is this how his commercial managers, at Adidas and since, had coached *der Kaiser*?

The Freshfields report looked at the Dempsey abstention, too, and cited his version at the time, which was that he was under 'intolerable pressure' the night before the vote. In some reports Dempsey was quoted saying the pressure was from 'highly influential European interest groups'; in another he was supposed to have complained that there were rumours he was taking money from South Africa, and he had wanted them to lose with his abstention. Both Radmann and Beckenbauer were interviewed, saying that Dempsey had never asked for money. Radmann had said the corruption allegations, of Dempsey being paid $250,000, were 'baseless filth'. Niersbach said that Dempsey had always said openly that he had wanted to abstain.

Dempsey wrote to Egidius Braun, then the president of the DFB, after the vote, saying the night before the ballot had been the worst of his life, then that he would like to meet them when he was next in Europe: 'It would be good to have a talk with yourself, Franz and Fedor about all the goings on, which I can't put on paper ...'

But Theo Zwanziger told Freshfields that in fact he believed Dempsey had been paid $250,000, by ISL. In the ledger of ISL payments, that figure was there, dated the night of the vote, against a recipient, E16, and Zwanziger said that he assumed it was Dempsey. The Oceania president had been mandated to vote for South Africa, and when he arrived home in New Zealand he faced a vote of no confidence for abstaining. His family have always denied that he was paid money for doing so.

It seems that in April 2005, with the Fifa executive committee's bare majority for Germany to host the World Cup long sealed and the preparations well advanced for the *Sommermärchen*, presided over by the now kindly figure of Beckenbauer, Robert Louis-Dreyfus was still 10m CHF overdrawn and wanted his money back. So, the DFB arranged to repay him the money, and did so via Fifa. Freshfields found that the DFB paid Fifa €6.7m, which was the value of 10m CHF. The DFB claimed, and even noted on the payment reference, that the €6.7m was a contribution towards the opening ceremony. Freshfields were not impressed with that at all, because it was for Louis-Dreyfus:

'This true purpose of this payment was knowingly concealed,' the report says, adding later that it was 'knowingly falsely declared' by the organising committee of the 2006 World Cup, of which Beckenbauer was the president and Radmann then a consultant.

Fifa then forwarded the money to Louis-Dreyfus. Blatter was informed about it, the report states.

'The payment amounting to €6.7m from April 2005 served as a refund of a payment previously made by Robert Louis-Dreyfus [to Mohamed bin Hammam's company],' the report concludes.

The report traced Wolfgang Niersbach's failure to inform the DFB's executive committee of these possible irregularities with the World Cup bid, after he became aware of them in June 2015, until finally he notified them in October, only after *Der Spiegel* had hold of the story and had made inquiries. Beckenbauer and Radmann were involved in a meeting with Niersbach about the issues, but still the DFB was not officially notified.

In June 2015, Niersbach had initiated a search of the archives and accounts, which was done by a female employee, unnamed. She insisted on doing this alone and refused any offers of help from colleagues, the report said, although she had told Freshfields she could not remember that.

'On 22 June 2015 she removed from the archives the "Fifa 2000" folder which could not be found during the course of the investigation,' the report said. 'During her interview with Freshfields, this employee of Wolfgang Niersbach denied that she had destroyed the file.'

Under a concluding section: 'How could these events happen?' Freshfields speculate on the factors. They are not pretty reading, for the German football establishment, for Franz Beckenbauer, its icon and elder statesman, for Fedor Radmann, his long-term fixer with the contacts and connections. The questions Freshfields raised were:

Unreasonable levels of ambition?
Dependencies, in an environment inclined towards
corruption?
A pronounced inclination to look the other way?
A lack of transparency?

In Beckenbauer's interview with *Süddeutsche Zeitung*, he admitted
that the contract with Warner 'looked dubious', saying: 'Looking at it
from today's point of view, many things look funny and you wouldn't
do it like that today. But we simply meant well at the time.'

He said that Warner, typically, had said to the Germans: 'If you are
friends, do something for my confederation.' Beckenbauer described
the resulting deal with Warner as 'a development aid package with
ticketing opportunities'.

He insisted: 'I know that I did nothing wrong. I gave my all to
bring the World Cup to Germany, which we succeeded in doing. I
have a clean conscience. We didn't bribe anyone, and we didn't have
any slush funds. We only meant well. Why do people always believe
negative things?'

But that blanket assertion of good intentions was not very
convincing in a scandal burgeoning into the biggest ever in the great
history of German football, of which Beckenbauer was the finest
living product. In January 2016, even before Freshfields produced
their findings, there were reports that the FBI was investigating
the Germany 2006 World Cup bid. The DFB itself was reported to
have commenced legal proceedings against Beckenbauer, Radmann
and the other former executives in the organising committee, for
repayment of the €6.7m.

Days after the report in *Der Spiegel*, the public prosecution office
in Frankfurt launched an investigation, reportedly into the tax implications of the payments, and raided the DFB's headquarters. On
22 March 2016, after reading the Freshfields report, the Fifa ethics
committee opened an investigation into Beckenbauer and other
members of the 2006 World Cup organising committee. It said in
relation to Beckenbauer it was investigating 'possible undue payments
and contracts to gain an advantage in the 2006 World Cup host selection, which could constitute … bribery and corruption'. Niersbach

was then banned from football for a year, for his failure to report the possible misconduct.

Then, on 1 September 2016, the attorney general in Switzerland publicly announced it had opened criminal proceedings into the DFB, in relation to the €6.7m payment, which raised allegations of fraud, criminal mismanagement, money laundering and misappropriation. The named suspects in the criminal proceedings were Franz Beckenbauer, Wolfgang Niersbach, Horst Schmidt, the DFB secretary general at the time of the payments, and Theo Zwanziger. The presumption of innocence applied to all four of them, the announcement said.

'In particular, it is suspected that the suspects wilfully misled their fellow members of the executive board of the organising committee for the 2006 World Cup. This was presumably done by the use of false pretences or concealment of the truth, thus inducing the other committee members to act in a manner that caused DFB a financial loss,' the attorney general said.

After all of this, it was another report by *Der Spiegel*, in September 2016, which finally turned the adoring German public against *der Kaiser*. The magazine reported that Beckenbauer had not, in fact, been the president of the World Cup organising committee out of the benevolence of his love for the mother country. In fact, he had been paid €5.5m for leading the bid and World Cup project, and that the money had been paid to the DFB bid from a betting company, Oddset, which had responded to requests for sponsorship of the bid.

In the detailed questions I sent to Radmann and Abold in preparation for writing this book, about their relationship with Beckenbauer, I put to Radmann the issues raised by the Freshfields inquiry, and the report that he is being personally sued for the €6.7m. Neither responded.

I called Beckenbauer's brand representative and agent, Marcus Hofl, to ask for an interview with Beckenbauer and an opportunity to discuss all these allegations. The press office of Camp Beckenbauer responded, and then I emailed them a request for an interview with Beckenbauer, at whose conference I had spoken of the toxicity and corruption of Fifa, with him looking on and listening quietly. I asked a series of specific questions; about all of these issues: his closeness to

Abold and Radmann, and whether there was a conflict of interest or improper commercial relationship in the huge money paid to them by Australia 2022. All the issues raised by the Freshfields report, in particular the contract he signed to grant benefits to Jack Warner, including 1,000 tickets, four days before the vote. I asked about his response to the criminal and Fifa ethics committee investigations and allegations being made against him, and the revelation that in fact he had been paid for leading the World Cup project. When I had contact with the Camp Beckenbauer people during the organising of the conference, they were highly professional, very capable and smart, and nice people to deal with. Now, really, all I wanted was for Franz to come back, and say it ain't so. But at the time of writing, they have not responded at all.

To refresh my memories of 1974, of being captivated by watching my first World Cup, in colour, at home, aged nine, I have had a look on YouTube, to see some of it again. I looked at the Cruyff turn, and gazed on it with an awe and appreciation I didn't have at the time. There is a gorgeous clip of Beckenbauer in the final against Holland, taking a free-kick from outside the penalty area. He had reached that time of mature authority when he seemed to stroke the ball in his sweeper role exclusively with the outside of his right foot, which increased the unruffled impression he gave of always having time. He looked like a veteran of a seniority above everybody else on the field, although, captain of his country, he was only twenty-eight. In the World Cup final, in his country, at the Olympic Stadium in his home city of Munich, full of German supporters willing victory, Beckenbauer took a stroll up to the ball, and chipped it with the outside of his right foot. It was a ridiculously sophisticated skill, of course he made it look so easy, and the ball rose and curled and dipped over the wall. It was dropping into the goal, as well, and the Holland goalkeeper, Jan Jongbloed, had to make an excellent flying save to tip the ball over the bar. It was, from Franz Beckenbauer, sublime – and so, to me, was football.

CHAPTER 18

Tainted History

João Havelange, the Brazilian president from 1974 to 1998 who oversaw Fifa's and football's transformation into packaged, sponsored, global television content, and started major development programmes too, died on 15 August 2016. He was 100. The official Fifa announcement was brief, really, for so gigantic a figure in its history, although it did pay tribute to his globalising of the game. There was a potted history of his remarkable life, career and achievements: a lawyer born in Brazil to Belgian immigrant parents, an Olympic swimmer, chairman from 1958 of the Brazilian sports federation including the CBF, where he organised Brazil's innate football brilliance into triple World Cup winning magnificence. Gianni Infantino offered a corporate thank you quote:

'During [Havelange's] 24 years as Fifa president football became truly global, reaching new territories and bringing the game to all corners of the world. Something the whole football community should be grateful for. I extend my condolences to his family.'

Yet none of the obituaries in the media for so dominant a global sports figure could hail his achievements without enmeshing them with his tainted record of proven corruption. There were always allegations, back in Brazil in his business dealings which reportedly included arms trading, and about his 1974 Fifa election triumph, when he paid several delegates' travel costs, and his lobbyist, Elias Zaccour, took care of some African FAs' debts. But Havelange reached the age of ninety-six before his entrenched bribe-taking at Fifa in Zurich was established as fact, in unforgiving global exposure.

Shortly after Havelange's passing, I happened to talk to Patrick Nally, the English pioneer of sports marketing, who worked with

Havelange, and Dassler, from 1974, at the beginning of it all. He said he had been reflecting on Havelange's tainted legacy, and he thought it terribly sad. He knew Havelange and believed he had great virtues:

'He was intelligent, a sports person, competitive, he had businesses in Brazil, he was sophisticated,' Nally said. 'He saw the importance of football in Brazil and big opportunities for it internationally. It was a good vision, with development plans. I think that was genuine. He wasn't seizing an opportunity to make millions – he didn't know how to make money from football, they didn't have money then and they couldn't see the massive increase in television rights coming.'

Nally believes Havelange was corrupted from the start by Dassler, a manipulator of the 'dark arts'. And that this corruption of Fifa, from early in the Havelange era, set the template for the system of bribes paid by marketing-rights companies more widely, including the endemic corruption in the Americas.

'João Havelange died on my birthday,' Nally said. 'He made it to one hundred. I was thinking of him and his legacy, and how it came about. Horst Dassler was most responsible.'

In the early 1970s, Nally had begun selling sports events for sponsors to brand in the UK, and Dassler sought him out to work with Fifa after Havelange's 1974 presidential victory. Havelange had promised much more dedicated football development and coaching programmes to Africa and the poorer countries' FAs, but TV rights were peanuts then and Fifa had no money to implement his election pledges. Nally worked closely with Dassler and his staff in the Adidas international relations operation, and with Blatter, who, remarkably, spent six months working and being trained at Adidas after he joined Fifa in 1975. Eventually they signed up Coca-Cola to sponsor the global development programmes, and Adidas took their name round the world supplying kit and balls.

Nally said that he and Dassler moved on together to package the rights to the next World Cup, in 1978 in Argentina, then for Spain, in 1982, for which greater money was needed because Havelange had promised it would be expanded to twenty-four teams. In 1978, when Nally was developing the package for the Spain 1982 World Cup, the corrupting of Havelange began, he told me.

'Horst Dassler asked for a sum of money to be put into the budget for Dr Havelange,' Nally said. This was for Havelange personally, from the rights which would be bought from Fifa, and sold.

'I argued, I said that was wrong, that the money for Havelange should be paid by Fifa. But Horst Dassler said no, I was being too Anglo-Saxon. He said Havelange "needs to respect us and stay with us". He said that if we made it easy, they would take it all away from us. Horst wanted to be the paymaster, so the federations would owe him, and that way he kept control. That was the sea change, the start of it, 1978. That became the template for ISL, and that was the model for Traffic, all working on the principle of kickbacks. Traffic was the Brazilian ISL equivalent.'

Nally and Dassler's partnership ended in 1982, after the proposed deal for Nally to buy him out was cancelled, with Dassler instead going in with Dentsu, the Japanese marketing company, in co-ownership of ISL. Nally said that Dassler's 'dark arts' were to 'back the right person in a federation, and make sure he stays loyal', which could be done in different ways.

'He would say that everybody was buyable, but people want different things: it might be money, some might be grateful for a sexual favour, some if there was something for their wife. He was a very, very shrewd guy.' Dassler would be at dinners and events, Nally says, knowing all the influential people, and he was 'very shrewd' at knowing how to control them.

'Writing payments into agreements became an integral part of his strategy,' Nally said. 'If he is the paymaster, it becomes less likely that the individuals would do things out of his control. Kickbacks were created to keep power, rather than have people paid salaries. Once that became the culture, it was very difficult to change it.'

It is true that as football was transformed from the 1970s into a more lucrative globally packaged business, the officials who ran the federations were mostly still expected to adhere to the old amateur spirit of being involved purely for the love of it. That culture can be seen to have stretched down the decades even into the modern scandals, where significant figures were still not being paid salaries. Although there is outrage at the scale of the wage packages paid to some executives in football, including Blatter once his was published by Fifa, you can argue that the lack of payment actually made people more susceptible to scandal, because everybody needs to earn a living. It was surely not sustainable for Franz Beckenbauer, handsomely rewarded throughout his life, to spend a great deal of his time working on Germany's hosting of the 2006 World Cup, for free. But he had said he would, true to the enduring pure expectations of national sporting figures; hence the outrage in Germany when it turned out he was well paid after all. Jeff Webb, as the president of Concacaf, is also reported to have not taken a salary, and to have been warned that by doing so at that time, in 2012, people might take it not as a sign of his pure dedication to football, but that he must be a crook, making his money in other ways.

Nally believes this jarring of the commercial forces seeking to exploit football then, and the amateur façade clung to at Fifa, was a crucial factor in Havelange's and Fifa's systemic corruption. Havelange acceded as some apparent father figure from the country of the beautiful game, and Nally argues it turned out to be a 'tragedy' that the president was not paid an official salary, hence was more likely, Nally argues, to pocket money illicitly. Dassler became busily involved with Havelange immediately after his election to the presidency, in trying to package the development programmes with a sponsor, then the rights to the World Cup. And he very quickly began to pay kickbacks, too, according to Nally's account.

'By 1978 and then 1982, João Havelange was totally in his pocket,' he said.

Once the bribery started, it would become soaked into the culture, on into new generations of confederation heads and marketing companies, as ultimately the ISL court document and US indictment chronicled.

'I saw Havelange not long before he died, and I told him I was sorry for him, for his legacy,' Nally told me. 'He was sad, a broken man. From a strong, proud Brazilian, a stiff-backed swimmer' – Havelange famously still swam every morning, into his old age – 'he was broken.'

Contemplating the history of Fifa since its watershed, its commercialisation, globalisation of TV rights and sponsorships was probably inevitable. From 1970 the World Cup was, after all, on colour television around the world, spending on sports equipment and brands was growing, and so was the appetite of sponsors to buy the game's image to sweeten their products. Yet from the perspective of forty years, during which Havelange was president with Blatter as his secretary general, then Blatter the president from 1998, corruption in various forms was endemic. So often, it is represented as a non-European, African, developing-world plague. Much of the suspicion of Fifa has focused on the GOAL project and other development money and the assumption, not borne out by too much actual evidence and giving too little credit for the committed work often done in developing countries, that a lot of is filched.

Fifa even made that case officially, in their submissions to the Zug prosecutions, arguing that corruption was a way of life in Africa and South America; that, 'bribery payments belong to the usual salary of the majority of the population'. Platini said similar in his breezy interview with me at Uefa's house of football by the banks of Lake Geneva, in clean and neutral, tax-lite Switzerland, about people in the Fifa executive committee, that 'they didn't share our philosophy, our morality, our policies because they are coming from another world, another morality.'

Yet the truth is that the corruption of Fifa was secured in Europe, in Zurich, Switzerland. Horst Dassler, the owner of Adidas, a great and pioneering German boot and kit company, the acme of sporting glamour to us as kids, selling the tracksuit and shoes with Beckenbauer's name on them, forged the system of corrupting sports governing body presidents. Havelange, undoubtedly, was served up with bribes by ISL through the 1990s, and from well before that by Dassler, according to Nally.

I asked the modern-day, Stock Exchange-listed Adidas company, still headquartered at Herzogenaurach in Germany, for their response to the stories about Dassler, and they do not deny it. A company spokesman confirmed that in Dassler's time: 'Adidas did run an international relations department, and they did seek to influence the politics of sports governing bodies, principally by having very close relationships.'

The spokesman said the company cannot confirm or deny the widely suspected and reported episodes of alleged bribery, or the detail of any 'dark arts', but it has now commissioned full research of its archives by the German society for company history based in Frankfurt, the Gesellschaft für Unternehmensgeschichte e.V. This is intended to establish more solidly what did happen during the Horst Dassler era, a culture which has wormed its tentacles so far and long down into the history of Fifa and football. The spokesman was at pains to stress that after Horst Dassler died in 1987, his sisters sold Adidas in 1990, and that the company now has no connection with that culture of the 1970s and 1980s.

'Times have really changed,' the spokesman said. 'The company is listed on the Stock Exchange since 1995, with no major shareholders. The leadership of the company has changed, and there have been very great changes to compliance procedures in companies over the last fifteen or twenty years. Here we are talking about a history, which goes back thirty or forty years, and we have commissioned this archive research to establish the facts.'

It is, though, notable that Fifa's major sale of the 2002 and 2006 World Cup rights to ISL was concluded by Havelange just before he stepped down in 1998, and that no similar allegations, of taking kick-backs on the sale of TV rights, have been made against Blatter. Nor has his name appeared on the US indictment or any other legal or ethics committee proceedings, accusing him of this practice. Blatter was paid a salary, which we now know to have been very handsome, and as he has repeatedly stated, he appears not to have indulged in this crude corruption, as his predecessor and many of his executive committee members did. The question asked of Blatter many times, though, is whether he knew about the corruption of others and tolerated it, because if they were happy it perpetuated his position in charge. He has always said that he did not.

This history of his organisation, though, shows that the rottenness did set in from the top, in transactions and relationships between Germany and Switzerland: at the heart of Europe. Yet still, there remains a complacent and suspect tendency among Europeans to blame corruption on parts of the world which feel strange and faraway, foreign, where the 'morality is different'.

CHAPTER 19

'And the Host of the 2022 World Cup Will Be ... Qatar!' (2)

In July 2011, seven months after Qatar's shocking, winning bid to host the Fifa World Cup in 2022, the official bid committee invited me to interview its chief executive, Hassan Al Thawadi, for the *Guardian*, at the operation's headquarters in Doha. The country to which Fifa's barons had casually sent the World Cup in the summer was suffocatingly hot, and like in Abu Dhabi, the only people out of air-conditioning and in the dusty tracts between the streets were the immigrant workers doing the tough and dirty construction work.

The campaign groups Amnesty International, Human Rights Watch and the International Trades Union Congress would mount fierce attacks on the country's *kefala* system of employing immigrant workers under the control of one company, the oppressive working conditions in Qatar and inadequate accommodation in 'labour camps'. Al Thawadi and his team would respond with a series of reforms and promise better conditions on their sites, and argue that hosting the World Cup was a catalyst for change because it subjected Qatar to fierce global scrutiny. Amnesty would welcome some reforms but persistently argue they did not go far or wide enough. The ITUC argued that Fifa sending the huge construction project to Qatar meant there would be more workers dying on building sites, although the bid committee, renamed the 'supreme committee' for organising the World Cup, disputed the ITUC's figures.

For Al Thawadi, the young, driven, English and American university-educated lawyer entrusted by his Emir to market the country's merits to Fifa and lead the bid, Sepp Blatter pulling the name Qatar out of that envelope – while seeming almost to hold his nose – was the most ecstatic moment of his life. Al Thawadi would tell me he had been highly emotional the day before, when they made their slick final presentation to the twenty-two voting executive committee members, to send the World Cup to the tiny Gulf state in the summer.

'Afterwards I broke down and cried,' he recalled, in his surprisingly spartan office on the twenty-sixth floor of a bog-standard office block in Doha. 'We had been all over the world, we took a bid nobody thought had much chance of winning on to a new level. I told my team on 1 December: win or lose, you should be very proud.'

Al Thawadi still could not dare to believe they would win, despite the huge money poured into his marketing budget, the involvement of the Qatari, bin Hammam, still in the heart of the executive committee, and his country's vast, coveted wealth in a credit-crunched world economy. A World Cup in Qatar would be played at a planned twelve stadiums, building nine and remodelling three, essentially in a single city, Doha, capital of a previously fairly obscure emirate with a native population around 278,000, in desert summer conditions of oppressive humidity and temperatures. Then, they did win the vote, and Qatar's delegation leapt and hugged each other delightedly in that stunned and sheepish hall.

On my trip, the bid's head of communications, Nasser al-Khater, who also went to university in the US, had explained the nation-building, 'Brand Qatar' elements which the World Cup and the country's other sporting, cultural and investment efforts were intended to promote:

'Warmth, hospitality, economic development beyond oil and gas, openness to the world and being a positive interface between the Arab world and the rest of the world.'

But the ecstasy of the victory for these young Qatari, Western-educated professionals was immediately devoured by a reputational firefight. The allegations that Qatar must have corruptly 'bought' the World Cup through bribery were instant, and this was before Blazer, Warner, Teixeira, Grondona, bin Hammam and Leoz, all of whom voted, were charged or proven to have been corrupt, and other voting members were sanctioned by the ethics committee for breaches of Fifa's own code of conduct.

Being there, in their Doha offices, I saw and heard how agitated and resentful they were. Work was going on towards the monumental construction project they had taken on, to be incorporated with a new metro system and other huge infrastructure which by 2022 was to transform Doha, still then a strung-out city with dusty, empty spaces between the skyscrapers. They did show me the engineers working on the air-cooling technology which they had promised could make a summer tournament possible – the bid had built a prototype stadium with just 500 seats for $27m – but they seemed partly paralysed, stuck on stemming the storm of allegations.

They had invited me over and the BBC's then sports editor, David Bond, for Al Thawadi to give a press and broadcast interview, in which he planned to be defiant, rebut all the claims, maintain their bid was clean. When we finally sat down for the interview, though, he went further than just that: he complained that in the relentlessly suspicious focus on Qatar, there was an element of racism, the assumption that Arabs with so much money must have been greasing palms.

'I do believe that there is a stereotype, and prejudice against the fact that we are a rich, Arab nation,' he said. 'Ignorance fed into prejudice and made it a more fertile ground for these rumours to take seed and grow. Maybe we are an easy target. Had England or Australia or the USA won the bid, would any of this outrage have occurred?'

There were strong rumours even then, since considerably strengthened, about the probity of Germany's campaign to land the 2006 World Cup and South Africa's to host the 2010 tournament, yet there had been no outcry on anything like this scale. Al Thawadi mentioned England's bid for 2018, particularly that they had been organising the friendly with Thailand, which the FA then cancelled after Worawi Makudi did not vote for them. There were also questions about Australia's bid by then, and the employment of the consultants, particularly Radmann, who was known to be so close to Beckenbauer. Al Thawadi asked furiously why all the attention was on Qatar. Responding to the calls for an investigation, he said he believed it would clear them and they had nothing to hide but, fiery, he retorted:

'Why do I have to take ten steps to prove my innocence when there is no shred of evidence available? Why should we have an investigation if no other country has one, even Russia, which won it on the same day?'

Every time the accusations came, including from John Whittingdale's parliamentary committee after they published the *Sunday Times* 'whistleblower' claims, Al Thawadi responded strongly and in detail, usually with lawyers' letters. When eventually there was the Fifa ethics committee investigation, by Garcia, the official Qatar bid gave him access to all their correspondence, computers, emails, and made themselves personally available for discussions and questions. Russia, which as Al Thawadi said, won a majority of votes from the same executive committee, including its corrupt members, the same day, had its explanation of leased, destroyed computers accepted without comment by Eckert in his summary of Garcia's report in November 2014. Yet Russia's bid, personally propounded by Vladimir Putin with all necessary state backing, has always escaped the relentless suspicions lasered on Qatar.

While David Bond and I were there, trying to understand this place where Fifa was sending its World Cup, the bid sprung on us that the 'whistleblower' had agreed to retract her claims. She was Phaedra Almajid, the woman who had worked on international media relations for the bid, left in March 2010 unhappy at some of her treatment, and gone to live in the US. She had told the story alleging that at the CAF congress in Angola, the African executive committee members had been offered $1.5m each for the vote, which they and Al Thawadi denied. Now, we were told, she wanted to withdraw it. She had even signed an affidavit, taking back that and other information she had given against the Qatar bid, saying the Angola story was 'fabricated and untrue'.

It was a fundamentally awkward and unsatisfactory position for us to be landed in. We were presented with this by the Qatar bid itself, which raised the clear suspicion that Almajid had been either threatened, or paid. The bid denied that, and so did Almajid, to us. Practically, as she was insisting she was retracting of her own free will, there was no way to further satisfy ourselves. Also, we were in Doha, and she was in the US.

The question of whether to tell this story at all, given the obvious questions about it, necessitated long calls on the phone to her, and to my editor in London. At home, by habit, I often walk around while on the mobile, and I found myself doing it in Doha, too, leaving the bid's office or my hotel and wandering around outside. It was ridiculously hot, and exceptionally humid. I remember talking through the knotty ins and outs of it with my editor for half an hour late morning one day, and bursting out sweating immediately, literally dripping, my shirt soaked within minutes. Of sending a World Cup to these conditions, I could just about accept that the hugely expensive air-cooling systems might work for the stadiums, to keep the players at ideal temperature, and even people in the stands. But the thought of fanzones, and tens of thousands of people wanting to mill about to enjoy a World Cup, in those temperatures, seemed ludicrous. As in Abu Dhabi, nobody really went outside in the daytime, unless they were going to and from their cars, except the immigrant workers in their boots, overalls and helmets.

Almajid repeatedly maintained that the bid had not put pressure on her or induced her to retract her stories; in fact she swore to that in her affidavit. In it, she said she had been bitter about the circumstances in which she left, felt the bid unfairly questioned her ability to 'control' the international media, and she had been told she would be replaced. She said she made up the Angola story 'to hurt the bid like they had hurt me'. But then, she stated, it had gone too far after the stories were printed and made such a huge impact, and when Blatter had said the whistleblower would be coming to Zurich and there could be a re-vote on the basis of her story. She said she then contacted a member of the bid team and voluntarily offered to retract.

'I want to make clear that Qatar 2022 bid committee never engaged in the behaviour I accused them of,' her affidavit concluded.

Ultimately, we decided to report this, with the circumstances of how it came about. Al-Khater, who had worked most closely with Almajid and been friends with her, had gone to the US to conclude her signing of the affidavit, just before they invited David Bond and me to Doha. We reported this retraction as she and the bid were presenting it, and made clear that the bid itself had delivered it to us.

Al-Khater and Al Thawadi were satisfied that Almajid's retraction removed the only solid allegations in the swirl of suspicion against Qatar since the vote. Al Thawadi made the point that his country was seeking the World Cup to promote a wholesome, friendly image to the world, and that would be endangered if they had sought votes corruptly:

'Even if we had wanted to do anything improper, which we did not, we could not risk it because if it ever came out, the reputation of our whole country would be in tatters, the absolute opposite of what we are trying to achieve,' he said.

I was surprised, then, when Judge Eckert's summary of Garcia's report was published three years later, in November 2014, that it cited a 'whistleblower' who had repeated stories to Garcia about the Qatar bid. Eckert said that Garcia had had 'serious concerns about the individual's credibility' because 'it' – an attempt to maintain the whistleblower's anonymity by not disclosing her gender – had previously retracted the allegations in a sworn statement. Eckert said Garcia had not relied on any information from her because her journals could not corroborate her story, and that the findings 'demonstrate the difficulty to establish reliable evidence, independent of the public opinion [sic]'.

The coy non-use of her name and gender worked for precisely nobody, and in the media everybody knew this whistleblower was Almajid, as she confirmed herself. She was furious with Eckert for referring to her, and for Garcia for allowing that to happen, when, she said, her confidentiality had been guaranteed. Eckert did the same with Bonita Mersiades in relation to her information about the Australia bid on which she worked, referred to 'a whistleblower', then questioned her credibility. It remains inexplicable why he went out of his way to do that; as Almajid said herself in a seething complaint to Fifa, Garcia was said to have talked to more than seventy witnesses anonymously, yet only she and Mersiades were singled out and dismissed. Fifa's ethics committee said it would not hold an investigation into that, and there has been no explanation as to why these two women, who helped Garcia, were publicly outed and undermined in this way.

Yet it was surprising to me that Almajid, having insisted in 2011 that her original story had been false and she was put under no pressure to retract, had gone to Garcia and, presumably, repeated the original allegations. So I talked to her again, to find out what had happened. Almajid now says that in 2011, after Blatter said that she would be coming to Zurich to tell her story to Fifa, the bid did threaten her with legal action, that it would invoke a confidentiality clause in her contract, which carried a $1m potential penalty for a breach. She told me she had never intended to be a public whistleblower in the first place, that she talked to the *Sunday Times* off the record and did not know they would then write to Whittingdale's committee, or that it would publish the claims. She says she did not even know parliamentary privilege existed until she saw the committee able to freely publish that story of hers.

Almajid told me she became scared of the situation she had found herself in, and felt vulnerable, so agreed to sign a retraction and go public with it. She also maintains that, contrary to what she said at the time, the Qatar 2022 bid had promised her something in return: to give her a commitment that they would not take a lawsuit out against her in the future.

'I felt terrified,' she told me. 'I have two kids, one is disabled; I was facing legal action and the loss of my income too. I agreed to sign that affidavit, and they promised to release me from legal action. But they never kept their side of the bargain.'

Al-Khater told me in response that the Qatar bid, now the supreme committee, did not threaten to sue her. He said that they have checked their records, and there are no confidentiality clauses in their employment contracts which carry a $1m penalty for a breach. Al-Khater has always said that Almajid contacted the bid committee herself, feeling that she was in over her head. He also denied having promised her that if she retracted they would provide a firm commitment releasing her from legal action. However, he did acknowledge that she asked for it, and that it was discussed, but then they never provided it.

'Although we initially discussed the possibility of providing her with assurances that we would not take legal action against her, we never agreed to do so,' Al-Khater said.

Almajid insists it had been promised, and says she felt betrayed immediately after swearing the affidavit, when she then did not receive a written commitment in return. Throughout this process, she says that while the Qataris had high-profile and expensive London lawyers, she had nobody advising her. Almajid began to demand the written commitment from them and to complain vehemently when they did not provide it. Finally, on 21 October 2011, she was sent a legal letter – but it threatened to take action against her if she continued to contact them.

The lawyers' letter said that the bid committee had never 'formally agreed' to give her an assurance of no future legal action against her, and accused her of being 'threatening and disturbing' in her communications with Al Thawadi and Al-Khater, when she had been repeatedly asking for the commitment. The lawyers said there was no 'wish' to bring a claim against her over the 'completely false' accusations she had made, but that if she made any further allegations to the media or other third party, or tried to communicate directly with any bid members, that would be different.

'In either such eventuality, legal action in respect of your past conduct as well as in respect of any further conduct you may have undertaken of concern to the Bid Committee and the Supreme Committee [organising the World Cup] would be very likely,' it said.

When Garcia began his investigation, Almajid still had no commitment from the bid to release her from legal action; in fact she faced this threat. Weeks after receiving it, in December 2011, she decided to talk to Garcia, in confidence, to tell him that in fact the story had been true and she stood by it.

'It was fifty-fifty if he would believe me or not; I accept that, it is my word against other people's,' she says. 'But I was promised complete anonymity, and I didn't get that.'

However, despite being a reluctant whistleblower, she maintains the story is true, except that what happened in Angola was more subtle than a story of straightforward bribery, which was the impression that came out in parliament. Almajid says the perception that cash bribes were offered to the three CAF voters is not correct. In fact, she says, there was a discussion about football development in the voting members' countries, an assurance that Qatar would like to make a contribution, and no explicit connection was made between such contributions and a request by Qatar for their vote.

They were all in Angola for the January 2010 CAF congress, which the Qatar 2022 bid had sponsored for $1.8m, in return for exclusive access to CAF, its executive committee representatives, and fifty-four federations, for the duration of the event. The bid team deny completely that any such meetings with the executive committee representatives took place at all, and that they made any offers for votes, whether linked to development or otherwise. They say they used the time to make their professionally produced pitch for a World Cup in Qatar, particularly emphasising it was an opportunity to have the tournament in the Middle East, in an Arab country for the first time. Almajid herself acknowledges that people in Angola were very supportive of that idea:

'Very many of the African journalists I was talking to were saying they agreed, that they had the World Cup in Africa in 2010, and it was time to have it in the Middle East,' she recalls.

One of her roles there, she said, was to provide reassurance that Qatar was not behaving detrimentally to African football via its 'Aspire' academy programme, which had been accused of trawling for talented African players and taking them back to Qatar.

There has been a culture at Fifa – for years, decades – of FAs in Africa and other poorer parts of the world asking for development funds, often legitimately, as they have always lacked anything like the resources of the wealthier nations. Yet the Qatar 2022 bid's position is that they paid $1.8m to secure days of exclusive access, when they wanted the votes of CAF's executive committee representatives, and they never discussed what their World Cup could do for development.

In the summer of 2014, just before the World Cup in Brazil was about to kick off, the *Sunday Times* made a huge splash with more stories, which it claimed showed 'how Qatar bought the World Cup'. It was almost entirely based on emails from Mohamed bin Hammam while he was the Asian Football Confederation president before, during and through the bid; the newspaper had been given leaked access to the whole AFC database. The emails and other internal AFC information had in fact substantially been made public already; they were what PWC had been given access to and reported on in 2012. The *Sunday Times* published more details of bin Hammam's regime of largesse – principally paying and entertaining in Doha the presidents and senior officials mostly of small African FAs, who had usually requested help with football facilities or resources. None of those people whom he paid had a vote on the executive committee for the World Cup host, and, despite the huge impact the *Sunday Times* coverage made, there was a general scepticism in football whether this did reveal a campaign to buy World Cup votes. Rather, it was felt to expose a culture of beneficence, and influence-buying, by which bin Hammam buttressed his personal stature in football and laid the foundations for his bid to become president.

Bin Hammam was, though, found to have paid two executive committee members who did have votes. One was Warner, but this was in July 2011, seven months after the vote, appearing to relate to bin Hammam's halted presidential bid and the pair's efforts to salvage their careers and reputations after the Trinidad scandals. The other direct payment was $262,500 to cover Reynald Temarii's legal costs, so that he could appeal his suspension from the executive committee after the *Sunday Times* 2010 undercover sting. That did directly help Qatar with the vote for the 2022 World Cup host; Temarii being able to appeal meant that he was not replaced by his deputy, David Chung, who was mandated to vote for Australia.

Al Thawadi and the Qatar bid always argued in the face of this next onslaught that it was naïve to believe that all bin Hammam's activities related to the World Cup bid, from which they said he had actually been semi-detached for a long time. He clearly had major ambitions of his own and was steadily building up his prospects for a presidential campaign. When Qatar first decided to bid for the World Cup, bin Hammam is said, not only by Al Thawadi, to have been sceptical, even worried that it could damage his own efforts and lobbying within the entitled world of Fifa. Al Thawadi said they had to work hard to convince bin Hammam, and that he only came round to properly supporting Qatar's bid in 2010, when he saw it gaining momentum.

'He had responsibilities with the AFC; there were three other bids from his confederation [Australia, Japan and South Korea] and his presidential campaign still out there,' Al Thawadi said. 'Don't assume that because we had the AFC president we didn't face difficulties. Mohamed bin Hammam went through significant efforts to show there was no favouritism to Qatar.'

The persistent rumours of a voting pact between the Spanish and Latin American executive committee members to vote for Qatar, and the Asian representatives to vote in return for Spain's bid, had been rejected by a Fifa investigation, but were reignited by Ricardo Teixeira in June 2015. He told the Brazilian website Terra:

'Spain needed votes [for 2018]. They had the three from South America, their own and maybe one more from Europe, but it wasn't enough. So we had a meeting. Me, Villar [the president of the Spain FA, Ángel María Villar Llona] and [Julio] Grondona [of the Argentina FA] got some votes from Asia thanks to Qatar. And what was the deal? Qatar would vote for us for 2018 and would, in exchange, receive our support for 2022.'

Although this alleged pact did not appear to figure in any of the emails in the whole AFC database to which the *Sunday Times* had access, it seems inconceivable if it did happen, that bin Hammam was not involved with it. It appears to be against the Fifa rules forbidding collusion between bids, but outrage about any alleged collusion should perhaps be tempered by the realisation that others did it. England's FA, which under the later chairmanship of Greg Dyke was relentlessly critical of Qatar's bid, nevertheless admitted that its own executive committee member, Geoff Thompson, believed he had a pact with Chung Mong-joon of Korea. England's 2018 bid were actually quite vocal about being upset when they discovered Chung had not kept to it.

The summary of Garcia's report published by Eckert in November 2014 crushed those hoping for Qatar to be 'stripped' of the World Cup, and for a re-vote, after the allegations. Eckert, publicly dismissing Almajid's credibility, did not uphold her story of development funds being offered in Angola. While he said the Qatari sponsorship of the 2010 CAF congress 'created a negative impression' because the total cost was unclear, such exclusive deals were, remarkably, not against the rules. He said Garcia's report found that the Qatar bid had 'pulled [the Aspire Academy] into the orbit of the bid in significant ways', but did not judge it to affect the 'integrity' of the bidding process. He also said that Garcia's report had highlighted the conduct of two people acting as advisers to the Qatar bid for 'questionable conduct', and that the relationship between them and the bid was 'characterised by a significant lack of transparency'. However, as they did not hold official positions, Eckert said it was difficult to bind them to the rules and sanction them, and, without elaborating, he dismissed this as an issue.

Eckert also addressed a friendly match played between Brazil and Argentina in Doha on 17 November 2010, two weeks before the Zurich vote, which some speculated to have been a sweetener for Grondona and Teixeira. Eckert found, however, that the money paid to each country's FA to bring the teams over to play the match was not excessive, but 'comparable to fees paid for other matches featuring similarly elite teams'. There were concerns over the money, but they were not focusing on the Qatar bid itself, rather on what happened to the $2m legitimately paid to Argentina, and whether it all went to the Argentina FA. The Swiss attorney general, following Fifa's reference to him of the issues raised by Garcia, did conduct an investigation, focusing not on Qatar, but on two unnamed companies in Buenos Aires.

On bin Hammam, Eckert found that the payment to Warner was not related to the World Cup vote, but to the Trinidad scandal. It was, he stated, 'in connection with Mr Warner's decision to resign from Fifa and refuse to cooperate in the proceedings against Mr bin Hammam'.

Eckert agreed with the view that the payments to small African FAs and presidents did not, as the *Sunday Times* had alleged, show a plot to buy the World Cup for Qatar, because those recipients did not have a vote on the World Cup hosts. Eckert did note that the payments were 'improper', saying it was more likely they were buying votes for the presidency, and had been dealt with during the previous investigation into bin Hammam, after which the Qatari was banned from football for life.

'The evidence before [Garcia's arm of the ethics committee] strongly suggests that Mr bin Hammam paid CAF officials to influence their votes in the June 2011 election for Fifa president where he was a candidate,' Eckert concluded.

Eckert did find that the payment of Temarii's legal costs did influence the vote, but decided that, as it was only one, it did not make a 'significant' difference to the bidding process.

The German judge accepted without criticism Russia's explanation about its destroyed computers, with no surviving emails or documents, and he concluded that, on 'the evidence available', there was nothing 'sufficient to support any findings of misconduct by the Russia 2018 bid team'.

It is still not known if Garcia's remarkable, outspoken objections to Eckert's summary of his report were related to the findings on Qatar, or if Garcia expressed his concerns about any bid more strongly. Dyke complained the Eckert report was a whitewash about Qatar, produced for political reasons, and exaggerated the issues with the English bid. However, that outraged response meant that the FA never engaged publicly with the genuine criticisms made. Again, as with Qatar, the Garcia and Eckert reports were produced following full cooperation by England's 2018 bid, whose officials felt they had done nothing wrong. It did highlight various concerns, principally that England's bid had linked offers of development to votes, and that they had sought to 'curry favour' with Jack Warner.

Garcia, Eckert reported, had concluded that Warner 'had considerable influence', that he 'sought to exploit the perception of his power to control "blocks of votes" within the Fifa executive committee,' and that he:

'Repeatedly used that power to exact personal benefits … Mr Warner's conduct demonstrated an expectation that bidding teams would react favourably and seek to curry favour with a voting member of the Fifa executive committee. According to the [Garcia] report, England 2018's response showed a willingness, time and again, to meet such expectation, thereby damaging the image of Fifa and the bidding process.'

England, the Eckert summary reported, had sponsored the CFU gala dinner at its congress in Trinidad in 2010, 'once again in an effort to curry favour with Jack Warner', paying the $55,000, which Warner had suggested. The England 2018 bid had also given 'substantial assistance' to a training camp for the U20 Trinidad and Tobago team in England in 2009, and 'appeared willing' to cater to Warner's demands for 'favours and benefits' for the club he owned, the 'Joe Public Football Club'. The England bid had also helped 'a person of interest to Warner', understood to be the son of a friend of his, to find work in football in England; the FA apparently helped him to gain an internship at a senior professional Football League club.

Eckert said Garcia had found that the England 2018 bid had also linked an agreement with Temarii for the FA to do development work in Oceania, to his potential vote for England to host the World Cup. Eckert's report said that the English FA's proposed deal:

'Raised the appearance of Mr Temarii using his position in Fifa and the upcoming 2 December 2010 vote in order to achieve a most favourable result for the OFC, and of England 2018 granting Mr Temarii (or the OFC, respectively [sic]) considerably preferential treatment in terms of allocating football development funds.'

The judge also referred to the Dingemans report, which Jérôme Valcke had told us in 2011 showed all the executive committee to have been 'completely clean'. In fact, Eckert said Garcia had found that three of the four executive committee members mentioned had 'made improper requests' to the England bid – and 'with regard to at least two of these committee members, England 2018 accommodated, or at least attempted to satisfy, the improper requests'.

The England bid appears to have stopped short of bribery, which remains unproven in relation to any of the 2018 or 2022 bids. However, they look to have found themselves with a £21m budget and high expectations, including from the British government, of bringing the World Cup to England, where there is a sense of entitlement in football. The voting system of the executive committee was far from an objective assessment based on Mayne-Nicholls' reports or openly stated considerations. Instead, it required bidding countries to win the votes of twenty-four, then twenty-two men, of unpredictable opinions and wants, several of them now known to have been corrupt. The England 2018 bid did want Warner's vote, and Temarii's, and did what they could to get them. Sources in the England bid say they always tried to do so within the rules, which were grey, particularly when it came to development projects, and that they checked ideas in advance with Jérôme Valcke. Overall, Eckert said of England's bid, there were 'certain indications of potentially problematic conduct of specific individuals'. At the time of writing, no ethics committee or other proceedings have been brought against any of them.

The Spain and Portugal bid for 2018, accused of colluding with Qatar in a pact of votes, appeared not to have cooperated at all with Garcia. Their bid was not included in Eckert's summary and the Spain FA president, Ángel María Villar Llona, was later given a warning and fined 25,000 CHF, apparently for not cooperating. The ethics committee stated that he had not behaved 'in accordance with the general rules of conduct applicable to football officials in the context of the investigations'.

The Korea bid had been led by the Fifa executive committee member Chung Mong-joon, a seriously wealthy member of the family which owned the Hyundai car and industrial manufacturing company, and a politician in his home country. Eckert said the Garcia investigation had found that Chung had written to Fifa executive committee members in late 2010 about a proposal to establish a $777m football development fund for confederations and FAs, to run from 2011 to the World Cup in 2022. The report said this proposed 'global football fund' was directly linked to the Korea 2022 World Cup bid, and therefore that it 'created at least the appearance of a conflict or an offer of benefits to Fifa executive committee members in an effort to influence their votes'.

Following an ethics committee investigation into the issues raised by the Garcia report, Chung Mong-joon was banned from football for six years after, the announcement said, being found guilty of infringing several rules in the code of conduct. On appeal, that was reduced to five years. Chung raged against it, calling it a political process, because he, like Mayne-Nicholls, had been considering standing for election as the president. But at the time of writing the ban still stands. I did contact Chung to ask for an interview in the preparation for this book, but after initially making contact, his team did not respond.

Then there was Australia's bid to host the 2022 World Cup, the rival to Qatar's, with its Fifa insider consultants close to Franz Beckenbauer. Bonita Mersiades, the former head of communications who did turn into a whistleblower, raising her concerns publicly, was also outspokenly critical of the Australia bid's payment of development money to regions with voting executive committee members. The FFA bid contributed to the Oceania Football Confederation when Temarii was the president, stated in the bid's final report to have been Aus$500,000; to the AFC's 'Vision Asia' development programme when bin Hammam was the president, Aus$1.25m, and paid Aus$500,000 to Jack Warner at Concacaf. That latter donation was intended to be for the upgrade of the stadium at Warner's Dr João Havelange Centre of Excellence in Trinidad. Warner had asked the FFA for $4m, and they agreed to pay $500,000 initially to fund a feasibility study. The bid also donated LapDesk computers to FAs throughout Africa, at a cost of Aus$90,000. These payments were part of much bigger contributions made in Oceania and to Vision Asia, including with Australian overseas aid money.

The April 2013 report into Warner's activities by the Concacaf integrity committee found that the FFA paid the $500,000 (US$462,500) by cheque made out to Concacaf, which was deposited at Republic National Bank in Trinidad, in which Warner also had personal money. The $462,500 appeared nowhere in Concacaf's accounting records and the committee could not identify any trace of the money. It concluded that Warner defrauded the FFA and kept the stadium donation for himself.

Mersiades, who has become a campaigner for wider reform of Fifa following her experiences working on the Australia bid, a founder member of the group #NewFifaNow, argues that the FFA bid was wrong to contribute to those confederations whose presidents wielded votes in the executive committee.

'The culture of Fifa was that there were expectations of favours sought and gained,' she told me. 'And while the guidelines warned bidders against seeking an "advantage", there was also an implicit understanding that potential host countries should be active in "development". Of course, "development" was targeted at the voters and their interests.'

Eckert's summary of the Garcia report is at its most forthright, of all the bids, not about Qatar, but when dealing with these payments by the Australia 2022 bid to the confederations. Eckert said Garcia had noted 'potentially problematic connections between financial and other support for "football development and the bidding process"'. Noting Temarii's requests for financial support, Eckert said: 'Australia's acquiescence helped create the appearance that benefits were conferred in exchange for a vote, thus undermining the integrity of the bidding process.'

Eckert noted the payment to Warner, too, and also said there were 'indications' that the FFA bid had 'attempted to direct funds the Australian government had set aside for existing development projects in Africa towards initiatives in countries with ties to Fifa executive committee members, with the intention to advance its bid'.

Eckert said the Garcia report found the FFA 'well aware of the ramifications such a pattern of conduct might imply'. But they went ahead anyway, to provide financial support 'under the title "(football) development projects" preferably in areas home to Fifa executive committee members'.

Eckert did say that according to the Garcia report on Australia: 'There are certain indications of potentially problematic conduct of specific individuals in the light of relevant Fifa ethics rules' and 'potentially problematic facts and circumstances'. He went close to calling for an ethics committee investigation into these issues, saying that he:

'Trusts that the Investigatory Chamber will take appropriate steps if it deems such measures appropriate and feasible ... and underlines that the Investigatory Chamber has full independence and discretion with regard to the initiation of proceedings against specific individuals.'

At the time of writing there has not been an ethics committee investigation announced into the Australia bid, however, or any action in relation to it.

Frank Lowy argued that the money for development was legitimate, demonstrated a commitment to international football and was the same approach used to win the Australia bid for the 2000 Olympics and for Australia to win a seat on the UN Security Council. It was, he said, 'consistent with what every other bidding nation was doing'. Of the Concacaf money, Lowy said Warner had 'stolen' it and the FFA had asked for it back, and had been advised by Fifa to wait until all inquiries were complete. Without expanding, Lowy claimed that Australia ran a clean bid, but it had not been 'a level playing field and therefore we didn't win it'.

Hence, following this clearance three years after I met him in Doha, Hassan Al Thawadi would feel vindicated, and he has since argued again that there was anti-Arab prejudice in the persistent accusations that Qatar could not have won the vote cleanly, with no similar focus on any other country.

Blatter himself, after his own suspension for the 2m CHF payment to Michel Platini, began to reveal his feelings about the votes for Russia and Qatar. In October 2015, he said that the executive committee had already agreed, before the vote, to share the next two World Cups with the world's 'two biggest political powers', Russia, then the USA. He bitterly regretted that the Qataris gazumped the USA, sending the World Cup to the Gulf in the summer and causing a fundamental credibility crisis for Fifa. But Blatter did not put the blame on still thin and unproven allegations of vote-buying. Instead, pointing to Platini switching his vote from the USA to Qatar after the lunch with Sarkozy, Blatter said World Cup votes were not 'bought', the real influence was geo-politics, that World Cups went 'where the higher political influences are'. He said that four European votes were lost from the USA to Qatar after Platini changed his mind. Otherwise, regardless of all the stories about how Qatar won other votes, in Africa, South America or elsewhere, the USA would have had a majority. Talking of his plan to have Russia host the tournament in 2018, then the USA in 2022, Blatter said:

'Everything was good until the moment when Sarkozy came in a meeting with the crown prince of Qatar, who is now the ruler of Qatar. And at a lunch afterwards with Mr Platini he said it would be good to go to Qatar. And this has changed all [the] pattern.

'If you put the four votes, it would have been twelve to ten [for the USA].' Arguing again that this had prompted the US authorities' investigation of Fifa, he said: 'If the USA was given the World Cup, we would only speak about the wonderful World Cup 2018 in Russia, and we would not speak about any problems at Fifa.'

One of the European executive committee members thought to have voted for Qatar, Marios Lefkaritis of Cyprus, chairman of the Uefa finance committee and a key ally of Platini, was reported afterwards to have sold some land to the Qatar Investment Authority for €32m. He has strongly denied any suggestion that it had anything to do with the World Cup vote. I did seek an interview with him for this book via the Cyprus FA, as recommended by Fifa, but I did not hear back.

For a full assessment of how Qatar claimed the World Cup, the eyes do need to be lifted from the Eckert summary of Garcia's efforts at unravelling the claustrophobic rumour mill within the corridors of Fifa. The global economic and political realities have to be considered, as well as their effect on football. According to the CIA's *World Factbook*, by 2007 Qatar had the world's highest income per head of population. In 2015, this figure was put at $132,100, when in total the tiny country, luxuriating in natural gas and some oil reserves, had $320bn GDP. Qatar was estimated to have $49bn directly invested overseas by the end of December 2015. The strategy for developing the country by 2030 includes, like Abu Dhabi's, being associated with cultural and sporting prestige events, tourism and education. After the new Emir took over from his father in 1995, and particularly into the 2000s, Qatar began seriously investing in sport, including the hosting of events. Speaking at the Institute of Foreign Affairs in London in May 2016, when he again suggested there was some racism in the constant accusations of corruption, Al Thawadi accepted there was 'an element of soft power' in his country's determined bid to host the World Cup.

While the Emir was putting his energy into wanting the World Cup for Qatar, for the prestige, exposure and power, and perhaps for the fun it could be, too, his country was reported to have concluded gas and pipeline deals with Argentina, Paraguay and Thailand. In England, while Greg Dyke repeatedly cast suspicion on the Qatar World Cup bid, the Gulf statelet was buying up some of the most coveted properties in London, including the Shard and Harrods. The government and trade missions were constantly seeking to interest the Qataris in buying more British assets and products, in a country which now relies economically on investment from overseas.

In football, there was in Europe a startling disconnect between the constant allegations of corruption about how Qatar won the World Cup bid, and the acceptance, hunger even, for Qatari and Gulf money in club football. Barcelona, whose legendary former player and coach Pep Guardiola had been a paid ambassador for the Qatari bid, ceded more than 100 years without commercial sponsorship on their shirts to sell it in 2013 to Qatar Airways, reported to be paying the club €96m over three years. PSG were one of the biggest club spenders in the world, and always in the Champions League group stage. BeIN were buying TV rights from dozens of countries besides France, including from the English FA, to broadcast England matches and the FA Cup in the Middle East and North Africa. The UAE, a rival to Qatar politically and religiously, also has huge amounts of its money in European club football: Abu Dhabi's Sheikh Mansour owns Manchester City, where he has spent around £1.2bn, and Dubai's state airline, Emirates, sponsors Real Madrid, Arsenal, AC Milan and PSG.

Europe, in recession and on its economic knees, was seeking cash in all areas, and Qatar had it. While Al Thawadi was still engaged in the diplomatic efforts to assuage the accusations about his country's ethics, Western construction companies were queueing for some of the $4bn to $5bn budget reported to be for building the stadiums alone, and $150bn for Qatar's general infrastructure projects. US masterplanners AECOM, Danish engineers Ramboll and British architects Pattern were announced in April 2015 as the contractors to build the 40,000-seat Al Rayyan Stadium. The main Al Wakrah Stadium has been designed by Zaha Hadid architects, of London. Other firms working on World Cup infrastructure projects include British architects Foster + Partners; Populous, largely US-based stadium designers; Besix, a major Belgian construction company; and the Italian contractors Salini Impregilo. When it comes to wanting to earn from the work of building a World Cup, there appears to be little British or European sniffiness about Qatar.

At the time of writing, the Swiss attorney general says he is still investigating the 2018 and 2022 bidding process. That followed the criminal complaint made by Fifa itself after Eckert's summary of Garcia's report, so does not appear to have Qatar in its sights. The US authorities have said they are also investigating, but have not so far made any accusations of wrongdoing by any bid.

Since the astonishing majority decision on 2 December 2010, seven members of that twenty-two-man Fifa executive committee have been charged or accused by the US authorities of criminal wrongdoing; another, Franz Beckenbauer, is under criminal investigation in Switzerland and Germany over the allegations relating to

Germany's 2006 World Cup bid. Six more members, including Blatter and Platini, have been sanctioned by Fifa's own ethics committee. So fourteen out of those twenty-two, the most senior administrators in world football, have since had a criminal or ethics procedure against them. Yet the decisions a majority of them took, after their mostly lazy and dismal approach to a flawed and wastefully expensive bidding process, to send the 2018 World Cup to Putin's Russia, and the 2022 tournament to the Emir's Qatar, still stand. No vote-buying allegations have been proven sufficient for a re-vote, the contracts with Fifa are signed, the Western companies are swarming in for the work, the immigrant labourers are being recruited, and a multi-billion dollar chain of football stadiums is taking shape in Qatar.

CHAPTER 20

The Boss

Sepp Blatter agreed to see me in Zurich in the summer of 2016, six months after he was banned – summarily expelled – from football's world governing body, whose inner workings and culture he had mastered over forty years. Looking at the long course of his time at Fifa, and talking to people about him and the organisation, I had seen that there was another dimension to Blatter and Fifa itself than the arch villains of popular caricature. That photograph of him marooned in a blizzard of dollars, thrown as a stunt by the English comedian Simon Brodkin, could now be endlessly reproduced as the defining image of his tenure, but I can recognise that his record is more complex. He had arrived at the old House of Fifa in 1975, at the start of the watershed João Havelange presidency, and become president twenty-four years later, when fistfuls of dollars were always going to rain on football. His first job had been to orchestrate Havelange's promised development programme, and, for all the scandals and criticisms, nobody can credibly deny that over his four decades there had been a major concrete legacy of global improvement. So far, through a ferocious and complete investigation of all Fifa's books, he was not accused, as he had maintained he would not be, of taking any money corruptly, while all around him football's chiefs were helping themselves to it. He was accused more persuasively of having known it was going on but done nothing to address it for many years, of keeping the crooks on the executive committee happy, and the cash flowing to the national FAs, to maintain his prime purpose: his own position and longevity as the head of Fifa. Personally, there seemed to be more to him as well, than the consiglieri-turned-don portrayal of him at the head of the Fifa family. People who knew him said that along with his wiles, ambition and ruthlessness were charm and a sense of humour, and that he did really love football.

Blatter and his press adviser, Thomas Renggli, had named a place we could talk and have lunch: Restaurant Sonnenberg, they said, at Hitzigweg 15. In the flurry of preparing, and noting down the long list of allegations I needed to put to Blatter, from his 'clumsy' handling of the ISL payment to Havelange, the alleged vote-buying in 1998, to the Platini payment and the general perception that he knowingly presided over endemic corruption, I didn't quite register the significance of the location. It was hot in Zurich, and I took a tram up the hill from Central, next to a couple of the private banks which stand impassive on every corner. The restaurant was a steep walk up from the tram stop, through a suburb of grand old Swiss-style houses with ample gardens, well settled, comfortable and quiet.

The restaurant staff knew I was meeting Mr Blatter there; we were expected. I was early, and they sat me on the terrace outside, looking down to the lovely lake and the beautifully appointed city around it, just so under a blue sky. There was a flag at the front of the restaurant I couldn't quite make out over the parasols, then I moved and saw it properly. Here, flying high at the top of the hill, dominant above Zurich, it was a Fifa flag, bearing its motto: 'For the game; For the world'. A smiling young waitress in the uniform of polo shirt, tracksuit and trainers brought me some water. It took me a while to click that the shirt had the Fifa logo on it, the interior was Fifa themed, and to realise this must be Fifa's own restaurant. This was Hitzigweg, of course, and next door, looking very 1970s in modernist lines, was the old Fifa House, where Sepp Blatter had arrived as a kipper-tied thruster, and made his considerable way in the world. After his ban, this was where he still chose to meet, at the place where he was king, before the fall.

He arrived a little late, driven up with Renggli in the back of a black Mercedes, to emerge and be greeted respectfully by the restaurant staff. He didn't look too great. Better than at that alarming press conference the day after his ban, a bit of colour in his cheeks, but shrunken, almost frail. He had let the shaving go, and his beard was white but very thin, so you could see his chin through it. The plaster from his cheek was gone, but the doctors had removed another growth from his nose and covered it with some skin from his ear, he would tell me; the graft looked like a fleshy plaster across his nose. He was wearing a waistcoat, over a blue-and-white striped shirt, on which you could just see, when he sat down, his initials: JSB. He looked his age, eighty; like an old granddad who had clearly been a twinkly-eyed rascal in his prime, currently recuperating from some troublesome ailments.

When we began to talk, he told me immediately, in English with that famous Swiss accent of his, in a tremulous voice, that it was true: under the pressure of the arrests and the ethics charge against him, he had suffered a breakdown.

'I had this collapse on 1 November and this was at the cemetery,' he said. 'The Catholics, we always go to the cemetery to pay honour to our parents, all the families in the same grave, and I was there, I felt very bad at that time. They brought me immediately back to Zurich in a clinic; they have realised that my immune system has collapsed.'

When I asked him about the arrests staged at the Baur au Lac, devastating the week of his fifth coronation as president, and whether he was bitter at the US attorney general Loretta Lynch's description of Fifa as a racketeering investigation, he replied: 'I was not bitter, I was shocked. And I have never recuperated about the shock.'

Now, he said, he was back up and battling; appealing to the Court of Arbitration for Sport against his ethics committee ban, defending his record to the Swiss investigators. He was that day off to prepare for a meeting with Fifa's lawyers about the alleged $10m bribe to Warner from South Africa. He had time on his hands now, though, for the first time in his life, and we would have three hours or so, with lunch in the middle. In that time, he would indeed be quite funny at times, sharp, scathing of some who had crossed him, like Michel Zen-Ruffinen, and tell me he had done nothing wrong. He would decry all his accusers, blame the investigations on the Qatar vote which he had not wanted, and on England and the USA being 'bad losers'; and denounce the very principle of whistleblowers. It would become clear to me as I listened, and when I thought about it afterwards, that his whole perspective, from commanding this remarkable, historic organisation for the promotion of football across the globe, was very often narrowed to its power political dynamics, and how he navigated them to remain on top.

He could not understand why the USA had gone for him, he said, when he had supported their bid to host the 2022 World Cup. Then he confirmed what had so often been speculated, that this plan was part of his ultimate aspiration, described as a fixation by some, to claim a Nobel prize at the end of his career, to be thereby recognised to have made a major contribution to world peace. Fifa began to work formally with the Nobel Peace Centre in 2014, agreeing a contract to roll out a 'Handshake for Peace' programme at the World Cup in Brazil.

'My idea then – and I had already spoken about it with high-level politicians,' Blatter explained, 'could we have Russia and USA in the World Cup. It would be good for these two countries, these powerhouses; they don't like each other – then with football they can make a handshake for peace. And this was the missionary Blatter was thinking about that.'

I asked him if it was true, then, that he wanted a Nobel peace prize, and he replied with all due modesty that it was not for him personally, but for Fifa, for the game:

'I have never – and this is even registered – we had meetings with the Nobel prize organisation, I was there, and what I was asking, really asking, was for the Nobel prize: for football, not for a man. It is the movement, for Fifa, what Fifa has done in the world, not for a man.'

Discussing Blatter's fall, one senior figure at Fifa observed to me that it was 'the greatest anti-climax possible'. There he had been at seventy-nine; still always conscious of his provincial beginnings, flourished and risen in a complex, cut-throat and intensely public arena, made it to the very top, prime ministers and presidents bent the knee to him, he survived every challenge. And he thought he was about to top it all by clasping his hands on the Nobel prize, when it was all snatched away, imploded in disgrace and he was out. The Nobel Peace Centre in Oslo, Norway, told me they cancelled the contract with Fifa in June 2015, shortly after the indictments.

On the terrace at the restaurant, the humid Zurich weather broke; there was a thunderstorm and we moved inside. Blatter hailed some people he knew at other tables – one, Renggli told me, was a very prominent banker in Zurich – and I sensed a slight discomfort in their parties as they stood and smiled and shook hands with him, now the tarnished former president, trailing scandal. He was quite cheery, flirted a little with the waitress, true to his reputation as an old-style charmer with the ladies, and we ordered. She recommended the côte de boeuf, and when it arrived, rare, it was a tremendous joint of meat, served with sauté potatoes and mushrooms, porcini, of deep flavour. Blatter ordered some white wine, and we carried on talking about the events of Fifa.

His chippiness about his provincial roots was clear after all these years, a need to show he had proved himself; even at eighty, he referred to being from an Alpine region considered a backwater. He believes some of his troubles stemmed from jealousy in his country:

'In Switzerland, you should never be too successful otherwise they don't like that,' he said. 'Especially in the German part of Switzerland [where Zurich is]. It is envy and jealousy, because we are in a paradise in Switzerland, if somebody is a little bit higher or gets a bit more attention.

'And I am from this part of Switzerland, the Valais, where they think we are still people from the mountains, mountaineers, and we are behind the moon,' he said, sitting in the smart restaurant in Zurich with the Fifa flag at the front. 'I have a better image in most of the countries of the world than here.'

It was instructive, when I asked him about his career and the early days, that the details he gave, for which he still had icy clarity, were almost all about the politics, as he worked his way up the network of sports administration bodies housed in Switzerland. After his first jobs in hotels and the Valais tourist office, then military service, he had two years as the secretary of the Swiss ice hockey federation. He described it as a 'terrible time'. That was because of the politics: three members of the central committee had gone for his job, he recalled of so long ago, and they had 'boycotted' him instead of working together. He went to the Swiss Olympic Committee, which was too much administration, then to become head of marketing at Longines, 'because the former boss had a problem with the director-general'. He told a long story about dealing with the watchmakers' union before the 1972 Olympic Games, and fixing the problem to everybody's satisfaction. He said that the president of Swiss Timing, Thomas Keller, who was also the president of FISA, the world governing body for rowing, had told him about the Fifa job in 1975, informing him: 'The new president at Fifa is looking for a man who knows football but who specifically could sell a development programme, because they have no money.'

Blatter told me one of his strategies for getting on in life, getting ahead of other people, and it was a little like the phrase from the Longfellow poem which Jack Warner had chosen as the title for his autobiography, reaching the heights by 'toiling upward in the night' while everybody else slept.

'I was a workaholic,' Blatter said. 'When I was in Zurich, I started at seven o'clock in the office; there was no need but it was a principle, and to be the last one who left the office. I liked this advance in the morning, waking up, listening to the news on the different radios, then in the office on the computer. So when people arrived in Fifa, they knew that I already had the knowledge of messages and information.

'And if you do that during so very many years, not only at Fifa, all my life; you have always a bit of an advantage of time, and also advantage of knowledge. This is important; this was my way.'

I invited him to talk about the record of development, the great progress around the world, whether he would argue this was his legacy. He said it was, and he told the story about meeting the Coca-Cola executives at the Parc des Princes, and going to Atlanta to close the deal. But he did not greatly enthuse about the development work itself, the houses of football they built all over the world, in some of the neediest and poorest of countries. He drifted back to the politics as if by reflex, referring to the involvement of Mohamed bin Hammam and Platini in the genesis of the GOAL project, then on to their support in the 1998 election.

'Bin Hammam was one of the supporters,' he said, 'but the biggest supporter I had in 1998 was Platini.'

On the vote-buying allegations of his first election in 1998, he flatly denied it, finally saying that nobody from his camp needed to pay anybody, because they had the votes pledged to them already. His European rivals had it wrong when they believed the night before that they had 110 votes – he did, he told me.

Now, Blatter blamed Platini, and the crucial votes from European executive committee members which Platini took away from the US, for, as Blatter saw it, the disastrous vote for Qatar. He, who knew Fifa and the executive committee best, argues that it is a distraction to look for bribery when it comes to the World Cup votes. His argument is that the confederation heads are accused of indulging in kickbacks on their own turf, when selling TV rights, but he did not believe such practices determined World Cup votes:

'The World Cups are not bought; they are influenced by political pressure,' he reflected. 'The brilliant French president Sarkozy changed everything. He asked Platini to look for the interests of France and vote with his colleagues. [Platini] informed me before, he told me three votes will change, but it was more, it was four.'

Blatter complained, seethed, that Platini should not have been influenced by his head of state, and he believed that had been Platini's only reason for changing his vote.

'Some weeks before that, he told me that we can't go to Qatar because everybody will say we [must] have been under pressure to go to Qatar – that we were paid, or pressurised. Then he comes with that ...'

I asked him how he had felt when he pulled the name Qatar out of the envelope.

'Look at the picture,' he replied, and grimaced. 'I haven't had a very smiling face.'

He is convinced that the US investigations began from then, and he railed at the Swiss authorities for cooperating so fully, at the unfairness of it all. He accepted that the American investigators appeared to have found major corruption, mentioning the kickbacks on the Copa America television deals with Traffic, but he argued that had nothing to do with Fifa itself, it involved the confederations, over which he had no control.

'So why the hell then should the Fifa president bear all the charges, the responsibility and the blame; how can he be the moralist to go into the conscience of these people?'

He singled out Jeff Webb, as many involved in Fifa do, as the most breathtaking scoundrel of all. Blatter recalled being at the publication of the Concacaf integrity report, which identified the alleged frauds of Chuck Blazer and Jack Warner, and that Webb presented himself as the president for a new era of fair play and respect.

'Jeffrey Webb was answering that [committee report]; he had tears coming down his face, saying: "I am humbled, I accept it; I promise I will do that."' Blatter, warming up, did a little impression of Webb, and mimed the weeping. He then gave a revealing insight into his regime of patronage, saying that after Webb became the Concacaf president, he put him in as the chair of the anti-racism committee. Webb asked for 'a better committee', Blatter said, so he 'gave him a committee'. Blatter said he promised Webb the development committee eventually, 'which is the big one, and you have privileges'.

Then, on that morning at the Baur au Lac: 'The first one arrested was him,' Blatter said. 'How can you be misled by that or by yourself to say this man is a correct man? I was already thinking that he could be tomorrow the president of Fifa, a good person, a strong man.'

Throughout the conversation, Blatter maintained that he did not know the people around that executive committee table, whose support he nurtured for so many years, were corrupt. He said that after the arrests he had thought he had been 'wrong to trust people', although he admitted that he was not surprised about some of them. Even then, talking about the compendious criminal charges against people with whom he worked so closely and was entrusted to run world football for so long, he diverted back to politics. When I asked about Nicolás Leoz, who took ISL bribes in the 1990s and is charged with having been the instigator of the corruption of Traffic in South America at the same time, Blatter instinctively recalled only that Leoz hadn't thought him the right candidate in 1998. Several of the long-serving executive committee members, he said, could not adjust to his move from being secretary general to president, from being at their service to being their boss; 'not directly, but you can feel it'.

Of Jack Warner, Blatter insisted he had not known or suspected him of wrongdoing either. Again, the point at which he said he stopped trusting him related to Blatter's own position when he was standing for the presidential election in 2011 and whether Warner was supporting him, rather than any of the alleged frauds:

'No, Jack Warner and his wife, both of them were schoolteachers, at the level of college, good educated people, and he was a good speaker also,' Blatter assured me. 'And I would say he was a pleasant guy in contact. All the pleasant guys from time to time they have a question mark – but I couldn't imagine the volume of problems he has created.'

I asked him about the handing out of the cash in Trinidad, which really generated the major US investigation, and Blatter's take on that was still electoral:

'At a certain time I stopped believing him, because he was saying that he did this special meeting there [for bin Hammam] but [said] it doesn't matter, [the Caribbean delegates] will all vote for you.'

Blatter said they did all vote for him anyway in the end, because the scandal had been uncovered and Warner had suddenly stepped down.

Asked about the alleged $10m bribe from South Africa to Warner, Blatter said that Thabo Mbeki had decided himself to have a legacy fund for the African diaspora, the Caribbean was the natural place for it, and Fifa did not pay the money itself, only deducted the $10m from the organising committee's budget. The idea had been a surprise to him, he said, and anyway the money was paid a long time after the vote, so was not connected to it. When I put to him that Chuck Blazer himself had told the US law enforcement authorities that it was a bribe, Blatter replied, quite quickly:

'I am not involved in this case. I have not even seen that [the money] has passed from Fifa.'

Asked about the ISL bribery, when he was shown the payment to Havelange, which Eckert said may have been only 'clumsy', Blatter pointed out that he had been cleared. He said he had not known Havelange, Teixeira and Leoz were being paid so much money.

'One amount came for Havelange and we sent it back the next day.'

Then he offered the longstanding explanation that, anyway, this was not a crime in Switzerland and then:

'At that time, it was so-called commissions – it only came in 2003 to forbid it. Not only was it permitted, you could deduct it from taxes. So come on ...'

He had an interesting way of dismissing Michel Zen-Ruffinen, and the litany of allegations made against him in 2002:

'Zen-Ruffinen? He is silly. He thinks he is a combination of ... James Bond and Don Juan, and he is the most intelligent man, best looking and so on. He's just a fool.'

He was not impressed with whistleblowers in general, even criticising Yuliya Stepanova, who had recently exposed the Russian state doping of athletes, the great scandal breaking over athletics.

'She wants to go to the Olympics, and now everybody says it is a shame she can't go because she is a whistleblower. Before long whistleblowers will be allowed to everything,' he sneered. 'Because if you are a whistleblower, it's not correct as well.'

I was quite shocked at that statement, and asked him to clarify it; was he saying that he thought whistleblowers were not correct?

'No,' he confirmed. 'At the school level, primary school, if you had somebody who was a whistleblower towards the instructor or the tutor, then ...' and he trailed off, as if it was obvious.

'Do you still think that about whistleblowers now?' I asked.

'Yes.'

'That they are like a snitch in school?'

'Yes, yes,' he said.

He was scathing about Blazer, and the US criminal investigation using him as an informer after his arrest: 'Blazer was at the Olympics as a representative of Fifa, and he was wired by the FBI. So, what is such a country trying to give us lessons in how to honestly do a job?'

'Do you think that is deceitful?' I asked him.

'How can you do that? [Blazer] accepted because it was his escape, but it is incredible.'

Of himself, he believed that the authorities, which were turning over every last document of his forty years at Fifa, would find nothing to incriminate him. He was still indignant and disbelieving that he had lost the position he worked so hard for, over that payment to Platini. He argued there was nothing wrong with the 2m CHF payment except a failure to note their oral agreement down at first. It had nothing to do with the presidential election of 2011; Platini had already said he was staying at Uefa, and the ethics committee found it was not corruption or bribery. He disagreed even that it was a conflict of interest at the time. He said Platini told them Fifa still owed him money, he had presented an invoice to Markus Kattner, Blatter had agreed they did, and they paid him through the books. He argued there was a pressure to get him:

'The day the media started to condemn the Fifa president to say he is a corrupted man. The payment to Platini was a payment which was due to an oral agreement. There is nothing wrong there. If I am using my prerogative as president of Fifa to use 2m for an item, and this has been registered through all the financial control system, so what is wrong then?'

The famous press conference he called for the day of the ethics committee decision, when he looked so suddenly ashen, rough-shaven, with that plaster on his cheek, he said he had called it because he was convinced that he would be cleared.

'When I was banned I was so much surprised,' he said.

I told him that he did seem quite relaxed, considering everything, the battalions of lawyers inspecting every step of his record over forty years with the money, issues and characters he dealt with, some of them now exposed as industrial-scale crooks. His reply was instructive, too, of how he sees himself:

'I am relaxed, because I would have stopped all the matters if I feel really guilty and that something could happen to me in a criminal case,' he said. 'I would have stopped everything, taken a rucksack, I would be somewhere in a Valais alp with my pipe or cigar, I would have radio and television, I would be there. I would be like the Greek philosopher when they come to visit him and they say: "Can we do something for you?" and he says: "Yes, you can go away, so the sun comes directly to me."'

That was his vision, and there was something a little odd that he pictured it like this, that if he was ever caught out, with his fingerprints or signature on some incriminating act, he would not be in jail, but it would just entail him leaving his adventures and successes in the world, and he could retire back to the obscurity of the Valais. Listening to it, I felt then as I have with many of the old football men whose careers and reputations I have seen curdle when they have stayed on too long: that he should have taken that option, retired, and lived that vision some years ago. A pipe, radio, feet up, a bit of sunshine in the Alps. Rather than be here at the age of eighty, his life in the hands of lawyers, using up all his resources still battening down against endless waves of allegations from the decades of buccaneering.

He had to be off, to his appointment at 2 p.m., and he called for the bill. It is always an awkward predicament, the bill when you meet for lunch as a journalist, when you are meeting somebody you have to write about as a subject, particularly in these circumstances of his. I had decided in advance that I would insist on paying – even at these prices, at Fifa's Restaurant Sonnenberg, at the top of the world above Zurich, where everything is expensive.

'No,' Blatter insisted, he had already paid the bill. 'No, it's done. Not in my restaurant.'

I said really I ought to pay, as he was giving me his time, for an interview for my book.

'No, no, not in my restaurant,' he said, and then, through gritted teeth, he added almost to himself as he stood up: 'Well, it's not mine, but I am still the boss here.'

When I had been sitting there waiting for him, on the terrace looking out at Lake Zurich and the wealthy city spread over the hills and in the valley, I had realised that a part of me wanted to believe in him, in Fifa. It is a phenomenal story, of football and this organisation, formed by seven earnest Europeans in 1904 to play a simple, marvellous sport, moved to Switzerland in 1932. From this most discreet of havens they could have nestled complacently in their plush and comfortable 'house', but they did not. They ventured out constantly, to the whole world, and saw football develop everywhere, while keeping it together as one sport, just one official FA affiliated from every country, participating together in one World Cup, just as the amateur founders envisaged all those years earlier. But in these decades of its modern development, since the World Cup was first broadcast in colour television in the 1970s, Fifa became bloated and had corruption woven in, throughout Blatter's forty years. It all culminated finally in mass arrests, criminal charges, significant guilty pleas, bottomless shame.

At the end of a pleasant lunch at which he gave his version of events – he had made a remarkable journey from a childhood in the Valais, where he is still a hero; smartly orienteered the politics of sports governing bodies, partly by putting more hours in than everybody else; he was guilty of no wrongdoing, he knew of no wrongdoing, he saw no wrongdoing; he had been a success and implemented major development work; whistleblowers are snitches, and England and the USA should learn to lose – Sepp Blatter said his goodbyes. The chef and staff of the restaurant loyally came out to line up and shake his hand, the ageing, tainted, one-time president. Then he was ushered back into the black Mercedes, and driven down the hill again, to face his meetings with lawyers.

Sepp Blatter's time is finally done; he is not the boss any more. And nobody can say what the future holds: for Fifa, for the game, for the world.

Bibliography

The Ugly Game: The Qatari Plot to Buy the World Cup, by Heidi Blake and Jonathan Calvert (Simon & Schuster 2015)

The Official History of the Football Association, by Bryon Butler (Aurora Publishing 1991)

'Stanley Rous's "Own Goal": Football Politics, South Africa and the Contest for the FIFA presidency 1974', by Paul Darby, in *Soccer & Society*, 9 (2008), pp. 259–72

Africa Football and Fifa: Politics, Colonialism and Resistance, by Paul Darby (Frank Cass 2002)

The Turbulent World of Middle East Soccer, by James M. Dorsey (Hurst & Company 2016)

The Ball is Round: A Global History of Soccer, by David Goldblatt (Riverhead Books 2006)

Futebol Nation: A Footballing History of Brazil, by David Goldblatt (Penguin 2014)

The Big Fix: How South Africa Stole the 2010 World Cup, by Ray Hartley (Jonathan Ball Publishers 2016)

Feet of the Chameleon: The Story of African Football, by Ian Hawkey (Portico 2009)

Das Reboot: How German Football Reinvented Itself and Conquered the World, by Raphael Honigstein (Yellow Jersey Press 2015)

League Football and the Men Who Made it: The Official Centenary History of the Football League, by Simon Inglis (Willow Books 1988)

FOUL! The Secret World of Fifa: Bribes, Vote Rigging and Ticket Scandals, by Andrew Jennings (Harper Sport 2006)

The Dirty Game: Uncovering the Scandal at Fifa, by Andrew Jennings (Arrow Books 2015)

100 Years of Football: The FIFA Centennial Book, by Pierre Lanfranchi, Christiane Eisenberg, Tony Mason and Alfred Wahl (Weidenfeld & Nicolson 2004)

Platoche: Gloire et déboires d'un héros français, by Jean-Philippe Leclaire (Flammarion 2016)

American Huckster: How Chuck Blazer Got Rich from – and Sold Out – the Most Powerful Cabal in World Sports, by Mary Papenfuss and Teri Thompson (Harper 2016)

Reforming Fifa, by Mark Pieth (ed.), Lord Peter Goldsmith, Leonardo Grosso, Damian Heller, Michael Hershman and Geuillermo Jorge (Dike 2014)

The FIFA World Cup 1930–2010: Politics, Commerce, Spectacle and Identities, by Stefan Rinke and Kay Schiller (eds) (Wallstein Verlag 2014)

Football Worlds: A Lifetime in Sport, by Stanley Rous (Faber and Faber 1978)

Pitch Invasion: Adidas, Puma and the Making of Modern Sport, by Barbara Smit (Penguin 2006)

Young Havelange : FIFA in the Third Millennium, by Edgard Soares and Sérgio Baklanos (J.S. Propaganda 1995)

Fifa: The Men, the Myths and the Money, by Alan Tomlinson (Routledge 2014)

Great Balls of Fire: How Big Money is Hijacking World Football, by John Sugden and Alan Tomlinson (Mainstream 1999)

Global Corruption Report: Sport, by Transparency International (Routledge 2016)

Angels with Dirty Faces: The Footballing History of Argentina, by Jonathan Wilson (Orion 2016)

How They Stole the Game, by David Yallop (Constable 2011)

Acknowledgements

Writing a book about the scandals of Fifa was a journey into the same maddening contradictions involved in any work investigating football's modern fractures, but on a global scale. The number of people making so much money out of the game is vastly outnumbered by those participating for the love of it. While the men who enriched themselves were always hard to reach, many other people gave up their time willingly to talk, and to help with research. I am grateful to all of them, and to everybody quoted in the book. Those thanks extend to Sepp Blatter, for agreeing to see me and answer all my questions in an interview, and to Thomas Renggli, who arranged our meeting.

Several Fifa staff were very helpful in responding to questions, however difficult, and I am also particularly grateful to Guy Oliver and Michael Schmalholz at the Fifa museum for providing so much fascinating material and insights into the organisation's history.

Fellow journalists whose help was very much appreciated included Steve Menary, Valentino Singh and Lasana Liburd in Trinidad, Mark Gleeson and Carlos Amato in South Africa and Jean-Philippe Leclaire in Paris. The encouragement of the legendary Fifa writer and reporter and former *World Soccer* editor, Keir Radnedge, was very much appreciated. The insights of Luiz Guilherme Burlamaqui in Brazil and Paul Darby of Ulster University, were very illuminating. My friend Don Bealing helped very much with translations from German.

Ian Prior, head of sport at the *Guardian* when I wrote the book, was very supportive, as always; his replacement, Owen Gibson, is a steadfast colleague and as the chief sports correspondent was a brilliant chronicler of the Fifa fall for the paper. Thanks also to the football editor Marcus Christenson and deputy football editor Jon Brodkin for their patience while I was away working on the book, and to all my colleagues at the *Guardian* for being good people and great to work with.

At Yellow Jersey Press, I am very grateful to Frances Jessop for commissioning this book and for all her hard work and care and attention on it. I'm also thankful to Bill Hamilton for his support, as ever.

Finally, my wife Sarah and lovely daughters Isobel and Emily put up with me again, writing another book, so the most thanks goes to them.

Index

David Conn is the author of *The Beautiful Game* and an award-winning journalist for the *Guardian* where he has been a key part of the coverage of the FIFA crisis.

Photograph by Andy Farrington

NATION
BOOKS

The Nation Institute

Founded in 2000, **Nation Books** has become a leading voice in American independent publishing. The imprint's mission is to tell stories that inform and empower just as they inspire or entertain readers. We publish award-winning and bestselling journalists, thought leaders, whistleblowers, and truthtellers, and we are also committed to seeking out a new generation of emerging writers, particularly voices from underrepresented communities and writers from diverse backgrounds. As a publisher with a focused list, we work closely with all our authors to ensure that their books have broad and lasting impact. With each of our books we aim to constructively affect and amplify cultural and political discourse and to engender positive social change.

Nation Books is a project of The Nation Institute, a nonprofit media center established to extend the reach of democratic ideals and strengthen the independent press. The Nation Institute is home to a dynamic range of programs: the award-winning Investigative Fund, which supports groundbreaking investigative journalism; the widely read and syndicated website TomDispatch; journalism fellowships that support and cultivate over twenty-five emerging and high-profile reporters each year; and the Victor S. Navasky Internship Program.

For more information on Nation Books and The Nation Institute, please visit:

www.nationbooks.org
www.nationinstitute.org
www.facebook.com/nationbooks.ny
Twitter: @nationbooks